A LIFE

LIVED

EMBRACING CHANGE,
CHERISHING MOMENTS,
AND EXPLORING THE WORLD

ERIC BERMAN

This book is written in the memory of:

LIVIA BERMAN—Who was my dedicated wife for 26 years

NADIA BERMAN—My loving mother

ARMAND BERMAN—My beloved father

Acknowledgements

I would like to thank:

Hailey Stone for her dedication and fantastic work. All the staff of American Pubishers Inc., in particular, Jerry Stevens and Conard Martin.

I would like to thank Ian Harel, Andy Waitman, Sorin Berman, Silvian Fiderer, Puiu Cohn, and Carol Hoffner for their inspiration and facts update.

Also, many thanks to Eden Stewart for her inputs and valid remarks.

Thanks to Iris Stewart for her patience during the many days she was left alone.

"Always Look on the Bright Side of Life."

From Monty Python's *Life of Brian*.

Contents

PROLOGUE 1

CHAPTER 1 Birth and Early Years 3

CHAPTER 2 Early School Years in Romania 19

CHAPTER 3 Israel—Arrival and School Years 36

CHAPTER 4 Israel and the 1973 War 59

CHAPTER 5 Trip to Europe Before the Studies 65

CHAPTER 6 Italy—University First Year 77

CHAPTER 7 Milan, Italy—Second Year 88

CHAPTER 8 Milan, Italy—Third Year 95

CHAPTER 9 Switzerland and the Surgery 100

CHAPTER 10 Travel Industry—Israel 108

CHAPTER 11 American Trade Show 127

CHAPTER 12 A Beginning: the USA Adventures .. 134

CHAPTER 13 New Starts 145

CHAPTER 14 Starting a Life Together 158

CHAPTER 15—Pt 1 The Years Following 177

CHAPTER 15—Pt 2 1993 189

CHAPTER 16 A New Life in 1994-1999 196

CHAPTER 17 The New Millennium—2000-2004 .. 220

CHAPTER 18 My 50th Birthday—2005 235

CHAPTER 19 The Years 2006-2008 240

CHAPTER 20 A Very Significant Year—2009 257

CHAPTER 21 A New Period in My Life—
2010-2013 264

CHAPTER 22 Livia, Livia, and Livia Again—
2014 283

CHAPTER 23 Life After Livia, Meeting Iris—
2015-2019 294

CHAPTER 24 Eden, Wes, and Lilith—2019 315

CHAPTER 25 COVID-19 Years: 2020-2022 322

CHAPTER 26 A New Beginning—2022 337

CHAPTER 27 A Year Not to Be Remembered—
2023 341

CHAPTER 28 The Current End 348

EPILOGUE 352

PROLOGUE

Before we dive in, let me introduce myself. I'm Eric Berman, and I'm on a mission to compile my memories into an autobiography. Writing has always been my passion, and now I have the perfect opportunity to pursue it fully. After a lifetime of devouring books, exploring different genres of music, and watching countless films, I've decided to start fresh and embrace a new beginning.

I've led an adventurous life, and I believe it's worth sharing—not just for myself but for others to enjoy as well. Now that I'm nearing the third section of my life, the stories of my journey are captivating, and I hope that by sharing them, others will be inspired to look forward to a good life. My tales will stir emotions and make you laugh, cry, and reflect. Travel was and still is my ultimate passion, and the stories are also related to my travels and experiences during these times.

One of the funniest moments I've witnessed in my family was during a road trip my father took us on in early 1971, just after our arrival in Israel. We were heading to the Sea of Galilee, and my father, insisting he knew what he was doing—despite all evidence to the contrary—set about changing a flat tire. He emerged from under the car a few minutes later and announced he couldn't find the tire iron, saying he was sure it was there when he started. Finally, with a triumphant shrug and a smug grin, he held up a tool. I broke out into laughter when I realised he was holding a barbecue grill, tool! It was quite a sight to behold.

Telling this story has become a ritual at family events, each retelling accentuating our appreciation for each other's foibles, deepening our family bonds, and celebrating the funny mistakes of our loved ones. Retelling that memory boosts my feelings of well-being, and every time I reminisce about it years later, I add another layer of context that suggests inconveniences are transient and a good laugh can emotionally free you, even if temporarily.

Laughter is one of the best antidotes for stress. The flat tire was a bump in the road, but laughing about it helped us turn an impending crisis into a cherished family story—a marvelous skill for coping with the inevitable curves' life throws our way.

Looking back at that family road trip, it's clear that humor allows us to see our lives, friends, and family through a lighter, more pleasant, less daunting filter. It welds bonds, provides pleasure, and makes life—with all its terrors, pains, and sorrows—seem more manageable.

CHAPTER 1
Birth and Early Years

I was born in the summer of 1955 in Bucharest, Romania's capital, during some of its darkest years. Though the city was the arts and culture hub of Eastern Europe under communism, and much of the madness of those years cloaked the streets with a heavy pall, the metropolis was bursting at its seams, vibrant with the mirth and mess of urban living. It was a fortress, and it was a funhouse, a capital city teeming with all kinds of contradictions: Bucharest, in its time of suffering, was also a boomtown. Construction workers paved and rebuilt the damned city; their shadows spread long across the dusty avenues preparing for sunrise. Neoclassical and Art Nouveau buildings were scattered across the once-grand city, interspersed with modernist structures built after the Second World War. Much of the city centre had been levelled by Allied bombings, but what lay in ruins was now being rebuilt into a socialist 'wonder,' as Stalinist as they come.

I was born into this family regime. A typical Romania childhood was shaped by the Securitate,

Romania's secret police, since that's the only reality my parents knew. Growing up, I learned very quickly that life in Romania was not as it might be in the West. It was normal for families to have only one child because they couldn't afford more. Therefore, we learnt early on to be content with little. We soon realised that dreams were constrained by what we knew was possible with the limitations of this regime.

My Parents

My mother, Nadia, was born in the industrial town of Ploiesti, 56 kilometers north of the capital Bucharest, known as the 'Capital of Black Gold' because of its enormous oil industry of interest to the Germans in wartime. The town had also become an interest for them because it was the largest oil producer in Romania, a country that would soon crumble at the Germans' feet. In 1943, my mother's grandfather was sent to a concentration camp in Braşov, and, with my mother and her sister, my grandmother lived in one apartment or another for two years.

My mom was a beautiful woman. She had black hair and bright green eyes—eyes that popped against her pale skin. At 168 cm, her height was commanding for a woman of that time, with legs that went on by her quiet strength. Before she got pregnant by my father, she had trained as a registered nurse.

Every month, a package arrived, sent from my family in Israel, containing clothing and chewing gum.

My mother kept what fitted me, and the rest went to the flea market on Sunday mornings, where she and my father went to sell the merchandise. The flea market was overblown smell of sweaty rags and survival mixed together with the smell of deals and trade.

But we got through it in the end, as everyone else did under the difficult conditions of communist Romania. Our story was a story of deprivation but also one of love, family, and ties that bridge boundaries.

My father, Armand, was born in the town of Craiova, where his parents had a crystal store, and there he had his childhood together with his older brother, Jack. This was before they had to move to Bucharest in 1938.

My father, Armand, called Bebe, was 175 cm, with a prominent forehead and black hair combed back behind thick brown (later green) rimmed glass lenses that made him look like a scholar. If he wasn't working, he was usually surrounded by friends, invariably couples who matched his effervescent intelligence. An engineer at a Romanian factory and professor at the local university, his reputation grew after he won Romania's State Prize for his book, *Heating and Drying with Infrared Radiations*, which literally broke new ground in a field in which he was truly a pioneer.

My father was a brilliant man, but aside from two favorite quirks (classical music listening and photography), he displayed little curiosity about the world outside his study. So immersed was he in his thoughts and work that he rarely appeared to be aware of what was going on at home; certainly, my mother must have managed things here while he was 'elsewhere.' "Your father's head is in another place," she would say. ("I'm not in his class," she'd add with characteristic modesty, but she was the one we all looked to. "Remember," she'd tell me, "I run the show.") "Hard work done sincerely and with kindness will make a difference to others," was another of her gently proud adages that I always strove to emulate. She placed a great store in this legacy.

My father had very particular tastes when it came to music. He adored classical music but disliked attending concerts, as he could not stand the inevitable interruptions—murmurs, coughs, and rustling sounds that disrupted the flow. Instead, he preferred listening to Bach's piano sonatas in the quiet solitude of his own space, often with headphones. In his later years, he had developed such a refined ear that he could even distinguish between different pianists based on their unique interpretations. He went as far as purchasing multiple recordings of the same pieces, each performed by different artists, to explore the nuances.

Opera, however, was another story. He found it hard to enjoy because he felt that the performers—especially the sopranos—were often too old or physically mismatched for their roles, which made it difficult for him to immerse himself fully in the experience. The main operas he enjoyed listening to were those by Richard Wagner. Yet, it was in this world of refined preferences that I was raised. I learned to appreciate music, to seek out its nuances, and to open myself to diverse styles. This intellectual approach to music became, in a way, my bridge to understanding my father and connecting with him on a deeper level.

In addition to music, he also had a passion for reading, which intensified in his later years. His literary journey took him from Hermann Hesse to Thomas Mann and from Albert Camus to Aldous Huxley, each author adding new dimensions to his perspective on life and the world around him.

The state was making it harder and harder for us to emigrate to Israel: when my family first tried, his salary had been reduced by two-thirds, and our total income had fallen by 60 percent (all that due to the fact that the Romanians did not want to have such a brilliant mind leave Romania). To make up for the shortfall, he worked a second job: during the day, he was an engineer; at night, he became a university professor.

Gradually, the strain of it all led my dad to smoke himself into a case of tuberculosis and hospitalization, my mom coming every day, sometimes with me. These were days of silent misery for her. The financial strain, the absence of the man she loved, and the burden of being in charge of me—all of this meant she started taking the odd Valium.

When my father was released from the hospital a

year later, she got depressed and took a year and a half to recover. For most of that time, I was under the supervision of my grandmother, Omama.

Life in Romania

Life under 'communism' held many contradictions for Jews and Jewish families such as ours in Romania. Communism's ideological commitments to the end of class stratification—and even the abolition of class— were subverted and undermined in the daily reality of state socialism.

Religious communities, including Jews, were often relegated to enclaves, their communal canters kept under surveillance and subject to infiltration, their religious education truncated, and the open expression of their cultural distinctiveness stymied. And yet, the regime's liberatory myths of social justice and meritocracy theoretically permitted Jews, like other social groups, to rise on the basis of their abilities, if not their talents (on paper, at least).

Me, Myself, and All About Me

I was the sort of child one, at an early age, often hears about. I was not one for chasing a ball or playing cops and robbers with the neighborhood gang. I was in my own world and invented my own games, filling all those long hours with tales made up as I went along. My room became a kingdom, the living room a battlefield for knights, and the back garden an unknown planet.

It's not that I didn't want to be outside with all the other kids. I just never felt like I belonged with the other kids. I was happy being alone—to invent, to dream, to think.

My imagination was boundless, always brimming with ideas. I invented games and refined them to suit my tastes—like button football, a version of soccer played with custom-made buttons. But just inventing the game wasn't enough for me; I had to change almost everything besides the core idea, making rules on the spot. I created teams by cutting buttons from the backs of family coats and jackets: one set for Rapid, another for Dinamo, and one more for Steaua Bucharest.

Thick buttons from a winter coat became my goalposts and defenders, medium ones from jackets formed the midfield, and particularly flat ones played as attackers. Even the substitutes had their own 'bench'!

I crafted a special wooden board, painted green to resemble a real soccer field. It was much larger than the standard button football game board—about one meter long and 80 cm wide, approximately 10 percent the size of an actual soccer field.

During the day, thanks to the hat that had been given to me by a trolleybus driver. I used to sit on a little stool, the wooden chair beside me being the brake and the traction steering wheel, and 'drive' the tram for hours, completely absorbed by this fascinating occupation.

Every summer, for a month, at the early ages of two and three, my mother and I would go to Bușteni, a mountain town in the Carpathian Mountains in Romania. The landscape was harsh, juxtaposing the impoverishment of life under post-war communism and the splendor of the natural surroundings. The summer air there was clean, a bit crisp, redolent with the fragrance of the surrounding pine trees. The mountain breeze brought earthy notes: the damp smell of moss, the smell of freshly hewn wood from the logging, and the vaguely sweet aroma of the meadow flowers.

The town was shrouded in green—the thick fir and spruce forest that rose up the steep mountainsides. The light filtering through the leaves brushed in golden patches across the forest floor. The 'Caraiman Cross,' a large, cross-shaped memorial that towered over Bușteni, shone in the sun.

My father couldn't afford to come for the whole month, so he commuted by train every weekend. He was an avid amateur photographer; he took a hundred snapshots or more of my mother and me on each of those trips, and sometimes, he'd develop the film, too. I remember those summers with great fondness, and these photos allowed me to revisit those memories in miniature.

Learning French With a Nanny

My parents believed in the importance of speaking

as many languages as possible, so they decided I should learn French (in those days in Romania, French was the second language). Feeling that a tutor would be the best way to help me speak French quickly, they hired a nanny named Madame Silvie. She taught me and four or five other children, all roughly my age, during the summers when I was four, five, and six.

Throughout those three summers, Madame Silvie took us on walks through parks and organised picnics with sandwiches made at home. While we hiked outdoors and enjoyed our time together, she insisted that we speak only in French. These experiences were educational and culturally enriching, but I liked every second of them.

My Grandparents

There was an uproar one day when I was about four or five years old. My mom took me from my room to the center of the apartment and told me to sit down. People were all weeping. My mom took me outside, and we went for a walk in the park, but the tears continued. My grandfather, Melech (father's father), had passed away from cerebral attack.

My grandparents on my father's side, Esther and Melech, were old Jewish people who had opened a shop in Craiova selling crystals. Craiova is the largest city in southern Romania, the seventh largest in Romania, and the capital of Dolj County. It lies on the east bank of the river Jiu in central Oltenia, close to the border with

Muntenia. The large city of Craiova (population 170,000 in 1943) lies in the middle of Romania. The two of them were where Ashkenazi Jews came to work in Craiova in the middle of the nineteenth century, but the community was not officially set up until 1913. Many of the Jews in Craiova were impoverished following the onset of the Holocaust that began in Romania in 1940, including my father and his brother, and in 1938 the Romanian Nazis burnt down the shop, exactly like they did in Crystal Nacht. They moved to Bucharest and took a flat on Mântuleasa Street 31 and started selling all kinds of glass products in the Obor market.

My grandmother, Omama, became a very dominant figure in my upbringing and throughout my childhood and my early years as an adult.

The apartment had three rooms in a row, like train compartments: to go from the first room to the second, you had to go through the first; in order to go from the second to the third, you had to go through the second. My parents lived in the first room, my grandmother's sister, Dina, and I lived in the second, and my grandparents had the third room—the closest to the kitchen and bathroom.

My Other Grandparents

On the weekend, I went to my grandparents, from my mom's side, to spend a day in Cişmigiu Park, a public park in the center of Bucharest, spanning areas on all sides of an artificial lake. The gardens' creation was an important moment in the history of Bucharest. It is the largest park in the city's center. The park has a lake that, back then, seemed endless to me.

Every appearance at my grandparents meant an event, especially because of the trolleybus that I liked to ride on and to look at the driver—I simply absorbed his technique. My mom would walk me to the trolleybus station, and I would then board it alone, getting off at my grandparents' stop where they were to be waiting.

For about five to six years, my father did not speak to my grandparents. My grandparents always wanted my mom to marry a doctor. Before she met my dad, she had this boyfriend—his name was Ionel, and they pushed her so much to marry him. But when she met my father, she found out he was the one she was supposed to marry, so they got married. My dad heard them still pushing her to change her mind, so since then, he did not want to talk to them.

My grandmother, Albertina (Tusca), was obsessed with cleanliness and employed a woman named Maria, who helped around the house and cooked. Maria had also raised my mother and her sister, Miricel. She was a simple but loving woman, dedicating her heart to my grandparents, especially since her husband was a drunk who drank pure alcohol and was difficult to be around.

My grandfather (Papi), Marcel, was a building engineer who studied and graduated in Vienna. After enduring time in the ghetto in Braşov, he remarkably rebuilt his life from the ground up. He was meticulous about punctuality and routines, making mealtimes at their home formal and structured. Each meal required white cloth napkins and wine accompanied by the multi-course menu, which always finished the meal with a salad served after the main dish and before dessert.

The best lesson I carried through life was sitting at the table, being present, and respecting those around me. Those early years—the 'basic seven years from home'—were basic. Stay at the table, no matter what, until the head of the table is done eating. That taught patience and good manners.

One of my grandmother's specialties was stuffed grapevine leaves filled with a mixture of meat, rice, and raisins, always served with yogurt. They were delicious.

Here is the recipe:

Ingredients

- One kg of chopped meat (pork and lean beef)
- Two large yellow onions, finely chopped
- 100 g vegetable oil
- 100 g tomato paste
- 50 g round rice
- 50 g yellow raisins
- One teaspoon oregano
- One teaspoon thyme
- 30-40 grape leaves
- One cup of white wine

Preparation

- Boil the grape leaves for 5 minutes, then prepare a filling using the meat, rice, tomato paste, raisins, onion, salt, pepper, oregano, and thyme to create a well-seasoned mixture.
- Fill the grape leaves one by one and place them in a pot.
- Add oil and wine, cover with water, and cook on the stove for one hour.
- Transfer the pot to the oven and bake for an additional hour at 175°C (375°F).
- Serve with cold yogurt.
- You will not be disappointed—it is delicious!

Moments and Flashbacks

I remember going out with my parents in the afternoons. With a sweet tooth, I loved gazing at the enticing pastry shops in Bucharest and often asked, "Can you buy me a pastry?" They always obliged, and I would dash off to get my treat while they sat at the table. My father would look at my mother, and she would return the glance, both smiling at me. Yet, I could sense that their smiles masked deeper sadness.

I recall the grandmother who, every second morning, went to buy the 1-meter-long, 20 cm-diameter ice blocks for carrying home in one of those cloth sacks, as we did not have a refrigerator at the time, and we used to keep the food in a huge metal box where it inserted the ice blocks to serve as a refrigerator.

Once, I remember running to the kitchen. My grandmother had just come back from the market and left a bag of tomatoes on the floor. I was running and obviously slipped on the tomatoes and hit my head on the soapstone. Hospital, stitches, a beautiful head scar.

Another vivid flashback is from a cold Sunday afternoon when my parents and I took a walk in the fields near the railway tracks. A sharp piece of metal struck my right eye, and I immediately cried out in pain without fully understanding what had happened. Eventually, I pointed to my eye, prompting my parents to rush me to the hospital. The doctors decided to extract the metal using a strong magnet, which hurt immensely, and I got no anesthesia with the procedure.

My grandma made fish with tomato sauce for dinner one day. Accidentally, I swallowed a big bone, and since then, I did not dare to touch fish until the day I arrived in Italy. They never told me, and I didn't know how to clean the bones.

My parents were strict with money. They only bought groceries when it was needed or available. On Sundays, a woman would come with a horse and carriage, delivering milk, cheese, and sour cream. She sold white cheese, cottage cheese, milk, feta cheese, and yogurt. Those Sundays were the worst for me because I dreaded having to eat white cheese and sour cream every week.

My mom also used to prepare—only for me—

spinach with oranges (oranges were a very rare and very expensive fruit in those days in Bucharest).

I remember when my mom used to go to buy food, "What is the line for?" was the question my mom was asking all the time. To buy cheese and meat, in the evening, you used to queue to make sure to get something the next day. People used to buy what was available, not what they wanted to buy. No one knew, but everyone queued because they had something. My mom, who was friends with the butcher to make sure she had whatever she wanted (from whatever was available) put aside for her, always used to bribe the butchers or the fruit sellers. That was the rule in Romania in those days. Just imagine. If you wanted to buy meat—anything that was available on the day—a line would form, and without knowing what animal it was coming from or how it was slaughtered, you bring it home to cook for your family.

There was a little outdoor cinema in our neighborhood, which showed films under the stars in the summer. My mom took me every week. I think Ivanhoe was the first one I saw. I loved Westerns and historical pictures. My mom loved Elizabeth Taylor. She'd pack sandwiches and feed me during the movie. It was always a big occasion, something to look forward to every week.

Later on in my teens, we did go to the seasonal taverna, and the movie theatre became a place to catch up in the early fall. The undisputed attraction was the 'must,' freshly pressed grape juice about to transform into wine, often still with its seeds and skins. Chilled and fresh, before it fermented, must was a seasonal pleasure. 'Must' was sipped, along with fresh cheeses and grilled meats, in a simple, memorable dinner that you could enjoy only at that time of year.

One year, one of my parents' friends made their own tiny Christmas tree with lights, Christmas music, gifts, the whole nine yards. We did all of it and had a blast. I received and gave presents to other kids in attendance. It struck me as very odd that both Jewish groups would celebrate Christmas. When I think about how we were honestly so excited by all the Christmas decorations, and so happy and thankful for the presents, it seems fuzzy brained that we never once thought, 'Hey, these rules must not really apply to us.' Going to a Christmas Eve celebration was unheard of. And my mom never told my grandmother where we had gone that night.

CHAPTER 2
Early School Years in Romania

I was starting the first grade in the Mantuleasa district of Bucharest, a city caught between its majestic past, marked by splendid architecture, and the harsh, gray reality of its communist present.

Bucharest

The winter air in Bucharest was a curious mix of old-world and modern scents. In the morning, the sweet aroma of freshly baked bread from local bakeries filled the air, mingling with the fragrance of lime trees along boulevards like Calea Victoriei, especially in spring and early summer. These calming smells often clashed with the acrid scent of coal smoke, exhaust fumes from the growing number of private cars and trucks, and dust from numerous construction sites as the communist regime pushed forward with its modernization plans.

In the evenings, the air carried the scent of cheap beer and tuică, a rough spirit made from plums.

Drinking was a popular pastime, and payday excitement often led to many getting drunk.

The city's former opulence was visible in the flaking paint that revealed cracked plaster and faded pastels— yellow, pink, faint blue. Even amidst the imposing Stalinist concrete blocks, the grand architecture's splendor was undeniable.

As spring arrived, Cişmigiu and Herăstrău parks burst into colour with tulips, roses, and poppies. Children played by the fountains while older folks sat on benches, gossiping or reading newspapers. Yet, the beauty of the parks contrasted sharply with the harsh, regimented atmosphere of a city reshaped in the Communist Party's image. In autumn, the trees turned golden yellow and orange, and the winds carried the earthy scents of wet leaves and chimney smoke. This combination of smells reflected a city proud of its past yet uncertain about its future.

Bucharest was grim, characterised by gray skies, the tram and trolleybus traffic turning snow into slush, and the air thick with coal fumes.

School Days and Friends

When I started school, I quickly got to know all the children in the district, especially the girls. I often carried their bags home after school and formed close friendships with two in particular: Anca, the thin, short one, and Monica, the tall girl with nice breasts. I secretly liked both of them, and they became my best friends.

For my first two years of school, my best friend was a Jewish boy named Gerard, the only Jewish student in our class. Our families became friends and spent weekends together. Eventually, I also became close with his younger brother, Martin, and their friend, Silvain. The four of us were like brothers. When Gerard and Martin emigrated with their family to Israel, we kept in touch.

Monu, Silvian's dad, taught me to ride a bicycle, although I never quite mastered it. I spent countless hours with Silvian, either at his home or mine, getting into childhood mischief and giggling. Silvian had a peculiar habit of punching anyone close enough to him, usually without warning. Once, he punched me from behind, and when I complained, he ran straight to my grandmother, Omama, and reported, "Eric hit me!"

Omama, my dear grandmother, never seemed to consider that Silvian might be the troublemaker. Instead, she would take his word for it and scold or even smack me, regardless of whether I had actually hit him. It was a strange kind of justice, but I grew accustomed to it in my own way.

Another fond memory of Grandma Omama is watching a football match together. She'd sit beside me, her eyes fixed on the screen, and to my surprise, she even knew some of the players' names! I was genuinely impressed. This little glimpse of shared enthusiasm made those moments with her feel special.

Another long-lasting friend of mine was Daniela. Together, we fell in love with books and ideas. We read all the classics: John Steinbeck's *Of Mice and Men*, Jerome K. Jerome's travel tale, *Three Men in a Boat*, Emily Brontë's *Wuthering Heights*, and Mark Twain's *The Adventures of Tom Sawyer and Huckleberry Finn*. We even ventured into the controversial works of the infamous French novelist Françoise Sagan, absorbing *Bonjour Tristesse* and *Aimez-vous Brahms?* which were deemed 'amoral' at the time and blacklisted for their content. Around the time I turned 13, we explored other dimensions by reading Kafka's existential novels and Hesse's self-reflexive fiction.

Being a huge fan of Western music, Radio Free Europe became our salvation as it broadcasted to the Eastern bloc. We listened to *The Beatles* in silence, sometimes in the bathroom with hot water running to prevent any sound leakage.

Daniela was a striking individual. Her wide shoulders and robust body exuded strength and confidence. She had big, dark eyes that were playful and animated, and her facial features, though utilitarian and sparse, gave her a muted appeal. Her long dark curls framed her face starkly, aligning with her straightforward, no-nonsense nature. Standing at five foot six, she was both physically and mentally irresistible. Daniela was a controversial figure, especially when it came to politics, about which she held fiery but humorously sincere opinions. She was honest and blunt, but her candor was always tempered by her open-heartedness and the intimacy of an affectionate friend.

Playing Around the Mântuleasa Church

And then there were the neighborhood soccer matches, where everyone played regardless of skill. The streets were our stadium, and the rules were always flexible, allowing for the pure joy of the game. I was never the best player, but I loved being part of the action, the shared excitement as we chased the ball, and arguing over goals and fouls until the sun dipped below the horizon.

These moments formed the fabric of my early childhood, a time when the boundaries between reality and imagination blurred. Every day held the promise of adventure, and the world seemed endless, full of potential. Whether it was the simple thrill of riding a bike down a hill or the shared laughter of a broken go-kart, those memories stayed with me, shaping my sense of wonder and curiosity.

When the weather permitted, we played outside. We often met in the square in front of the Mântuleasa Church, a Byzantine Romanian Orthodox Church with a central dome, cylindrical drum, and smaller domes on either side. The church was not only colourful and imposing but also ornate, with a facade of warm-coloured bricks and stone elements and frescoes of saints and Biblical scenes.

We boys would play football there, and I broke my collarbone playing goalie once. I dived but flipped over, falling on my right side. Mom came to pick me up and take me to the hospital. My arm ended up in a cast so big that they missed the break, so the bone healed at an angle. That was my first operation, but there would be many more.

School Struggles and Teacher Support

My father, who spoke Yiddish, French, and German quite fluently, resolved to teach himself English with a reel-to-reel tape recorder—and he had it down pat in two or three years. He set goals high and met them. Likewise, he wanted me to speak English. When I was eight or nine, he hired a private English tutor. 'You could be successful,' he told me. I already knew more English than most of my classmates. I started skipping class. My teachers couldn't quite figure me out. I was always the smartest in my class, but what was the fun of that? Aside from being an awkward, shy kid, I was also a smart aleck. Wise guys, as it happens, are not popular in Socialist Romania.

The school was too slow for me. I liked sports and was sent out of math and English classes for playing football. My mom visited the school a lot because of me. I did well in English, but my uncooperative attitude over other subjects didn't go down well with the teachers.

Domnul (Mr) Popescu was my only teacher who

truly inspired me, and I held a deep admiration for him. He instilled in me a sense of self-control and creativity I never thought possible. Always impeccably dressed, he sported a bow tie and tailored jackets paired with neatly pressed trousers, exuding an air of class and sophistication. In retrospect, I suspected he was gay, a detail that added an intriguing layer to his personality. He often visited our home, where he would teach me all about world capitals, igniting my passion for travel and exploration. Each lesson felt like a journey in itself, filled with stories that sparked my imagination and fueled my dreams of adventure.

The atmosphere in school was not to my taste. I was out of any discipline and always got in trouble with the teachers. Sports were my passion. While in class, when bored, I used to go through a sports newspaper.

Flashbacks

I was nine when I got low marks in math, and the teacher took me to the blackboard and said: "We are going to call your mom."

And I just remember this wave of fear and dread. I don't know why, but I have this very clear memory of feeling like a line had opened into my soul and was now closing up on me, and I thought, *Oh no, I am going to flip out.* The whole idea of her getting angry was very frightening. And so, I made sure I didn't flip out. It was all so stubborn and stupid.

When I got home that afternoon, I cut the line and

taped it up, certain that my teacher wouldn't try to phone my mother again. My parents did not notice that the phone wasn't working until the next day. When they finally did, the walls closed in.

My dad, who had never ever hit me in all my life, got the belt and hit me until I admitted to the whole horrible thing. Unspeakable penalties were administered: one week of house arrest, no TV, and I was not even allowed to leave the house. It was a catastrophe.

In those days, summers found me at the lake, where I finally learned to swim. I took hours in that shallow water and acquired a skill that I would use and love for the rest of my life.

Winters turned the routine on its head, three times a week, to the ice, skates and scraping and smooth exhaling glides that became part of the winter air. At the age of 13, I got my own skates and did not need to rent them any longer. I was thrilled. Each season had a little excitement of its own to set a heartbeat to every year.

Some of the anti-Semitic incidents I experienced were routine. A classmate called me a 'stupid Jew.' When I countered that he was a 'stupid piece of trash,' he put me through a desk with the screws of the desk leg splitting open my head. I ended up in the emergency room. This type of thing happened regularly. I learned to button myself up, to be silent, to suppress the pain of the verbal assaults.

Once at the Winter Olympics in 1968, as I wanted to watch the day events, again my brain overtook me and decided to break off bits of chalk while feigning a fever and watching at home, fooling everyone. I felt like such a dork doing it, but I never got caught.

Jewish Holidays

Both my grandmother and my father observed the Jewish traditions and kept the holidays. Especially Passover—when all the dishes were changed with new dishes that were kept in a closed cabinet which was opened only ahead of Passover and afterward to put them back. I remember that the dishes also eventually traveled to Israel. Same for the high holidays of Rosh Hashanah and Yom Kippur (the Jewish New Year and, respectively, the Day of Attornment). Both went to the synagogue and prayed for the whole day—even if my father had to miss the working day, he did not care. The holidays were more important to him than work. I went several times with my father, but sometimes, I was a really uncaring person so once, my father caught me playing football in the street straight from the synagogue and dragged me home by the ear.

The Bar Mitzvah: When a Boy Becomes a Man

The following year, just two months shy of my 13th birthday, my father took me to the synagogue to mark my entry into Jewish adulthood—a milestone that would become one of the most memorable moments of my life, a true rite of passage. I wore a crisp white shirt with a black bowtie, a white jacket, shiny black trousers, and brand-new black shoes. The most important part of my preparation was learning specific sections of the Torah, a challenging task that I undertook with the guidance of an elderly teacher. For two months, he grilled me relentlessly, drilling each verse and phrase into my memory. It was rigorous but necessary.

When the big day finally arrived, the ceremony was unforgettable, filled with warmth, joy, and a sense of significance. Fifty guests gathered to celebrate, offering gifts and heartfelt well-wishes. I could not stop smiling for days; it felt as though I had stepped into a world of connection and festivity, which was entirely new to me. The choir sang traditional hymns, their voices lifted by the soft tones of the organ in the background, creating a sense of grandeur that elevated the occasion to something truly special. Yet, despite the beauty and tradition surrounding the ceremony, I felt a certain distance from the Jewish rituals that shaped it. In the years that followed, each Rosh Hashanah and Yom Kippur, I would find myself in the synagogue, doing my best to connect with the prayers. But each time, I would stumble, struggling to keep pace, as if these ancient words were always just slightly out of reach, their rhythm somehow uncoordinated with my own.

Changes

After my mother started working at a dental clinic

when I was seven, our family income improved significantly. This change brought a wave of new possibilities for us. By the time I turned eight, we could afford new home appliances, which marked a significant shift in our daily lives. One of the most exciting additions was a refrigerator, allowing us to store food more efficiently and enjoy fresh produce longer. We also bought a TV set, which became a source of entertainment and a window to the wider world. My father also got a new tape recorder, so he could listen to classical music in his free time.

These new appliances symbolised more than just convenience—they represented a newfound stability and progress in our household. The refrigerator meant we no longer had to rely solely on daily trips to the market, and the TV brought us together in the evenings, creating shared moments of joy and learning. This period marked the beginning of a more comfortable and connected family life, thanks to my mother's hard work and dedication.

In the summer of 1968, my parents decided to go on a holiday to Neptun, a city on the Black Sea. Neptun was a dusty village on Romania's Black Sea coast, where every summer, you could embrace your childhood's freedom face to face with the blue sea.

It smelled of salt from the sea and pine resin from the dense green forests that lined the coast. On sunny days, the walls of water churned up in deep azure and emerald shades, reflecting the sunny skies overhead. A light breeze blew in from the sea, carrying mossy smells of seaweed and sand, and pine groves strewn with hot dust and high grass offered shade and a cool, woody smell.

The tastes were of fried dough, crisp on the outside, soft within, sprinkled with powdered sugar or fresh jam, the sweet smell wafting in the air; mititei, the small, spiced sausages served sizzling and smoky, with bread and mustard; the smell of sizzling meat, garlic and vinegar, the salty sea air. The shoreline was a hodgepodge of beach umbrellas in bright reds, blues and yellows—dots of colours in an otherwise beige sea—making broad swatches of colour on the sand. The beaches tended to mix both sand and small pebbles, glinting in the sunshine, turning a section of the shore into a mosaic of colours as the waves rolled in. The hotels and villas that lined the beach were low-rise and painted in pastel colours—lighter blues, pinks and yellows, colours that reflected the light and heat of summer—and the bordering pine forest further enhanced the green colours, natural boundaries to the seaside town.

By afternoon, the town was abuzz with locals and holidaymakers alike, but as evening fell, the sky would turn purple and orange, and the only sounds you could hear were the odd whiffs of folk music or laughter from nearby restaurants and cafés.

It was my first visit to a seaside resort, and I was captivated by the new hotels, restaurants, and swimming pools. We rented an apartment for two weeks, and it was a remarkable experience for my parents, who had never seen the sea or felt the sand in their lives.

That summer, I enjoyed two holidays: one at the seashore with my parents and another in the mountains with my grandmother.

Sinaia

Sinaia, a mountain resort town located in the Carpathian Mountains of Romania, was, or at least was supposed to be, a place of ubiquitous, vintage charm. It was quiet and lively at the same time, especially in the summer months when the city's residents would come up to breathe the cool mountain air. The air itself was fresh, with the smell of pine trees, damp soil, and moss, mixed with the wood smoke from the chimneys during the summer when city residents would leave their houses open throughout the warm nights and the occasional smell of new-baked pastries or food coming from the inns.

The colours of Sinaia were vivid: the deep green of the fir trees against the blue of the sky or the mist that enveloped the mountains, or else the gold, oranges and reds of those same trees in autumn. In winter, everything was covered in thick, powdery white. Snow made the whole town a white wonderland.

Sinaia's old-world architecture—filled with traditional wooden houses with delicately carved details, as well as its more imposing Neo-Renaissance Peleş Castle—lent it a sense of refined beauty. The dirt streets were nearly silent, save for the clap of horses' hooves landing on cobblestones or the distant murmur of strangers' voices, locals and tourists alike. And looming over everything was the unhurried, natural energy of the nearby Prahova River.

It was cool in the evening, with a heavy stillness that sank down as the sun fell behind the mountains and long shadows spread across the valley. There was a chill in the mountain breeze as it blew in at night, and the time to make a fire or get under a blanket had arrived.

We were lucky to find a decent family—the Maneas—with whom we stayed for a month in the summer and one month in winter. Constantin, the father, was tall, with white hair, and looked to be a very strong man. His wife, Rodica, mother, was an excellent cook and homemaker. Their son, Nicu, was a nice guy who had just started medical school in Bucharest. Before Airbnb existed, we rented an apartment in their house.

I liked it because there, I was never asked to leave, to mind, or to know better—I was free to mount up and fly, even if my grandmother kept a leash. She could barely keep up with me. I climbed the mountains, and I went up to Peles Castle, which is a two-hour walk on foot. And other mountain trails. I skated on the lake in the winter, and I played chess in the 'casino.' As I walked or tracked the deep green woods, I would feel so quiet and relaxed to be there.

A couple times a week, on my way to Bușteni, I went to the train station and bought two or three cigarettes (they sold them one at a time in Romania). Then I started walking to Bușteni, smoking those few cigarettes I had bought. It was 12 km. For two or three hours, I walked on the road, always facing the coming traffic, and then, when I got to Bușteni, I took the train back to Sinaia. I tracked the trails in the mountains, singing to myself, happy and full of energy.

Another Sinaia memory was New Year's Eve 1968, when Nelu, the houseboy at his parents' house, six or seven years or so older than me, held a New Year's party. The food was ready; the music had started with all the oldies and the hits of the decade. People were trickling in.

"Do you want to party?" he asked me.

Out of pity, I suppose, I was invited. I jumped at the opportunity to broaden my horizons. I went wild that night, gorging on Tuică (a traditional Romanian spirit) on tap, sarmale (stuffed cabbage leaves) like God had ordained, mititei (grilled ground meat rolls), the best. But most of all, the girls! The girls—all beautiful 18 to 20-year-olds. They were nice to me, danced with me a little, and touched me gently; those were my first adult experiences. The next day, I got a hangover and the first ciorba de burta of the year. Ciorba de burta, a traditional Romanian food, tripe soup.

I drank hard liquor for the first time. I ate for the first time a morning soup. I partied with girls. What a great time! I forgot what time it was. I forgot any manners my parents had ever taught me. That was the end of the fun. The day I came back from Sinaia, I had to go back to school, and I was pretty devasted. I did not like the immediate change, and I was angry with the whole world.

The same year, again in Sinaia, we all watched the landing on the moon. I remember that summer day of the 20th of July 1969. It was nighttime in Romania, 3:14 in the morning, when Neil Amstrong and Buzz Aldrin were the first human beings to step on another world. It was so exciting and fulfilling. It was a historic moment that I will never forget.

The Departure From Romania

One night, in mid-December, my father went to the foreign ministry to ask again the permission to go to Israel. Fifteen times now my father had asked to go to Israel, but they refused him. They told him he was not allowed even to go to Bulgaria. He stayed at home and was depressed and very angry. He took a walk somewhere for three or four hours and came back home at around 2 am. He tried many times, but he could always get only one answer from them: NO.

The very next day, the mail carrier brought a letter saying that we could leave Romania for Israel (Tusca and Papi, my grandparents, had paid the Romanian government $5,000 each for us to leave the country). He was happy. We would leave Romania in 10 days.

We started to prepare. Omama had left us three months earlier to visit my father's brother in Israel. The preparations, in the middle of winter, were hectic for all of us. We started to sell everything we owned. One person was allowed to take 70 kg of luggage, so both my parents quit their work and spent their days at home, packing and sorting things. I was done with school because of the holiday, and I spent almost all my free time with Daniela.

We sold everything for practically nothing; my father couldn't care less. All he cared about was leaving. I felt torn and excited but also sad, especially as I had to leave behind my whole stamp collection. I spent my last days with Daniela, spending my money on restaurants and sights we had only ever talked about visiting and experiencing before. Romanian money wouldn't be accepted in Israel, so we lived it up for those last few days, and I even got to spend the night at Daniela's house, thanks to her parents. The last thing my father promised himself was no matter what, he would not step back on Romanian soil.

On December 31, 1969, a significant turning point came for our family. We left Romania in search of better opportunities and freedom, emigrating to Israel.

CHAPTER 3
Israel—Arrival and School Years

Upon arrival, overwhelmed and tired, we were welcomed at the airport by the whole family, and the scene was pretty hard to take. There were tears and emotions all over, and after we succeeded in relaxing a little bit, we went to my mom's sister's place in Haifa, the third-largest city in Israel, with a population of 190,870 in 1970. Haifa forms part of the Haifa metropolitan area, the third-most populous metropolitan area in Israel.

Haifa

In 1970, Haifa was a vibrant tapestry of sights, sounds, colours, and aromas, reflecting the city's rich cultural blend and its picturesque Mediterranean setting.

The landscape of Haifa was painted in a palette of sun-soaked colours. The blue of the Mediterranean Sea contrasted sharply with the white and pastel facades of the Bauhaus architecture that lined the hills. With its vibrant purples and pinks, Bougainvillea cascaded over the walls while the bright greens of palm trees swayed in the warm coastal breeze. The golden hues of the sun setting over the bay cast a warm glow on the city, creating an ethereal charm as day turned to night.

The air was filled with a medley of scents. The salty tang of the sea mingled with the fragrant spices wafting from street vendors selling shawarma and falafel. Citrus blossom trees added a sweet and zesty aroma to the atmosphere, while the rich, roasted coffee beans from local cafes provided a warm, inviting scent. Walking through the bustling markets, the pungent smell of fresh herbs and spices, especially za'atar and sumac, filled the air, promising delicious meals to come.

The culinary offerings in Haifa were as diverse as its population. One could savour the fresh taste of grilled fish caught that morning and serve it with a drizzle of olive oil and lemon. Falafel, crispy on the outside and soft on the inside, was often served on warm pita bread, bursting with fresh vegetables and tahini. The sweetness of ripe figs and juicy pomegranates was a delight, while rich, creamy hummus served with warm bread offered comfort and satisfaction. In the evening, the local cafes were filled with the aroma of strong, cardamom-infused Arabic coffee, a perfect companion to the sweet pastries that were divided among friends and family.

Walking through Haifa in 1970 was an immersive experience. The vibrant colours of the city, the alluring scents of its markets and cuisine, and the delightful tastes of its rich culinary tradition came together to create an unforgettable atmosphere. It was a place where cultures intertwined, and every corner offered something new to explore, making it a cherished memory for those who lived there.

Meeting Family and Our First Month in Israel

In Haifa, we met Jack, my father's brother—a pharmacist—his daughter, Lilana, and my grandmother, Omama, who had traveled to Israel earlier and never returned to Romania. We also met Miricel (Mihaela), my mom's sister, her husband, Matei, and their children, Ariel and Dani, my direct cousins. Other cousins were also present, as my grandmother, Omama, had four other sisters, all living in Israel, most with husbands, kids, and grandchildren. It was a reunion with many family members, though sadly, most of them are no longer with us today. We had a fantastic dinner, and we reminisced about the years we passed in Romania. As it was New Year's Eve, I remember going to sleep at once after midnight after the usual glass of sparkling wine.

Arriving in Israel meant adapting to a new country, language, mentality, people, and climate. We had to understand all these changes within a few days because everyone was busy and did not have time to explain everything. Speaking Romanian was limited to within the family, as we had no clue about Hebrew, and

English was not as commonly spoken then as it is today.

My father was quickly offered a job in Israel's nuclear research institute, so we had to find ourselves a city near Tel Aviv for him to get started. I found myself questioning schooling with this new possibility. So, to get out of it, my parents decided that we would go first to my grandparents, Tusca and Papi, who lived in Qiryat Yam, in Haifa's suburb of Qiryat Yam. My father had reconciled with them after they left for Israel in 1964, so it was something familiar and supportive to live with for a time.

Newcomers would generally live for six months in an 'ulpan,' where they would study Hebrew and become integrated into Israeli society. But because my father already had an appointment at the Yavne research institute, and it wasn't as important to him that he learn Hebrew immediately as he got off from work, we skipped the ulpan phase.

The position also had a major catch: because his work was so sensitive and privileged, my father was told he would never be permitted to return to Romania or to any other communist country. Such a ban gave our arrival a further measure of certainty and an acknowledgement of the journey we were beginning in Israel.

Moving to Holon, Meeting Friends

After a month of living with my grandparents, we finally moved to Holon—a city on Israel's central coastal strip, just south of Tel Aviv, and part of the bustling Gush Dan metropolitan area. Holon in the 1970s was alive with energy, a place where the brightness of progress mixed seamlessly with a strong sense of tradition. The city was full of life: vibrant colours painted the streets, scents of fresh bread drifted from the bakeries, and gardens burst with greenery. Its warmth and diversity made it feel inviting, like a place that promised new beginnings, friendships, and memories.

Gerard's mother, Sofi, helped us find an apartment to rent for six months, conveniently located just across the street from Gerard's family. This was a huge relief, as it allowed us to feel a bit at home. We spoke Romanian with his parents, Sofi and Fritz, which eased our transition into a new culture. My father was thrilled with his new job in Israel, commuting on the buses provided by his work. At the same time, my mother took on the many bureaucratic tasks involved in our move— applying for ID cards, enrolling me in school, setting up medical care, and everything else that came with adapting to life in a new country.

My mother began working at a dental clinic in Tel Aviv, and since it was about an hour away by bus, her days were long and tiring.

My own school experience was a mixture of pride and nervousness. After weeks of doing anything but studying, I finally walked through the doors of my new high school, filled with a mix of excitement and dread.

The principal greeted me and personally took me to my ninth-grade class, where I was immediately overwhelmed. Everyone spoke only Hebrew, and beyond English, math, and sports, I understood almost nothing. Classes in Torah, Talmud, Hebrew language, and literature were completely foreign to me.

Despite my struggles with the language barrier, I found myself fitting in socially. Every Friday, there was a party at a different classmate's home, and because I was the DJ who spoke English, I became the 'cool' one. My accent may have been foreign, but it only seemed to draw people in—especially the girls, who had a hard time understanding me but still flocked around. It was an exciting, intense time, even if I couldn't fully adapt to the Israeli mindset.

Slowly, I started to pick up Hebrew, but by the end of the school year, I was told I'd need to repeat the grade. It was embarrassing for both me and my parents, though my father's happiness with his work seemed to make everything else secondary.

Afternoons and evenings were spent outdoors, playing in the sandy lots near our apartment. At night, I often joined Gerard's family—his parents, Sofi and Fritz, and his younger brother, Martin. Gerard and Martin had recently adopted the more common Israeli names Gadi and Moti.

We'd gather in their living small room to watch Israeli TV, usually the news, but if we were lucky, we'd catch an imported show. American hits, like *Mission Impossible,* and British series, such as *The Avengers* and *The Prisoner,* became part of our routine, giving us all a way to bond and escape for a while. These cozy nights of TV with Gerard's family became a comforting ritual, grounding me in the unfamiliar yet growingly familiar world of Holon.

Summer Ulpan

That summer, I took a beginner's Hebrew ulpan, joining a colourful cast of characters who later became dear friends. An ulpan is a short-term intensive language course in Israel, aimed especially at new immigrants (olim) and foreign residents, meant to accelerate their grasp of Hebrew. Ulpanim provides classes at different levels, ranging from beginner to advanced, and they are often found in cities as well as on kibbutzim and even online. For many new immigrants, it is one of the first steps in their integration into Israeli living.

At the ulpan, I reconnected with Daniela, who had noticeably changed, now taller and more confident. I also met new friends, including Ian (Iulian), the energetic one, always wearing a shirt unbuttoned down to his belly button; Ivan, a cheerful, full-of-life guy; George, known as 'the bump' of the group; and Pepita, the girl everyone admired and was eager to be around. Then there was Lucian, tall and bespectacled; Luc, known for his intelligence; and Dinu, the music enthusiast. Along with many other teens my age, they were all navigating the same path of new beginnings and adaptation.

At the same time, my parents bought a new home for themselves—a three-room flat in Bat Yam, a seaside town just south of Tel Aviv on Israel's Mediterranean coast. Suddenly, I spent more time with my new friends outside the ulpan, had a somewhat normal social life outside the ulpan, and was happy again for the first time since I moved to Israel.

New Apartment

We moved into this completely empty apartment, which became the foundation of my adolescent life. I never had my own room until the age of 18. The apartment had two bedrooms: one for my parents and the other for my grandmother (Omama). Looking back, I realise that I was very frustrated by my parents' decisions, but I never fully understood them until 40 years later. Although my desk was in my grandmother's room, where I was supposed to study, I never actually studied there. I preferred sitting at the table on the balcony. The apartment also had a large living room, a dining area, a kitchen, a bathroom with a separate restroom, and a porch, which we eventually used as a service room. My parents slowly started to furnish the apartment and get everything new as we only owned some clothes and dishes that we had brought with us from Romania. So, everything was getting in place slowly but surely. I had bought a tape recorder with which I used to play music while I studied.

In the summer of 1970, I eagerly watched the World Cup from Mexico in the evenings. Although my family didn't have a TV set yet, I would visit my parents' friends, Jack and Dani, to catch the matches. Their son, Sorin, sometimes joined us. I later met him again in Milan. He was a not-so-tall guy with glasses, almost always smoking, and he had the attitude of a prima donna, giving the impression that he knew everything in advance. He was a sound engineer for some very famous artists, a role he genuinely enjoyed. After spending time at home, he would often go out again, adding to his air of confidence.

Now, I had a new set of friends from the Ulpan in Tel Aviv, the Romanian bunch, and my old friends from high school in Holon. This blend of new and old friendships enriched my life and helped me navigate the challenges of adolescence in a new country.

By now, the school was going fine, but, as an outsider, the Bible and the Talmud were not required subjects, so I was not studying either of them. I needed to go to a private school in order to get a maturity diploma as I had already lost a year repeating the same class twice. But I had time to do that in the near future.

In principle, the best part of my life now was the life after school hours were over, as I started to get very busy with the extracurriculars—partying two to three times a week. Every night, I would either hang out with the Romanian crowd, with school friends or sometimes with my best friend, Ian (Iulian). For a few months, it was all fun: the music, dancing, and making new friends.

Because of my old fears about trying new things (which I still have today), I never took hashish or grass, so I was a good boy in this sense—apart from the smoking.

It was during these years that I also started smoking excessively, successfully hiding it from my parents for about a year until we moved again. I kept my cigarettes in a secret hiding place, a big hole in the wall near my building.

The second significant touchstone in my life was transferring to a high school closer to home, which spared me from the long bus rides and left my friends in Holon behind. I made new friends in Bat Yam, very many of whom I met either by accident or through my new classmates. There, we, too, were divided into two groups: the Romanian-born and the Israelis. We sometimes switched from Hebrew to Romanian when talking to each other.

I became a mail carrier in the summer of 1971, and it turned out to be fun. I woke up early, around 6 am, so I could be at work by 7. From 10 am until 2 pm, I'd walk the streets, handing out letters, seeing every kind of man. It was also a social aspect of work; I'd catch up with the neighbors and meet a lot of really nice people. Sometimes, I would meet married women who seemed...well, sexually adventure-seeking. I was only 16 years old and wanted to keep my job and not get into a scandal, so I stuck to the straight and narrow!

Every other week, I would go to Haifa to see my grandmother and cousin. Since my grandparents lived in the outskirts of Haifa, we would use public transport—something that was available on Saturdays in Haifa (no other city in the country left public transport open on the Sabbath, from sunset on Friday until the stars became visible on Saturday. That would have been seen as violating religious precepts). The whole family came to see us at least once a month; our day was never quiet on a Saturday.

It was another year, and while school was OK, I was a very good student again. But all the general knowledge I'd accumulated was still so overwhelming that most of the Israeli kids had never heard of it. I continued to go to parties every weekend. A pattern was set during school seasons.

I got mixed up in the Romanian-born and in the Israelis, and we alternated between the two in a Hebrew-Romanian. I made friends with other boys who loved sports, especially basketball, and some who were into music. We spent many afternoons listening to Roxy Music, Creedence Clearwater Revival, David Bowie, and Brian Eno, all of which were blending into the fabric of my teenage years.

And then, the summer of 1972 began. My friends and I would go to the beaches; Bat Yam's beach is 2 kilometres away or half an hour by foot.

The Bar-Barim Club

During that vibrant period of my life, we stumbled upon a gem of a club called *Bar-Barim,* nestled in the bustling downtown area of Tel Aviv. This club became our sanctuary for music and live entertainment, a haven where the rhythm of life pulsed with every beat.

Every Tuesday evening, we eagerly made our way there, drawn by the promise of fresh rock and jazz performances. Bar-Barim was legendary, a hotspot highlighting a different group each week, transforming the space into a lively jam session that echoed into the early hours of the morning.

The atmosphere was electric, filled with the energy of enthusiastic musicians and eager fans. We lost ourselves in the music, revelling in performances by local legends, like *The Churchills* and *Platina*, as well as talented solo artists who brought their own flair to the stage. It was a fantastic place, alive with the sounds of creativity and camaraderie, and we soaked up every moment of that musical magic.

The Kibbutz

One winter December day in 1971, the school announced that we would go on a week-long trip to work in a kibbutz. The week would run from Sunday to

Friday, which frustrated me at once since it fell during the New Year celebration and would ruin my planned party. Nevertheless, we went. Upon arriving, we were given rooms with four beds, each suitable for four people. The kibbutz had all the facilities: tennis courts, an indoor basketball court, a football field, a beautiful dining room adorned with flowers around the windows where all meals were served, a small disco, and a shop where anyone could buy extra necessities.

A 'kibbutz' (plural kibbutzim) means grouping or gathering in Hebrew. It is a community where people voluntarily live and work together on a noncompetitive basis. The first kibbutzim were organised by idealistic young Zionists at the beginning of the 20th century. Despite many hardships, they succeeded in creating a social system and a way of life that has played a crucial role in the development of the State of Israel. Most kibbutz members work in some section of the kibbutz economy or in one of its maintenance units. Routine jobs, such as dining room duties, are rotated among members. When too few members are available for a particular job, outside workers may be hired and paid wages or given room and board on the kibbutz.

Kibbutzim, like any other society, is made up of individuals who are all different from one another. Some members of the kibbutz are strongly in agreement with the pioneer spirit that founded the kibbutz. Many others, if not pioneers themselves, are the children of those pioneers who are now grown up and have families of their own. They are called 'sabras' or people who were born in Israel. ('Sabra/tsabar' refers to a type of cactus fruit, which is hard and prickly on the outside yet sweet and tender on the inside.)

Many kibbutz members, however, do not fit this stereotypical image. Lots of 'kibbutznikim' (plural of kibbutznik—a resident of a kibbutz) look like people from your hometown. They may, in fact, even come from a place like your hometown! Many members of kibbutzim are 'olim' (immigrants) from foreign countries, such as the United States, Australia, South Africa, Russia, and many countries around Europe. Hebrew may not be their native language, but they all speak Hebrew, as it is the primary language spoken in Israel.

Some older members of kibbutzim were true pioneers in the early days of the founding of the state. Try meeting someone who was a founding member of the kibbutz where you are staying and ask them to tell you stories about the early days of the kibbutz. It is a great way to practice Hebrew.

Because I came from a different culture, I viewed the grounds and facilities of the kibbutz differently than the members. For the kibbutz members, the entire kibbutz is home rather than just a house with four walls. This is where my issues started. First, I brought a bottle of vodka from home for the New Year celebration. We were then assigned jobs to do from 5:00 am until 2:00 pm. My job was to pick oranges. I had a big sack and a schedule of two hours of work followed by a half-hour break, repeated throughout the day.

For the first two days, I worked hard. However, I soon noticed that the system was quite lenient, so I began to make my own rules. Breaks extended from half an hour to one or two hours. It was very pleasant to sit under the orange trees and feel the wind blowing gently.

The New Year party was not customary for the kibbutz, but we celebrated nevertheless. The next morning, I declared myself indisposed (I felt ill, as I had drunk too much) and didn't get into the fields. Bored, I went at noon to the tennis courts with a 'sick' fellow student—being sick myself—and started to play. The supervisor drove up on his tractor and yelled: 'Sick, eh? Next time I catch you, you will be sent home.' We hurried back to our room.

At some point, the afternoon would roll around, and we'd play a round of tennis or basketball. Then, in the evening, we all went to the disco to dance. If I remember it today, it must have been a good memory.

Insight of Israel in Those Days

A little about Israel in those years: The failure of the Rogers Plan led Nixon to halt efforts to reach a settlement with the Soviets, aligning with Henry Kissinger's argument against pressuring Israel for concessions while Egypt remained Soviet-aligned. In the summer of 1970, Nixon allowed Secretary of State

William Rogers to present 'Rogers II,' a plan to halt the Israeli Egyptian 'War of Attrition' along the Suez Canal, resulting in a three-month ceasefire starting 7th August.

However, Egyptian and Soviet military maneuvers, along with Syrian intervention in Jordan, diminished Nixon's appetite for diplomacy.

In September 1970, King Hussein of Jordan expelled the PLO, leading to Syrian invasion efforts thwarted by Israeli troop movements. This is how the 'Black September' terror group was created and acted in Munich the following year. The PLO then shifted to Lebanon, contributing to the Lebanese Civil War. President Nasser's death and Anwar Sadat's succession in Egypt coincided with a wave of Soviet Jewish emigration attempts to Israel, which were met with repression.

In February 1971, Sadat proposed reopening the Suez Canal if the IDF withdrew, but Israel opposed this, and Kissinger and Nixon provided little support. Kissinger prioritised avoiding Middle East discord before the 1972 Moscow summit. Sadat's 1972 expulsion of Soviet advisers and frequent Egyptian Syrian invasion exercises led to Israeli complacency and failure to mobilise despite warnings of an impending attack.

Jack Passing

That summer, we lost my dad's brother, Jack, to a long battle with lung cancer. He was only in his early

60s and had always been so vibrant, so the diagnosis came as a sudden, cruel thrashing.

From the day he heard that he had been diagnosed, he lived for about four aversive weeks, his final days in Haifa's Italian Hospital. The pain he was going through was awful to watch, and the whole family was gathered around him in love and despair.

Jack had been a sweet, lively person, and his death left a long trail. I remember my father and grandmother were devastated. They could not believe it; it was an agonizing experience watching my grandmother grieve her son, and it made the process nearly unlivable. As we reassembled ourselves, another terrible thing happened that made that period more devastating still.

The Olympic Games 1972

One of the most powerful moments in my early life happened during the Munich Games of 1972 when members of the Palestinian terrorist group 'Black September' took hostage 11 Israeli Olympic team members. On 5th September, eight terrorists broke into the Olympic Village, entered the Israelis' quarters, and shot and killed two of the team immediately. The other nine were held hostage, their lives promised in exchange for the release of 234 Palestinian prisoners in Israel and two German terrorists in Germany.

Over the following 20 hours, a tense standoff in the Olympic Village unfolded in full view of the world's media. West German authorities tried to negotiate with the terrorists, who, in turn, demanded to be flown out of the country to Cairo. It was agreed that they would be taken to the Forstenfeldbrück airbase, as was a group of hostages. The plan was to ambush them on the flight line. The rescue was poorly planned and communicated, made worse by a lack of training for counterterrorism.

In the ensuing carnage, the nine other hostages perished, along with five of the terrorists themselves and one German Polizei. The Olympic Games were put on hold temporarily, the world was shocked, and the very notion of terrorist violence on an international stage was given shocking new meaning. For us personally, our sports coach, Yakov Springer, a weightlifting judge, was among those who had been killed.

Indeed, the Munich Massacre provoked shifts in approaches to terrorism and to the security of major international events because it was an unprecedented accident that served as a wake-up call for world security. This attack profoundly affected me and our country. The day after, all the students from my school were standing proud in front of the German Embassy in Tel Aviv. I still remember how deeply we were hit by this atrocious attack.

My First Love

That fall, I met my very own first love. We were both

16. Her name was Lena. She was of Romanian origins, delicate and beautiful. I never had such a special girl in my life. *This is the real one,* I said to myself, after the party at my friend Daniela's, where I was the DJ. I played 'Across the Universe' by *The Beatles* and asked her for a dance. It was my first real woman since Sinaia.

Lena was tall, black-haired, and sportive in her grace, with warm olive skin, hazel eyes and a thousand stories in them. Her full, natural rose lips were the most beautiful I'd seen. She wore a deep burgundy sweater over dark jeans and thigh-high boots. She stood tall, and I was right. She was magnificent.

It was in that evening that I discovered she was going to Germany the next day. I was sad, but I took her to the taxi stand, the farthest from Daniela's home that I could find. We walked hand in hand, kissing each other passionately on the lips until we arrived at the taxi stand. We hugged and kissed until it was already 3 am. She asked that I let her go, and I did, but the pain was intolerable. I almost choked. We exchanged letters constantly for a year, and she told me that she could not continue the relationship anymore. She was my first love. Since then, I have always dreaded having a relationship for fear of getting my heart broken.

I have such vivid memories of those years spent at Daniela's place, in her tiny room, where we often squeezed in up to 10 people at a time. It was one big mess of a time, a huge period of happiness, an era of music that we lived as teenagers. We played the music legends of the time on full blast—Leonard Cohen, Janis Joplin, Jimi Hendrix, Neil Young, and Pink Floyd—letting the air of the room get stale with the smoke of cigarettes.

There, we spread out everywhere in that little room—on the floor, on the couch, and underneath the desk, sharing stories with each other over whiskey, beer, and cognac. This was cool, a slice of our childhood rebellion, and it was comfortable and so freeing. I enjoyed it when I did it, and so much of what was cool about it was because of my dad. He'd helped me fall in love with music and classical pieces that I still appreciate for their craftsmanship. So, those late-night sessions were, in some sense, an extension of that musical education. They were parties, yes, but they were more than parties. They were a continuation of my life's soundtrack, combined with our lives and friendship.

Gaby

But the attraction struck again at another gathering a year later when I encountered Gaby, a medium-height girl with vivacious blue eyes and great physique. Her mouth—broad and guileless—could tell tales that would seduce you into the furthest reaches of time.

Gaby had a slender build, smoky eyes, and was flat-breasted, with a certain radiance in her demeanour. What distinguished her, however, was the manner with which she traversed the room—this magnetic savoir-faire that left you no choice but to follow her defiantly swaying hips to the beat of her own enthralling music. I knew my parents were away that weekend, and she wanted to go home, so I offered to take her to my house.

"Do you mind if we go to my house?" I said. She was so lovely and such a giving and open lover, ready for sex straight away. My grandmom was sleeping hard in her room, and the door to her room was closed.

I will be quiet, I said to myself, *so she will never know.* We wanted to have sex. After we had just gorged on each other, we had a drink (whiskey) to get in the mood. Then, in my parents' room, I took her clothes off; mine were off already. She was ready to fuck very quickly, and we made love again and again. We ended up sleeping together. It was an event kind of a thing. That was the first time I had made love, at 16 years old.

At five o'clock in the morning, I woke up, moved Gaby to the living room, and went back to sleep in my parents' bedroom (so that my grandmom would not know what happened). In the morning, the first thing she did was check softly who was there sleeping on the couch in the living room and started shouting and screaming: "What are you bringing to our house, all the whores in Israel????"

I was so embarrassed that I had to take Gaby to a Taxi station and let her go to her home. My grandmother told my parents about me engaging intimately with her the night before. My parents were happy and said, "Good for him!" I was relaxed. I met

Gaby several times after; some led to sexual encounters, and some did not.

Ian

Yes, my friend Ian (really Iulian) was the best guy but also the worst delinquent. He was the only fighter among all the gangs of Bat Yam. My home was his only escape from his father, who was always beating him both mentally and physically. Many times, he escaped to my house and slept on the floor. I always had covers and blankets for him, but my grandmother didn't like him. Every time he was there, and she would pass by the living room, she would say, "Why do you bring home such a bum?"

My parents didn't mind if he was there.

One night, I had a party at my house and invited all my friends. More than one incident happened that night.

One was when Ian and I had an argument, and I locked him in the kitchen. After 15 minutes, he managed to get out through my parents' room. He was crazy enough to go out the porch window and open my parents' room window (about 4 meters away).

The second incident occurred when some of the guests got stuck in the elevator. Daniela, who was in the elevator, started crying and shouting out of fear. When I finally succeeded in releasing the elevator, she fainted. Ian quickly brought her back to consciousness by giving her two quick slaps.

After completing 10th and 11th grade in Bat Yam, I decided I should quit school and go to a private institution to get my maturity diploma. This was a turning point in my life. During the day, I worked at the biggest record store in Israel called Alhut; they had three stores. I took over the main one, and I was in charge of managing one of the branches where my friend, Daniela, worked. The owner, Tommy, was at the second one. I would go there sometimes to help him, too.

In the afternoons, I did some study to prepare for the exams that would complete my university degree and kept up with the record store commitments that made my study possible. In the evenings, I was out and about, going to parties with friends and enjoying a social scene that made being young and free feel like a thrill. This was one of the happiest periods of my life. This might seem odd for someone, especially a student, but most nights, I was out with my new acquaintances, most of whom I first met in those years. Working, studying, and partying made for a vibrant, exhilarating life.

To make the long story short, I was having the time of my life (at that point), having fun, going to parties, smoking, and drinking. Girls were there for me to have sex with occasionally.

CHAPTER 4
Israel and the 1973 War

On Friday, 5th October, we went out to be together as it was Yom Kippur Eve. As we walked around, we noticed many cars moving, which was unusual because on Yom Kippur, all of Israel's stops—cars, buses, everything, even the airport—were closed. This did not move us much, but it did make us wonder.

October 6th, 1973

Saturday afternoon, 6th October, at exactly 2 pm, the sirens started sounding. I was home with my mom and cousin, who worked at the telephone exchange (all international calls went through them). She told us that something was going to happen. My father and grandmother were both in the synagogue, praying for Yom Kippur—the Day of Atonement, the holiest day of the year in Judaism and Samaritanism.

The Yom Kippur War

In 1973, a coalition of Arab states, led by Egypt and Syria, attacked Israel, sparking the Yom Kippur War.

Believing that the IDF would be unprepared to defend Israel on the holiest day of the Jewish year, the Arab states coordinated a surprise attack on Yom Kippur. The war ended 18 days later, on 24th October 1973, when a ceasefire was declared. The war began with Egyptian troops and armour crossing the Suez Canal in southern Israel and Syrian forces entering the Golan Heights in northern Israel. After three weeks of heavy fighting, the IDF overcame initial Egyptian and Syrian gains, advancing to the western side of the Suez Canal and approaching Damascus. This forced the Egyptians and Syrians to accept new ceasefire arrangements.

Historical Context

After the Six-Day War in 1967, Israel gained new territories and, therefore, faced new challenges. The IDF had to guard the Sinai border along the Suez Canal, where it installed many posts on what was called the Bar-Lev line. The Golan Heights was also added territory for the IDF to defend. After being swiftly defeated in the Six-Day War, the Arab countries surrounding Israel wanted to redeem themselves and looked to regain lost territories. In 1972, the Egyptian and Syrian militaries rebuilt themselves from the ground up. By October 1972, Anwar Sadat, President of Egypt, was already speaking about attacking Israel in private meetings with his army staff.

Negotiations in the following years led to disengagement agreements, under the terms of which

Israel withdrew from parts of the territories captured by the IDF during the Yom Kippur War. The Yom Kippur War was the third time in less than three decades since its establishment that Israel was forced to fight a war for its very existence.

For us new immigrants, it was the first war we were subjected to, and obviously, we were a little scared. My father was at once mobilised, and he drove to a military base. From there, they used our car to transport people in need. All the buses were mobilised for the war, so there was no public transportation. I started volunteering: in the mornings; I helped in the record store, which seemed unnecessary but had to be kept. In the afternoon, I worked at the telex exchange. In the evening, I patrolled the streets, telling people to close their blinds to avoid light exposure in case of an air strike. I worked tirelessly, holding down three jobs to contribute to the war effort. I was travelling by hitchhiking from one place to another, waking up at 7 am and going to bed at 2 or 3 am. This period assessed my resilience and determination, solidifying my commitment to making a difference in any way I could.

The war ended on 24th October, but life never fully returned to normal. It took months to restore normality. During this time, I continued volunteering at the record store and telephone exchange until the end of December.

Elections 1973

General elections took place on the last day of 1973, and for the first time, I was eligible to vote for parliament. Ian was working as a member of the election board in our sector. We celebrated New Year's Eve at a party of friends at someone's flat in Jaffa. Around 1 pm, but it was still buzzing with people: old friends and new friends lined up for drinks, life and laughter. As usual, I was the DJ.

Gaby had a new boyfriend with her, but as soon as we locked eyes, the flames of our old chemistry flared. We began kissing and touching right there, our lip locks and heavy petting revealing what we had been hiding. Ian brought a bottle of J&B whiskey. As his best friend, I took the bottle and shared it with Gaby, laughing and flirting with her increasingly.

After the midnight kiss, we made love in one of the rooms of the house. She closed her eyes, and mine, dark as treacle toffee, gazed down at her. We were high or drunk, or both

We were both naked, and our friends, in search of us, entered the room and found us. Gaby's boyfriend left without saying a word. Ian had to take a taxi to bring me home, making sure I was OK and not completely unconscious. The following day was a working day, and I had to call in sick. I couldn't go to work.

For the next two or three months, it was a routine of

working during the day and studying in the evening, with no special memories besides the growing boredom with my studies. I knew, however, that this would soon be the end of my school journey.

When it was time for the maturity diploma exams, I passed all the exams with decent grades and was ready to go to university. I applied for medicine school, knowing that my chances of getting into a program in Israel were slim. I wanted freedom and wanted to study abroad. I took the tests for medicine studies in Jerusalem and Tel Aviv but did not make the cut in either one. So, I started investigating where I should go.

New Start

After meeting Dan Radu, a new friend, we both decided to study in Milan, Italy. Dan was a new friend with whom I spent my first four years in Italy. Since then, I stayed connected with him in Germany, where he worked as a doctor. Dan was also born in Romania and was a newcomer to Israel. He finished high school at Neurim, a school near the city of Netanya that was like a college for new immigrants from Romania. He was smart and very funny, an expert at jokes and humour, and a particularly good friend. Unfortunately, he died in 2022 from Alzheimer's disease.

Through my mother's friends, we knew that a certain guy by the name of Andy would start at the same time at the university in Milan. So, the plan was to contact him as soon as we arrived in Milan. We started planning our trip before the studies began, travelling from Paris (where Dan had another friend) and finishing in Milan.

CHAPTER 5
Trip to Europe Before the Studies

We had risked our travelling plans before our application had been approved by the University of Milan; therefore, only after that moment did we purchase our tickets and move on. Eurail Passes allow for unlimited first-class travel between European countries for a fixed price (within a period of 21, 30, or 45 days) and is a beautiful way to visit more than one city in a short time, as travel nights aren't considered when it comes to ticket validation. We bought two one-way tickets from Tel Aviv to Paris and a Eurail Pass, valid for 21 days from the first day of use. Our journey was supposed to have started on a warm, sunny day in mid-August.

Paris

I was 19, and Dan, who was 21, had arranged for his friend, Radu, to meet us. Radu and his family—his parents and his younger sister—were in Paris and on their way to Canada, getting their papers from Canadian authorities. Paris in 1974 was the place where old-world charm and modernity, just starting to bloom, were harmoniously intertwined. You could step into the street, and the smells of fresh baguettes and buttery croissants from the boulangeries, bistros, and cafés with their foie gras, escargots and wine enveloped you. It seemed to be bathed in soft, gentle, weathered colours; the buildings, many from the Haussmann era, with their creamy beige facades, lined the broad avenues with green wrought-iron balconies brimming with plants. The streets in Montmartre and the Marais were abloom with colour, as artists dotted the corners with their small easels.

Mini markets on almost every corner sold fresh vegetables, cheeses, and pastries, their displays wafting the smells of ripe fruit over musty, earthy cheeses like Roquefort and Camembert. Paris in this era tasted simple and decadent: bread and soft cheese, coq au vin, red wine and herbs, and the heady kick of thick, dark, bitter-sweet espresso.

The Seine was alive with Parisians and tourists alike browsing through the books and artwork on offer in the bouquinistes' stalls along the quai—a damp stone smell heavy with earthy moss, softened by gardens such as the Jardin des Tuileries, where the scent of roses and greenery mingled with the city. In the narrow streets of places such as Saint-Germain-des-Prés, there was the slight smell of tobacco from sidewalk cafés, where

Parisiens with dark-rimmed glasses and insouciant trench coats sat at tables, arguing about books over a café au lait and in equal numbers observed the world go by.

Social currents were swirling through Paris in the first half of 1974, and modern art and music contributed to that period. Flavors, colours, and aromas of the earlier Belle Époque were fading. A revolution was beginning to infuse daily life. In-person, Paris was the archetype of this transformation.

We went from from the airport by bus and eventually got to Radu's apartment in Montmartre. We finished dinner and began to search for a room where we might stay. We looked for the best deal close to Radu's home, which we found for the sum of about 25 francs (or 5 US dollars). The location provided six or seven floors, and we ended up with a room on the fifth floor with no elevator, two beds, a table, and toilets in the corridor. There was no breakfast option. The huge window looking across a Montmartre street was the highlight. We did not mind the street noise. We were youngsters then. The location and the room offered a place to fall asleep, and that was all.

It was the first time I had been alone, abroad, in a foreign city, but I wasn't scared; I was convinced that we would be getting wasted and having the time of our lives, and that was exactly what we did. We had stared at the obelisk at Place de la Concorde before returning to Radu's flat to avoid going up and down to our hotel room too often.

After dinner in the evenings, we left Radu's family, and took to the Paris streets together, singing in English Louis Armstrong tunes. The next day, in Saint-Germain-des-Prés, we visited the ancient church, one of the first to be built in Paris. There are two main roads near the church: Rue De l'Abbaye, which leads to Rue de Buci, one of the most bustling eating and drinking streets in Paris. We went through St-Michel and Rue Soufflot to Notre Dame de Paris, browsing the area and lying down on the grass in front of the Gothic cathedral. There, we napped. After that, it was on to the Panthéon, where we hiked up Montagne Sainte Geneviève and then walked through the beautiful gardens of Jardin du Luxembourg, with the Senate enthroned within its walls. We would end the day with another dinner followed by another walk, a gift that just kept on giving.

Having spent a glorious five days in Paris, it was time for us to begin our travels. We chose to start in Munich, Germany. An overnight train was booked, leaving Gare du Nord in Paris at 8 pm and arriving at Hauptbahnhof in Munich the next day around 10 am. Upon arrival in Munich, we made our way to the tourist board to enquire about accommodation. After a little time, a very pleasant young lady found us a budget pension in the city center. This was our kind of place; being on such a small budget, the cheaper the accommodation could be, the better. It could be walked to most places; we weren't too bothered about the view, just a clean and secure bed for the night.

Checked in and freshened up, we were ready to explore.

Munich

From the windows of St Peter's Church and the Neues Rathaus (New Town Hall), two of Munich's most beautiful towers have been at its centre for centuries and still shape the city's skyline. The surrounding area—such as Marienplatz, Munich's lively central square, which is full of goings-on all through the year—is one of the city's busiest spots. The other seething traffic hub is Karlsplatz, although it's so much more than just a place for crossing off your shopping list. Locals love it and simply call it 'Stachus.' If something in Munich is busy, you'll hear it being described as 'like Stachus.'

The half-circular square is full of hustle and bustle in summer as the fountain down in the middle attracts people from all points of the compass. At any time of the year, the surrounding stone seats offer weary feet somewhere to stop. In summer, the square is the place to see and be seen; but in winter, a short detour takes you up to the atmospheric half-timbered houses of the Rose-Insel housing estate. At the western end of the pedestrian zone, you'll spot some strange-looking characters in summer, too—but not just any kind of strange. Anyone who walks through Stachus will see the walls of the old Karlstor city gate, complete with smiling faces—something the city fathers had added in the early 20th century to lighten the spirits of those entering or living in the city. A little northwards and eastwards from Stachus, you find Odeonsplatz with its monumental Feldherrnhalle looking more Italian than Teutonic. Further eastwards, the view along Ludwigstraße towards the Siegestor arch needs no embellishment however often it may be seen.

That night, we had our first genuine Bavarian beer gardens, and we ate a lot of pretzel, wurst, and beer. The next day, we checked out of the hotel, stowed our luggage at the train station, and wandered more of Munich, drinking coffee and more of the beer and wurst until it was time to get on our train directly to Copenhagen, Denmark.

Train Adventure

There was an empty compartment in the train, also with wonderfully retro seats that could be unfolded into beds. Two American women were in one compartment with their children. Dan and I had the luxury of one compartment to ourselves. One of the women came over and asked if I wanted to join her and her little boy in her compartment. I thought: 'Yes, I'd quite like that.'

It struck me as very strange. Here, she was confiding to me about her marital problems, and then suddenly, we were going at it like wild animals on a train. It was one of the most memorable sexual experiences of my life, and I still wonder how she could have done something like that with a man almost 15 years her junior and with her small son sitting right there. It was pretty challenging but full of sex, and I loved it.

It was an experience I could not fully grasp at the time. Later, I realised why an affair had such appeal when I found myself in the vicarious grip of forbidden desire. My surprise grew even further when I later discovered that Dan had found himself in precisely the same situation.

Copenhagen

The following day, we checked into a hostel with an eight-bed dorm and curfew. We saw the two women again that afternoon, walking through Copenhagen, but without acknowledging each other this time. From the outset, we liked Copenhagen: it was a beautiful city of palaces, museums, parks, and waterfronts. A haven of counterculture and permissiveness, it felt sunnier and more congenial than anywhere we had been before.

The highlight was the Tivoli Gardens Amusement Park; oh, how delightful it was. We found the city's attitude towards sex liberal in a way that surprised us: in the center, every other shop seemed to be a sex shop. We visited Nyhavn Harbor, famous for its coloured houses and many restaurants and bars. A highlight was the autonomous neighborhood of Freetown Christiania, which had a strong hippy culture.

While strolling around the quaint City Hall Square and the inside of Copenhagen City Hall, we finally had the chance to indulge in people-watching in the true Copenhagenian spirit, feeling the relaxed vibe of the city and catching a glimpse of the Danish way of life. We also visited Amalienborg Palace, the official winter residence of the Queen, where the Danish active royal family was on clear display. On our final day in Copenhagen, we returned to Tivoli Gardens, this time experiencing it at night, all lit up.

Onward to Düsseldorf

Next was a wedding in Düsseldorf, Germany, of Dan's friend (whose name, incidentally, was Anca). We took the night train. We travelled part of the way by ferry from Neustadt to Puttgarden in Germany, between these two countries in the Baltic Sea. In addition to the fun though the decidedly unromantic allure of ferry travel, is the crossing between the two countries—where travelling by train, instead of by whatever wheels the ferry employs to transport a large, flat, metal structure, becomes a vivid moment in the otherwise more or less prosaic feeling of long-distance travel—offers a bit of unlikely adventure.

Düsseldorf

Upon arriving in Düsseldorf, Dan's friends met us at the train station and drove us to their apartment. They generously provided us with a room that had all the comforts we hadn't experienced since leaving Israel.

Düsseldorf in 1974 was a city embracing post-war modernity, blending German structure with a deep-rooted sense of tradition. Its architecture ranged from sleek, modern buildings with sharp lines and large glass facades to sturdy, pre-war stone structures in grey and beige. Although the city had an industrial feel, tree-lined streets softened the landscape, especially along the Rhine River—a silver-blue ribbon cutting through the city, casting a cool glow along the bustling promenade. In quieter residential neighborhoods, the fresh scent of rain on stone pathways was common, as the city's frequent drizzle gave the streets a crisp, clean fragrance.

We prepared for the wedding, a wonderfully elegant celebration in contrast to the more casual weddings we were used to in Israel. We had a fantastic time, enjoying the festivities with dancing, food, and plenty of drinks—perfectly fine since we were only guests. We stayed for another two days, exploring the local stores and indulging in a bit of carefree fun, just like we had in Paris.

Frankfurt

Instead of an overnight train, we traveled to Frankfurt by day, staying with Dan's friend, Dan Lazarovici, who lived on the outskirts of the city. During our two or three days with him and his family, we visited Frankfurt twice. We explored the Opera House, the main shopping areas, and the old town, which was filled with lively bars and music venues. One unique experience was visiting Frankfurt's regulated red-light area, housed in specific apartment buildings. Each room had an open-door policy for available rooms and closed doors if occupied, with the workers undergoing regular medical checks.

Frankfurt in 1974 was a blend of traditional German charm and modern financial vigor. Rebuilt after wartime damage, the city had become Germany's financial powerhouse. The skyline hinted at the future 'Manhattan' with its emerging skyscrapers. Along the Main River and the city's older areas, industrious energy filled the air, especially near the Hauptbahnhof (Central Station), where travellers, commuters, and international visitors crossed paths. This area was vibrant but had a gritty edge, reflecting the city's working-class roots. We enjoyed local fare, including Frankfurters and goulash soup, making for a uniquely memorable experience.

Amsterdam

Our last stop was Amsterdam, a city in 1974 brimming with freedom, creativity, and an unmistakable Dutch charm. The scent of the canals, a mix of damp stone, moss, and earth, felt uniquely part of Amsterdam's character. Bicycles filled the streets, and the scent of rain on metal frames and a hint of motor oil lingered near busier areas, like Central Station. There was also an undeniable sense of liberation in the air; coffee shops, new icons of the counterculture movement, emitted a light aroma of herbal tobacco and coffee.

Amsterdam, founded at the mouth of the Amstel River, evolved from a small 12th-century fishing village into a major port city during the Dutch Golden Age. Known for its openness and tolerance, the city had become one of the world's most multicultural hubs, home to about 180 nationalities.

Once we checked into the Eden Hotel, conveniently located on the riverbanks, we received a room on the fourth floor with no elevator—a good warm-up for exploring the city. We ventured through Amsterdam's historic canals, Dam Square (home to the Royal Palace), and the Anne Frank House. We also walked through the Red-Light District, with its unique atmosphere, and even found ourselves in a cannabis coffee shop, entirely unaware of what was being sold inside as we'd entered looking for beer.

We took a short trip to see the famous Dutch windmills and the countryside outside Amsterdam. Just 20 minutes away by train, Haarlem offered a rich landscape of culture, shops, and cafes. We also visited The Hague, the Netherlands' official capital, where we strolled through the Hofkwartier, a shopping district filled with charming boutiques. Our visit ended with a brisk walk along the North Sea beaches, a beautiful, rugged shoreline that stood in contrast to the warm, turquoise waters of other European coasts.

Reflection

This journey through Paris and other European

cities was filled with unforgettable experiences, marking the beginning of an adventure that would soon take us to Milan and beyond. Looking back, it was the start of a deeper transformation into a true traveller, not yet fully aware of the path that lay ahead but beginning to embrace the unknown with open arms.

CHAPTER 6
Italy—University First Year

As soon as we arrived in Milan, we headed to a sublet apartment in Città Studi (the City of Studies). This apartment was a sublet from Nadia, a friend of Dan's. Dan had many friends who proved to be extremely helpful to us in every city and all over the continent. I was so jealous of this.

Milan

In the autumn of 1974, Milan was full of life, a riot of cultural attractions and architectural treasures. The leaves were just starting to fall from the trees, their smell mixing with the earthy autumnal air as they scattered themselves across the pavement, picking up the smell of focaccia and coffee from the trattoria on the street corners nearby.

There was something nice about the smell of the city. Pleasant, suggestive, inviting. Coffee wafted from busy cafés, mingling with the sugary scents of pastries drifting from bakeries—especially the warm brioche and cornetto. There were roasted chestnuts with warm notes that you could smell in the street. There was even, on occasion, the scent of leather, especially around the fashion districts, where the precious alchemies of high-end shops were displayed.

Milanese fall cuisine was a rustic delight, full of sustenance, and representative of a bountiful season. Risotto alla Milanese, creamy saffron-dyed rice, was a local favorite, best consumed in a warm, cozy, laughter-filled trattoria. Seasonal radicchio (chicory) and pumpkin lent hearty flavours to many dishes; they added colour to this typically monochrome season. Fall meals were accompanied by the consumption of full-bodied wines, with Lombardian varietals being the best local bet.

In Milan in the fall, the colours were warm and glowing. The golden yellows, deep oranges, and rich reds of trees lining the streets added a dramatic counterpoint to the grey and beige stone of the city's architecture. The Milanese liked to dress for the season, and earth tones were combined with bright scarves and accessories that punctuated the urban landscape with splashes of colour.

Shop windows crammed with seasonal colours advertised this city's style to the world. Fashion, art, and creativity boomed in Milan in 1974, turning the city into a nexus of cultures:

'The Milanese were sharply dressed, in tailored suits or feminine skirts and blouses. 'Everyone spoke with a different accent. You could hear people meeting for coffee or an aperitivo or chatting about art, politics, football, and the latest fashion shows. Street performers often played their instruments in front of crowds in the squares.'

Foreigners rubbed shoulders with locals, and the diversity of languages, cultures, and sensibilities lent vibrancy to the urban fabric. Art tourists eagerly explored the collection of the Pinacoteca di Brera or the graceful Duomo, while visitors from abroad interacted with Milanese residents, swapping stories and suggestions over shared plates of food.

To sum it up, Milan that autumn day in 1974 was a feast for the senses: the smells of food, the colours of fall, and the energy of the city's residents was remarkable and still remain in my mind's eye, ready to embrace my next visit to this remarkable city. After a relaxing evening pausing and unwinding following a month of travelling, we at once started looking for an apartment to rent. Being quite naive and not fluent in the language, we learned some basic Italian phrases to ask the women who managed the buildings if there were any apartments for rent.

Looking For an Apartment

In Italy in 1974, each building typically had a caretaker, often a woman, responsible for monitoring who entered the building, supporting the premises, and keeping everything in order. In exchange for their work, these caretakers usually receive a free apartment.

So, the phrase we learned was "scusa signora—avete un appartamento per affitto?" It meant, "Pardon me, madam; do you have an apartment for rent?"

We systematically went from one street to another, asking this question in our search for an apartment. In continuation of the earlier knowledge, we contacted Andy, so we teamed up and began looking for a three-room apartment.

The trio—Andy, Dan, and I—finally found a beautiful apartment on Via dei Cibo 1, at the corner with Via Venini. It was not exactly in Città Studi, but it was centrally found, and we all decided to take it. The apartment consisted of a hall with the biggest room on the right (which Dan took), a well-equipped kitchen, a bathroom on the left, an average-sized room on the right (my room), and a smaller room on the left (Andy's room). Later, as the rent was high, we added Carol (who shared Dan's room) and Sorin (my parents' friend's son, who shared my room and was learning at the time to be a dental technician). So, we ended up with five people in a three-room apartment.

University

We then started attending our classes in the large lecture halls. We had lunch every day in the university dining room, where everything was self-service. The first course was always a different type of pasta, risotto, or polenta, followed by a meat course and dessert, with wine and water. The cost of such a meal was around three US dollars per day. After lunch, it was back to studies.

I must emphasise that we did not speak a word of Italian, and all the courses and exams were in Italian. After a short while, I felt lost in the classes as I did not understand anything. I would go back home and start reading the sports newspaper in Italian, which helped me start understanding the language better. Additionally, I watched TV every night to improve my Italian. This helped immensely.

After a couple of months, I took my first exam in biology. The teacher was furious that I could not speak perfect Italian and said, "Who the hell let all these foreigners into medical school without learning perfect Italian?" Despite her anger, I passed the test with merit, as I did with the other tests.

Centro Sociale Maurizio Levi

Meanwhile, we discovered a Jewish centre in Milan, Centro Sociale Maurizio Levi, named after Maurizio, who was killed in the Six-Day War in Israel. I became the DJ there, working on Saturday evenings and sometimes for unique events on Sunday afternoons. I was on cloud nine, doing what I loved and getting paid for it. That was only the beginning. It was then that we met Carol Hoffner (who later became a full part of the 5 Marvelous). He introduced himself as a fantastic cook and poker player, so we took him in.

We decided to take over the bar in the centre, giving us a part-time job every evening from Sunday to Thursday, from 6 pm until 11 pm. On Saturdays, I continued working as a DJ until 1 am. We involved all our friends, taking turns participating in the bar activities.

The centre itself was quite expensive. Besides the dancing room, there was a large room for playing table tennis, two big rooms for playing cards, and an exceptionally large kitchen with all the necessary utilities. There were also restrooms. Located in the centre of Milan, it was quite easy to get to. Nearby, there was a parking lot that was free at the time and some shops on Via Larga, one of the major streets in the centre of Milan. The centro was in a basement, chosen for security reasons. The entrance was on the first floor, and stairs would bring you down to the public area. On the top floor were a double security door, a security person—an Israeli who had finished their army service—a hall, and a manager's room.

The only times we had to go there in the morning were on delivery days when we received supplies, like soda, Coke, coffee, and kosher items, for preparing food and snacks. Carol managed to prepare the food.

Cars

Now to our cars. We needed them to move around the city, drive to the university, go to the centro sociale, and for little escapades out of town. We were busy in those days.

Andy got a car from his uncle, so we only had to pay for insurance and gas. It was a large Fiat 1500, part of a series of front-engine, rear-drive automobiles manufactured by Fiat from 1961 to 1967. That car was used for the transportation of goods to the sentro sociale and for long trips, as it had six seats.

Sorin had a Ford Capri, a fastback coupé built by Ford of Europe and designed by Philip T. Clark, who was also involved in designing the Ford Mustang. It used mechanical components from the Mk2 Ford Cortina and was intended as the European equivalent of the Ford Mustang.

I bought a grey Fiat 500, the successor to the 500 'Topolino.' It was an inexpensive and practical small car, measuring 2.97 meters long, and originally powered by a rear-mounted 479 cc two-cylinder, air-cooled engine. The Fiat 500 had two doors that opened in the opposite direction, so when I had brake problems, I could open the door and stop it with my foot. Later, I exchanged it with Puiu and got a red Mini Minor with USA plates instead. That was a great car, and I used it for a couple of years.

Carol had a Fiat 1100, a small family car produced from 1953 until 1969 by the Italian company Fiat. He changed to a green Giulietta 1300 after we went to a football game in Torino, having an accident coming back home, resulting in a total loss of the car.

Only Dan did not have a car then. When the streets in the city were being cleaned, we had to put all the cars on the sidewalks to leave the street open for cleaning. It was a big job.

I remember going to the centre every evening to be with the other Israeli guys and gals, as it was the main reunion point for us all.

Poker Nights

On Friday nights, when the centre was closed due to the Sabbath, we played poker at home. Sometimes, we had another 2-3 guys joining us, so we opened two tables. The other players were all Romanian guys: Puiu Cohn, a medical student who started his studies in Siena and moved to Milan; Puiu Hutter, who was studying architectural engineering. We had a full evening schedule for the whole week. We were so happy, and the only fights we had were about who would clean the dishes and how fast.

One night, we—Andy, Dan and I—headed to the ice skating rink in Milan. I, of course, needed to perform 'professional' on the ice, flying around like a master (well, I thought so). And then, voilà! I made a stupid play that I'm sure even I didn't catch. And boohoo! The agony hit me like a curse. I was in so much pain.

Andy and Dan sat there, probably debating whether to laugh or panic. Eventually, they decided on taking me to the 'hospital.' That was the real challenge. We stumbled into the ER, and a young med student—

clearly under his PPE—attempted to diagnose. For his frayed English and for our torn Italian, it became charades, us miming and gesturing until we finally got something across that I could handle the pain—for then.

When the pain finally started to ease, I finally understood this was my hernia acting up.

Enough about my pro skating!

Weekly Calls

Every Saturday morning, we had a call with Israel to speak with our parents. The one who made it happen was Vanda, a woman I got to know through my mom's cousin. She worked for the Italian telephone exchange and arranged for us to speak at home for free every Saturday morning, each taking our turn. It was such a great gesture on her part. Regardless, it was 1 hour, and she opened the line for us. Then, it was time to clean the house, another chore I disliked.

My studies went well at that time. I engaged in school and got good grades in the first year. During those years, I met many new people and got friendly with part of them. I did help some Israeli guys get to work for centro sociale (most in security positions).

Trips

We took quite a few spontaneous trips, especially on Friday nights. One night, around midnight, the five of us, plus Puiu Cohn, piled into the car and hit the road.

The original plan was Paris, but somewhere along the way, we changed course to Courmayeur instead.

Courmayeur, Italy's premier ski town, welcomed us with charming streets and Alpine views. After an early coffee and pastries, we indulged in chocolate for lunch (no protein bars back then!) before heading back to work that same afternoon.

Another time, we set out on a snowy Friday night to Cortina d'Ampezzo in the Dolomites. The snow was so intense we could barely leave the car; the biting cold was brutal.

It was then summer vacation, and I somehow broke my own misfortune record. I had a ticket from Milan to Rome, then Tel Aviv. Easy enough, right? And then, the next morning, like all good ones, I slept through my alarm and missed the flight.

I was so angry with myself that I called my parents (who were less than pleased) and ran to the airline office, begging them to alter my ticket. After what felt like a million years and several weary sighs from the staff, I found a seat for the next day.

The next morning, not wanting to make a mistake again, I rode a bus to Bergamo for the train to Rome, which was then finally to Tel Aviv. My fear turned into rage, then frustration, and then home was the sweetest relief—for me and my parents (who were probably just so happy I finally got home!).

That summer, I started working as a night shift

nurse at Belinson Hospital. They taught me how to take blood pressure, measure the pulse, give shots, draw blood, make hospital beds, and arrange patients for the daily visit of the Doctors. I worked in the Endocrinology department, with shifts starting at 11 pm and ending at 7 am every day, five times a week. My father never used the private car for work, opting instead to take the bus provided by his workplace, giving me access to their car all day long. I worked throughout my vacation to earn money and save for my expenses in Milan. During the day, when I was not sleeping, I met up with old friends like Ian or Daniela.

I often went with my family to see family on weekends or days off and drove to Haifa to visit my grandparents. Unfortunately, my grandmother, Tusca, died that fall and her absence shone bright in the family. She'd been sick with cancer, and my grandfather had taken care of her at home. Grandmother Tusca, filled with all that energy and style earlier, was refusing to go to the hospital, proud as she was of her appearance and her dignity. My mother was especially hit hard by her death, and it was during this period that I came to understand the distinction between grief and mourning.

Eventually, I had to leave and return to Milan.

CHAPTER 7
Milan, Italy—Second Year

Bureaucracy

The second year of our studies began, and we all returned to the apartment to restock the bar. Carol and Dan, who didn't go to Israel, had everything ready for our arrival. One of the first things we had to do was register with the police a yearly procedure, which was particularly annoying because of Italy's strict system for foreigners. This registration was necessary before we could start university.

The second year was focused mainly on human anatomy. There was a lot of reading material, and it was very complicated since we had never seen human parts, only read about them. We didn't have the opportunity to visit a morgue and observe post-mortem surgeries, which made it challenging, but we had to overcome it.

The studies were boring, so we started to invest more time in activities like travelling and side hustles. For example, Sorin had a side business involving arms brokering with a guy from Greece. Since Sorin didn't speak English well, I had to accompany him to various meetings as a translator.

Trips

At the end of the fall, we travelled to Greece to visit Sorin's business partner. We drove to Brindisi, a beautiful port town in Puglia, and caught the night ferry to Patras. From there, we continued by car to Athens, where we spent three days exploring the city while Dan stayed behind in Milan to manage the bar.

Athens was a treat, especially the lively Plaka neighbourhood. Nestled at the foot of the Acropolis, Palka's narrow, winding streets were lined with quaint shops, cozy cafés, and traditional tavernas. The pastel-coloured buildings, flowering balconies, and cascading bougainvillea created a vibrant atmosphere. As the sun set, locals and tourists gathered at outdoor tables, sipping ouzo and enjoying meze as traditional Greek music filled the air. Street musicians added to the charm, making the evenings especially memorable.

We stayed in a two-star hotel with a spacious room, perfect for the group, and relied on Sorin's Capri to get around. After finishing the meetings and some sightseeing of Athens, and after visiting the famous Acropolis and visiting the parliament, we were ready to go back to Milan. On the way back, the car broke down in Brindisi. While the car was repaired, we passed the time with a Bruce Lee double feature at a local cinema. After a long 10-hour drive with a couple of stops along the way, we finally arrived back in Milan at 4 am, completely worn out.

Gaby

Winter arrived, bringing with it a pleasant surprise: Gaby flew in from Israel for a wedding in Florence. She requested a couple of days of bed and board, and I was more than happy to oblige. That Saturday, we set off for a drive with Puiu Cohn to St. Moritz, eager for her to experience the magic of snow once more. St. Moritz, nestled on the southern flank of the Albula Alps below the towering Piz Nair (3,056 m), overlooks the breathtaking glaciated high valley of the Upper Engadin and the serene lake of St. Moritz. It's renowned as one of Switzerland's premier ski resorts and holiday destinations.

We travelled in my trusty Mini Minor, making the 175-km journey each way, which took about seven hours round trip in the winter chill. As we meandered through the snow-covered landscape, we enjoyed leisurely strolls along the sidewalks, admiring the stunning hotels that seemed out of reach for us. Puiu indulged in some energizing Swiss chocolate, savouring the rich flavors as we soaked in the atmosphere of this winter wonderland.

Gaby was utterly enchanted by the experience, her eyes sparkling with delight. It was as if the beauty of St. Moritz had awakened something deep within her. After returning to Milan and enjoying a casual dinner of pizza, we decided to settle back at the apartment. I discreetly asked Sorin to give us some privacy, sensing the electric tension in the air.

Once alone, Gaby, full of energy and desire, moved with a palpable eagerness. In a bold moment, she removed her panties as we drove, leaning over to surprise me with an intimate act that heightened the thrill of our adventure.

When we finally reached the room with its inviting king-size bed, I felt a rush of anticipation, knowing exactly what we both wanted. The night unfolded in a flurry of passion, but all too soon, it came to an end. Gaby had plans to meet her boyfriend in Florence the following day, leaving me with a whirlwind of memories from our enchanting winter escape.

New Year Dinner

On New Year's Eve, we decided to host a full Romanian dinner at the bar, charging an amount equivalent to 25 euros today. The menu included mititei, sarmale, dessert, and prosecco at midnight—all of which had to be kosher. We bought kosher meat and all the necessary ingredients, starting at midday to prepare the food in the club's kitchen. Suddenly, a fire broke out. I don't know what caused it. Not being sure what to do, I used a fire extinguisher to put it out. This was not the smartest idea since it was already late, and the kosher butcher had closed. Faced with a dilemma, I went to the butcher across the street and bought fresh meat, which we used along with the kosher meat that hadn't been touched by the flames. By 9 pm, we were ready to serve the food; it wasn't entirely kosher. Everyone in the club thanked us for the fantastic meal—nobody knew the truth except the five of us, at least not until today. I played music of different Janer with a very special attention to the Disco. I loved to play, especially Barry White and Donna Summers. After the event, we got home around 5 am, and we all sat on the edge of the bathtub with our feet in cold water.

Florence Easter

In the spring, during Easter, we took a train to Florence for four days. We rented a room in a charming pension with a fantastic view of the Duomo. I recall the room especially after seeing the movie, *A room with a view.* We walked through the city, soaking in its beauty and history.

On Easter night, we went to the Duomo and listened to the prayers and beautiful music. The next morning, we were spectators to a ceremony that has still been largely unchanged for centuries.

Starting around 10 am, a priest rubbed Pazzino's three flints together until they sparked and lit the Easter candle. This candle then lit some coals placed in a container on a cart. The procession delivered the Holy Fire to the Archbishop of Florence in front of Santa Maria del Fiore, better known as the Duomo. The cart was accompanied by drummers, flag throwers from the different neighbourhoods of Florence, and figures dressed in historical costumes, along with city officials and clerical representatives. We also visited the fabulous Uffizi Gallery, admired the Ponte Vecchio, and explored the Pitti Palace. We truly enjoyed the Florence experience, feeling deeply connected to its rich culture and history. After our visit, we took the train back to Milan.

Apartment Fights

Tensions were raging in the apartment, most notably between Sorin and me. As the older man, Sorin had decided that his life was devoted to teaching me how to wash, where to keep things, and basically how to act like an adult (a topic that I wasn't really interested in then). The bickering got so ridiculous that we could no longer communicate directly with each other and instead had Andy or Carol be our 'sentry.' It was like a tiny soap opera where all of the characters can't talk but must arrange laundry—and it was as frustrating as it sounds. So, I started preparing to move away.

I began searching for a new flat and a new job as the Jewish centre seemed less and less like my kind of place. Soon, I was renting a tiny room in the two-room apartment on Piazzale Susa with a guy called Salo Marcus. Salo was older, framed by glasses and a falling hairline that made him look like a scruffy old college professor. He was a silent guy who did not judge me for all my wild thoughts, which was nice after Sorin's 'command centre' vibes.

After paying a deposit for the property, I gathered my things and travelled to Israel—fortunately, without any travel misfortunes. Back in Israel, I continued working for a month at Belinson Hospital, the same job as the previous year. Having passed the anatomy classes with merit, I was ready to work as a full nurse. In the second month, I returned to working for Tomy at Alhut because I missed the store and the atmosphere. This arrangement allowed me to spend more time with my friends and avoid being tired from evening shifts. The summer passed with ease for me as I was already concentrating and looking forward to my move in September.

So, I flew back to Milan.

CHAPTER 8
Milan, Italy—Third Year

After arriving in Milan, I settled into my room in the new apartment, giving it a bed, a desk, and a large closet. Since I didn't own much besides my clothes, the move was straightforward. My parents, who could finally afford to travel abroad, came to visit for a few days. We decided to take a trip together with Sorin's parents, Jack and Dani, who were wonderful company. They took Sorin's car, and I drove mine.

Charlie

After moving into my new place, I got a dog—a small mixed breed named Charlie. He was one of the puppies from Puiu's friends, Roby and Paula. One Sunday morning, after playing tennis at Roby's home in Lainate (a town near Milan), I got Charlie back with me. At first, my roommate, Salo, was mad, but he relaxed when I assured him I would take care of the dog. Charlie was so small and cute, and although I didn't know much about taking care of him, I tried my best. The only issue was that Charlie would get overly excited and jump on and pee whenever someone rang the doorbell.

Derby Club

At that moment, I was recommended to be the DJ at Milan's Derby Club, the biggest and best cabaret in the city. I went for the audition. During that time, they said I'd spin records, but they'd also run the lights and announce the shows. But the rewards were good: nice pay, dinner on the go, and all the free alcohol any teenage DJ could desire. I was like, *'What can go wrong?'*

The first night was a revelation. The hours? Brutal. Six nights a week, I'd be at work from 9 pm till 3 am, and I still had to squeeze in some studying time (and miraculously managed to pass a couple of tests). The Derby was pulsing with artistry, craft, and an eclectic mix that felt like Milan in motion. It was where newcomers met eccentric regulars; it was where everyone could get a foot in the door. The most known artists of Italy were performing in the club and the ones less known made a mark for their future carriers.

But there was a darker side. The longer I'd been there, the more whiskey I drank as my 'coping mechanism' every night. I would mix records for a couple of hours before the shows started in a tiny little DJ booth with artists walking in and using everything from cocaine to last-minute weed smokes. I would be in search of the ultimate (and more frequent) 'subtle escape' when I needed to get away from it all: a glass of whiskey.

The club was managed by Gianni and his wife, Angela, and the members were as gregarious as you could hope to find—Gianni's cousin, Rosa, who was the mother of Diego Abatantuono, a renown Italian actor. Rosa handled the wardrobe and 'extras' for the actors and sold them to the customers in need of a hit; every detail was perfect. It was like one big dysfunctional family in which everybody played a part, even if sometimes it was untraditional.

On my free nights once a week, I would go to the movies. I was especially impressed by Federico Fellini's movie *Amarcord*, which was such a vivid and intimate experience that I will never forget it. Although I missed the centro sociale, I was content in my own way. During that year, I had the chance to see many other movies as well.

Funny trip

One Sunday morning, after an overnight layover, I drove with Puiu and his roommate, Tibi, to Bellagio on Lake Como. For those who are unfamiliar, Bellagio sits on a triangle of land at the bottom of the lake's iconic Y-shaped form, where the northern branch meets the Alps. It's one of those places where you get so caught up in the scenery that you don't even remember you haven't slept in 24 hours. Almost.

After lunch, we discovered that I would need to return to Milan for work that evening. But the traffic?

Pure chaos. Puiu had an idea (or, perhaps, it was sleep deprivation)—we'd play 'emergency ambulance.' What was he going to do? I was to sit in the backseat, arms flying through the window, waving a white handkerchief as he plowed along like a man, honking and weaving on the wrong side of the road. Individuals fled, frightened and worried.

In a sense, we made it home in time. We all laughed the rest of the time, not sure if it was the adrenaline, the lack of sleep, or the fact that my 'emergency handkerchief' was flying out the window.

Eventually, the toll of the job became too much, and I had to stop working at the end of the winter. I returned to a more normal schedule and resumed my studies in earnest.

Sima

I ran into an Israeli girl one night in Milan. She was beautiful. We ate out and then went back to her flat, which was huge and in the north of the city, with a very large, very nice living room and an even bigger bedroom.

We drank some prosecco because I wanted to stop drinking the whiskey. She was an innocent-looking woman with sharp tiger-like eyes, a straight nose, a long neck, and gorgeous, medium-length hair framing her ears. She had a beautiful mouth with full lips and seemed to always want to be kissed. We touched and kissed, slow and tender. It was a slow, languid rhythm—

effortless for both of us, as if we were shredding whatever we were before, and simply being in the moment. She was very gentle with me, and I with her. The sex was just as excellent, and throughout the evening, we found ourselves together more than once. This was the most amazing experience I had up until that point, one I would never forget. And when she woke up, she seemed transformed, as though she was a swan.

Thus, I started on the path to abandon the theoretical branch of medicine and enter the fourth year, the practical one.

CHAPTER 9
Switzerland and the Surgery

Travelling to Israel With Charlie

Of course, upon arrival in Israel, I resumed working at the same place, but this time, I shortened my vacation as my parents and I decided to take another trip abroad. Charlie would stay with them during this time. Our plan was to start in Rome, take a train to Florence, and then head to Milan. From Milan, I would drive us to Lake Maggiore, then onward to Switzerland. We intended to tour Switzerland, drive to Austria, and finally return to Milan at the end of the trip.

Trip to Switzerland

However, as we all know, reality doesn't always align with our plans. We began as planned, flying to Rome and enjoying the city. We found a small, cozy hotel near the train station called San Remo, with small rooms, including a triple room with single beds. The room had a desk, a telephone, and a radio but no TV. We attended an opera, Aida, at the Caracalla Terme amphitheater. It was a fabulous experience. I visited many different places. Since it was my parents first time in Rome-the Coliseum, the Roman Forum and the Titus Gate, we walked to Piazza Navona, The Pantheon and the Spanish steps. We also saw the Fountain of Trevi and the Barberini square and walked along the Via Veneto with its famous cafes.

Next, we travelled to Florence, where we visited the Uffizi Gallery and the Accademia Museum, home to the statue of David. We continued to the Duomo, the Baptistery, and the Ponte Vecchio. We stayed in a nice three-star hotel near the city centre. While visiting Palazzo Pitti, we were caught in a summer rain in the park and got soaking wet before we could get inside. Most of our dinners were in self-service restaurants, where the quality of the food was, at best, mediocre.

Then we took the train to Milan, stayed at my apartment for one night, and began our road adventure. During this time, I developed a painful abscess on my rear end, making sitting very difficult. Despite this, we continued driving towards Lake Maggiore. We stopped in Arona for accommodation in a hotel on the lake's shores and later visited Isola Bella and the town of Stresa.

Surgery

We headed north into Switzerland, stopping briefly in Interlaken and continuing on to Lausanne, where my parents had friends. By the time we got there, I was fairly ill, running through a series of red lights as we pulled up in front of the hotel. By the evening, I was fighting for my life, my fever reaching a dangerously high 39°C. My parents met with their friend, Leni, an anesthetist at the hospital of Lausanne, and I started my miserable evening. By 1 am, exhausted, I made my way into bed. I remember falling asleep to the sounds of the torrential rain on the roof. The next morning, I woke up feverish and spinning. That morning's news was on. The first thing I heard was: 'Elvis has died today, here in Memphis, at the age of 42.' I fainted—not because of the tragic event but because of my illness.

When I eventually woke up, two or three days had gone by, and I was in a hospital bed, my head bandaged, with a thick sucking tube running from my skull and into a bottle on the wall, draining blood slowly. I felt muddled and confused, my thoughts floating in a grey mist. The room was shared by a young girl, paralysed and completely immobile, following a motorcycle wreck. I couldn't move much, but I did have the slightly absurd ability to wiggle my fingers and toes, which contrasted strongly with her immobility. I remained unconscious for several more days, but when I regained enough consciousness, I recognised my parents, along with my aunt and uncle, Miricel and Matei, who had cut short their trip to the US to be with us.

Gradually, I returned to the land of the living, with the drainage bottle removed and only a few wires and IVs remaining. My mom told me how she'd been the one to wake up and find me gone. She immediately called an ambulance and managed (rather miraculously) to call Leni so she could join me in the ambulance. Surgeons later explained that they had found a large abscess in my brain caused by an infection originating in a back sore. The infection had travelled to my lungs and then to my brain through my bloodstream. Because of a small heart defect I was born with, there is something called VSD or Ventricular Septic Diseases that bypass the bodies' natural filters, and the infection was able to take advantage of this and travel straight up to my brain. The doctors did not see how I could possibly be moved back to Israel as my condition was too critical.

My parents had been assured by doctors in Israel that this heart defect, very small and hardly clinically noticeable, did not require any intervention, but now it had caused trouble for me. Basically, I was getting sick in one or different situations, and I have and still am blaming my parents for listening to doctors instead of getting the heart fixed once and for all.

For three weeks, I lay in a hospital room with a paralytic girl; she was mostly a piece of furniture because she lay there totally motionless. It was eerie. That time was like an eternity for me, being in that cursed room of the hospital, seeing that girl every single time I opened my eyes, being alone since it was the ICU. My parents were allowed, one at a time, and for no more than 5 minutes each. At that point, I don't suppose I would have said I wanted to be a doctor. Those weeks were my first clue that medicine was not for me, but I did not express those thoughts out loud.

Recovery

Recovery was a slow and steady process. I walked around my hospital room initially before taking a few tentative steps onto the balcony. What hit me nearly as hard as any other tumour blow was the shocking sight of my deeply incised-shaven head after the first surgery: clearly visible still are the incisions on my skull where a large piece of bone had to be removed for the biopsy, hindering all attempts at hiding the signs of my sickly state. Two weeks later, I was back in the surgery room for another operation to put the bone back where it belonged. And then I was finally discharged. As I was to stay in the area around the hospital, my parents found one of the cheapest hotels around. We relocated there for the next month.

In the morning, every day, I crossed the road and entered the cool green forest beside our hotel. At first, I could go only 50 or 100 metres, and then I had to turn back. After a few days, my father started accompanying and encouraging me. Gradually, I was able to go a little further, then a little further, until finally, I made it to the far edge of the forest three weeks later. And that became clear to me there: if I wanted to be in a state of recovery, perhaps medicine wasn't my path. I felt more strongly, day by day that I wanted to travel the world, and that was taking me in a completely different direction.

Andy and Carol made the 6-7-hour drive from Milan out to visit, which lifted my spirits greatly. To thank them, I invited them to join us for an early dinner so they could return while there was still daylight.

We ended up heading back to Israel, cutting our planned trip short and facing massive medical expenses. I hadn't thought much about travel insurance when I was 21, but now it all fell on us, with the full cost of the surgery to be paid by us. Leni managed to set up payment delays and instalments from Israel for my father, but almost all our income went to the bills.

Post-operatively, I received a prescription for lifelong anti-seizure medication, a necessary evil as a result of brain surgery. The medication saved my life, but it had terrible side effects: my teeth became brittle, my stamina and libido diminished, and over the years, other health issues appeared. It took me two years to be re-licensed to drive. Two years of seizure-free, as specified by the law, earned me the right to sit behind the wheel of a car. The entire experience upended every aspect of my life: my career plans, the way I viewed life, myself, everything. After spending a couple of months at home, I started working at the International Telephone Exchange in Tel Aviv where I showed all my skills in languages and then at a recently opened tour operator. My knowledge of many languages and extensive travel experience made me well-suited for these roles. During my recovery, I realised that my true passion was elsewhere. I decided to switch to the travel industry, a field that combined my love for exploration and my desire to connect with people from diverse cultures.

This meant leaving my studies in Milan and returning to the tourism field in Israel.

Me and My Father

That was a shock for my father, who couldn't accept that I was not continuing my studies. One October day, while walking down a bustling street, I nervously told him about my decision. His reaction was immediate and harsh. He stopped, looked at me, and shouted, "What did I make all those efforts for? To have a loser son?" The sting of his words remained in my memory till this day.

I tried to explain, my voice trembling, that my experience in the Swiss hospital had been a turning point. I told him how, lying in that hospital bed, I had come to realise that becoming a doctor was not my dream any longer. The constant exposure to suffering and pain had been too much for me to bear. I admitted that I couldn't see myself as a great doctor, capable of handling such immense responsibility and emotional weight.

"Dad," I said, pleading with my eyes for understanding, "I can't see people suffer like that. It's not in me. I want to help people in other ways, ways that don't involve so much pain and sorrow. That's why I must give up on this path."

Despite my heartfelt explanation, his disappointment hung in the air between us, a palpable barrier that would take time and understanding to break down.

But I was determined, so I started my new road.

CHAPTER 10
Travel Industry—Israel

PTC

In early 1978, I started working for a company named PTC that aimed to offer the best tours in Europe for the elderly. My role involved creating itineraries, calculating costs, and setting prices for each tour. PTC's specialty was to have a doctor on board and to ensure the tours were paced leisurely. This was the beginning, but soon, I started the expansion into individual land arrangements. For this, I brought in Gadi, my friend, to help us secure contracts and negotiate better prices for hotels worldwide.

We started working together, but it eventually proved to be a challenging partnership. The team included George, an older guy with vast experience in travel and aviation, and the original owner, Mr Osterer, who still worked in a travel agency in Tel Aviv. Later, Mr Osterer brought in his son, Dave, who was an architect but bored with his profession—he liked trying new things and still runs the company today. We all shared a vision to excel, starting from a modest three-room apartment on Dizengoff Street in Tel Aviv.

Our efforts paid off, and success started coming our way. Since PTC was in the beginning, the importance of every step taken was critical. The work was satisfying, even though most of my earnings went to my parents to pay off the debt in Switzerland. That summer, I flew with my mother to Switzerland for a check-up at the hospital. By then, all the money was paid back. All our incomes that year were allocated to this purpose. After a long series of exams, I got the thumbs up that everything was perfectly fine, allowing us to finally relax a little bit ever since I had to go for a yearly check up in Israel for about five years.

After our return, I continued working at PTC (Pan Trading Company) for another 6 months or so.

Social Life After the Surgery

Socially, my escapades were quite limited since I didn't drive. This made me heavily reliant on my friends Gadi, Ian, and a few others. My movement, especially on weekends when public transportation was scarce, was constrained. However, I managed to carve out a vibrant social life within these limitations.

I developed a keen interest in poker, and every Friday night, we would gather at Ian's home for lively poker games. These nights were filled with laughter, friendly banter, and the thrill of the game. We relished these gatherings, creating a little oasis of excitement amidst our routine lives.

Almost instantly, moviemaking grew into an aspect of my social life. My office sat in the middle of a bunch of theatres, and I'd often duck into a show before boarding the bus home, which meant that nearly every new release I saw felt like a bit of a chore. Each film provided a portal, a range of experiences that fed my imagination—a window upon some possibilities for the adult I might become.

At home, I would read other books that would expand my eyes and my mind, page by page. Music was also a constant presence, filling the hours both at work and at home, enriching my days with rhythm and inspiration. Together, movies, books, and music were my daily companions, shaping my thoughts and dreams.

Every other Thursday night, I went to see the basketball game, the best show in town for me. This is when I met my school friend, Yoram, and watched Maccabi Tel Aviv in the stadium. There, I became infected with the energy of the crowd, and I mingled with fans who mirrored my mentality, waiting for the players to come out of the stadium and cheer them up.

Weddings were a staple of my social life during that period, with Israeli kids marrying and starting families in their early 20s, sometimes divorcing and remarrying while young enough to begin again. Weddings are parties, joyous, noisy, dancing affairs. I often served as

DJ at weddings, spinning tracks that kept the dance floor moving and the drinks flowing.

Along with poker nights, movie nights, and thrilling basketball games, I added items to my social calendar. No matter how challenging it could be to get to a social function, community and excitement were there to stay. It was a time of continuous connection, of colour and warmth stirring, event after event.

Charter #1

In the spring of 1979, a new company called Charter#1 started in Israel, pioneering the first outbound charter flights from Israel to West Germany. On May 6, 1979, they ran their inaugural flight, and the novelty of this venture intrigued me. I eagerly applied for a job as a tour operator at the company. To my surprise, a few days later, I was asked to come for an interview with the owner of the company. Although I had applied for a tour operator position, I was offered a role as a flight control manager, to which I agreed at once.

In those days, Ian also started his studies in Bucharest, Romania, to become a dentist.

Starting a New Job

Excited about this new opportunity and the higher salary, I explained my decision to the PTC team and resigned from my position there. Joining Charter #1, I soon realised I was only the second employee, working alongside Bluma, the first employee. She was in charge of all the booking and payment aspects, and I was in charge of the ticketing and making sure no overbooking on our side was made. We handled about three or four flights a week, managing all reservations on a large white chart (for both departures and returns) and issuing tickets for approximately 50 passengers per flight. In the beginning, my workdays extended until 10 pm daily, including the weekends.

As the company grew, things got even more hectic. We launched the first charter flights to New York, accommodating two hundred passengers per flight three times a week. My duties included seat control to prevent overbookings or underbookings, handwriting all the tickets (since everything was done manually at the time), and sending telexes—telex was a major method of sending text messages electronically between businesses during that period. This involved typing all passenger names into a telex system, creating a yellow ribbon that could then be sent via telex—a precursor to modern computers but entirely controlled by humans.

The early days at Charter #1 were intense and demanding yet incredibly rewarding. The excitement of being part of something new and groundbreaking, coupled with the challenge of handling increasing volumes of passengers and flights, made it a vibrant and fulfilling experience.

Between 1978 and 1980, I oversaw the check-in process for US-bound flights with Evergreen Air, which departed Israel at 11 pm and were handled by a company called Maof Ground Handling. And since Charter #1 was owned by the same owner of Maof, it was easy for me to be in charge of the whole operation. Maof also looked after our flights, and they needed me out at the airport by 8 pm to make sure everything went well.

It was my job to check that my passenger lists matched those of the ground staff, whether to open three or more check-in counters, to set the boarding priorities, and to manage Israeli passengers, especially with constant overbooking. Overbooked passengers were sent to an airport hotel and rebooked on the next day's British Airways flight to New York via London. By 1 am, after finalising the lists, I would call a travel agent to secure their bookings, and by morning, I'd have their tickets ready for delivery.

Because Maof's offices were close by, I often slept from 1 am to 5 am in the manager's chair instead of heading home. It was a crazy schedule, but it was fun to check people in, try to overbook and deal with last-minute issues. It forced you to think quickly and do your job fast.

Visit to New York

The owners of Evergreen Air invited me back two years later to New York to review how things were going. It was my first trip to the city, staying at a hotel on Madison Avenue and 38th Street and commuting daily to Brooklyn to the charter offices—a large open space with no walls or private offices—and experiencing how much my world was expanding and coming up close and personal with Mr Nachmias and others who would eventually own Tower Air. Although I was sick upon arrival and had to rely on deli food from across the street while watching baseball and American football on TV, I recovered and began travelling to their other offices at day time and exploring the city in the evenings. The grandeur of the buildings and the beauty of Central Park left a lasting impression on me. I also visited my friend, Nanu, who was studying in Buffalo. We spent time together, listened to Bob Dylan and Janis Joplin, and visited Niagara Falls, only from the American side. After three weeks, I returned to Israel.

Ingrid

In those years, I also ran into another girl, Ingrid. She was very tall, about 1.85 metres, and came from a family known for their rare triplets. We met at a party, and from the very beginning, we hit it off. By the end of the evening, we were already friends—or something more.

I had never felt so complete the way I did when she was with me. I remember feeling so physically united—when our bodies were apart, our limbs would reach out and entangle, our bodies melding together, reaching out as though we were one, with no boundaries or divisions. I felt utterly intertwined with her, without boundaries or separations. The closer I felt to her, the more primal and instinctive our connection became. When I climaxed, the sensation was profound, as though we'd become one, and I longed to stay close, to hold on to that unity. That was my first sexual encounter since my surgery, and it was not so easy to perform.

We continued to see one another often, and the connection between us grew deeper until one day, I learned that her family was moving to Canada. Suddenly, she was gone, leaving me with the memory of a bond that had been as intense as it was brief. To be honest, all my romantic flings were short-lived, as the girls always left the country.

Omama Passing

It was the summer of 1980 when Omama died in a hospital. I was 25. All through my childhood, she'd been my solid rock. Omama had raised me. With all her quirks and flaws, she was a remarkably intelligent and wise woman, and her strength left a lasting imprint on my heart.

My father was struck by grief. His brother had died only a few years earlier. Now, he was truly alone in the world. She was buried in the cemetery in Holon. Deeply affected by the bereavement tradition, he visited the temple twice daily to pray according to the Jewish ritual. He began doing this after my operation in Lausanne as if it gave him an extra commitment. He had also sworn not to eat any pork product as long as he lived, and indeed, he kept his promise.

Maof Airlines

Its annual growth rate in the first two years of operation was a staggering 120 per cent. We moved address several times before 1981 when our parent company, Maof—using three B720 aircraft purchased from Monarch Airlines in Israel—started to operate charter flights between Israel and London. After long legal battles against the ministry of transport, we were granted a license on 15 June 1981 to operate charter flights. The first company flight commenced on 26 October 1981, with a fully booked 166-seat flight from London Luton Airport to Ben Gurion Airport.

At this point, Isaac Gadish, the owner, made the decision to run the company as a family business, restructuring it with himself as the general manager. His daughter, Orit, was placed in charge of seat control along with four additional staff. I was also moved into the position for which I had been hired, that of tour operator, creating itineraries for travels for Israeli clients. I discovered in this work that I had found my 'calling,' and I soon became a major player within the company.

In 1982, Mr Gadish came up with the idea of a weekly flight to Palermo, Sicily, and sent me to handle the project. I flew to Palermo to meet our local agent, Gianni Castellucci, who would take care of land for each flight. We drove all over the island. We visited the home of the perfect family holiday, the Cefalu's Costa Verde Resort. Here I was, flying and handling land in Italy. Finally, I'd live the Italian dream.

My parents went for a sabbatical year to London, Ontario, in Canada, and left me alone in the apartment. Sicily became one of the first destinations for Maof Airlines, and I worked hard to develop the destination.

Summer of 82

It was around the time of the first Lebanon War which started just before the 1982 World Cup, and my friend Ian, home from studying in Romania, moved in. That summer was a busy one, time-wise.

Ian's parents were on a sabbatical in Guatemala, and he needed a place to live, so I had him join me in my parent's apartment.

The 1982 Lebanon War, also called Operation Peace for Galilee, was launched by Israel on June 6, 1982, in response to escalating attacks from the Palestinian Liberation Organization (PLO) based in southern Lebanon. Israel aimed to remove PLO forces from Lebanon, end Syrian influence there, and establish a friendly government in Beirut. The operation succeeded in expelling the PLO leadership but led to unintended consequences, including a prolonged Israeli presence in Lebanon and the rise of Hezbollah, a new militant group. The war impacted regional dynamics and Israeli domestic politics, with many debates surrounding its objectives and outcomes.

The other big event that took place contemporarily was the 1982 World Cup, held in Spain. It was dramatic, highly competitive, and produced many memorable performances. Italy won the tournament, beating West Germany 3–1 in the final in Madrid on 11 July.

Life at the apartment was full of action and non stop adventures, as Ian's married girlfriend, Pitty, came frequently and cooked for us. We watched the war developments and the World Cup, sometimes favouring football. While watching TV, Ian also played backgammon with some friends, and we went out at night in Tel Aviv, too. Though tense politically, this was one of the best years of my life that I still remember.

Sicily Affair

At the end of that summer, after Ian moved out, I embarked on a group tour to Sicily. It sparked a brief but intense love affair with a 45-year-old married woman named Anat, who was 20 years my senior. She fell deeply in love with me, but for me, it was a fleeting connection. Anat was captivating—she had long, flowing hair, a willowy figure, and long legs that exuded elegance. Her shyness only heightened her allure, making her even more irresistible. We met more than 20 times during the next two years, in her apartment in Tel Aviv, consummating our passion—always when her husband was on duty in the hospital.

Winter, 1983. I went to see my parents in Canada.

They had an apartment with a living room, a kitchen, and a bedroom on campus; my father had an office in a lab where they fed squirrels on the windowsill. My father used to like throwing peanuts at them from time to time and watching them enjoy it. My father made new acquittances and some friends from Japan and Sweden. We took walks under a biting cold, and it almost blew us over when a blizzard was picking up. It wasn't a bad time. I tried to get in touch with my friend, Ingrid, in Toronto but couldn't.

The Rise and Fall of Maof Airlines

Meanwhile, El Al, Israel's national carrier, had long dominated the skies in Israel and had zealously held on to them. Each flight Maof undertook had to start from Atarot Airport outside Jerusalem in a small Cessna and, from there, continue on into Ben Gurion with the associated cost to every journey. El Al workers started a long strike to improve their salaries. During the strike, El Al cancelled all its flights, and the government asked Maof to try to operate flights on as many routes as possible, which helped its reputation tremendously. The call sign of Maof became that of El Al during this time, and it flew to different European destinations such as Basel, Trieste, Palermo, and more. A slogan was born: '*And thank you for flying Maof.*' It was a golden era for Maof Airlines. That was the way to end Maof's future since we did hurt the big bear.

Maof Germany

In the same spring, Maof asked me to go to their office in Frankfurt to take care of seat control, sales, and marketing for Israeli flights to the German clientele, as well as manage the office.

After making all my preparations, I left for Frankfurt.

Frankfurt—My Home for the Next 2 Years

The air was often infused with the hearty aroma of Frankfurter sausages sizzling on grills at street vendors, mingling with the sweet, nutty scent of freshly baked pretzels and the enticing wafts of roasted chestnuts in colder months. The bustling Römer area and outdoor markets were alive with the fragrance of spices from international cuisines, hinting at the city's diverse culinary influences. As for tastes, visitors could indulge in the local specialty, Äppelwoi (apple wine), a slightly sour beverage served in traditional ceramic pitchers, paired perfectly with regional dishes like Handkäse mit Musik (a marinated cheese) and hearty potato salads. The city's bakeries tempted passersby with delicate pastries, such as the rich, creamy Frankfurter Kranz cake. Overall, the sensory experience of Frankfurt in 1984 was a delightful blend of tradition and modernity, offering a unique culinary journey.

Upon arrival, I stayed for three weeks in a hotel near my office, which enabled me to look for an apartment, and I found a studio in the city centre. It had one big living/sleeping room, a kitchen, and a bathroom. Since it was unfurnished, I bought basic furniture and kitchen essentials from IKEA. It was a cute, small place on Kenney Alle, just a 10-minute tram ride to my office. The neighbourhood had a large supermarket, a fresh produce market, a butcher, and a bakery nearby, so I had everything at my fingertips.

I worked hard, often until 8-9 pm daily. After a while, I started using the company car, a BMW 318. It was a very fast and beautiful car. Although I didn't drive much, it was a nice bonus from the company. There were seven people in our office: our secretary, Mrs Gabriela—a mature blond lady with blue eyes and a perfect body; two reservation agents: Gaby, a beautiful girl, engaged to be married, and Anika, a tall girl but really insecure; Monika, a very charismatic girl, with dark black hair and very green eyes, long legs and medium-sized breasts, who was in charge of the land arrangements in Israel; Freddy, a tall guy with blond hair, skinny and very relaxed, a pretty heavy drinker in charge of the seat control; Ron, an Israeli accountant who was married and had 2 kids; and the office general manager, Tzvi, a really interesting man, tall, well-built, attractive, and full of good spirits—he was married with children but living by his own rules, having affairs every week with women.

We, the Israelis living and working in Frankfurt, met up regularly at the Kur-Royal Day Spa in the Kurpark in Bad Homburg, a well-planned centre of recreation and our favorite weekend pastime with a beautiful villa in its oriental style, the Kaiser-Wilhelms-Bad. It was here that the structure's historicism aroused the senses, with its high halls and blinding tiles and mosaics.

We usually began with the sauna, where colour-changing light therapy and uplifting scents created the perfect environment to induce a feeling of well-being and improve circulation and metabolism in an 80°C sauna. Essential oils were used for increased indulgence. And finally, the hay steam bath: 'By drying vegetation, nature transmits its healing power into the air.' Dried grasses, herbs, and flowers from the gardens of Bad Homburg were heated 'to release their soothing, medicinal power' in order to relax the shoulders, back, and pelvic region of those who sat inside. Finally, we smeared pieces of ice from the fountain on our bodies to warm up and roused our skin with slightly chilly bubbles. We ended this wonderful ritual with an ice mist, an ice shower, or a dip into the cold-water pools among many naked people. Another way of entertaniment was going to bowl. We went every other week to the bowling alley and spent time there.

After a year, I moved to my first real apartment: a fifth-floor, two-bedroom mansard in the trendy neighbourhood of Sachsenhausen. Gutzkowstraße, where I found the place, was a historic part of the city, full of bars, restaurants, and jazz joints. The apartment was located on the fifth floor of an old building with no elevator and steep stairs leading up to a charming flat with sloped roofs that created a slide-like effect in each room. I turned one room into a bedroom and the other into a living area, and the kitchen and bathroom were across the corridor. I took the furniture from the place I had before, and since it was partly furnished, I didn't have to add much.

A Turkish vegetarian restaurant in the yard became my regular, and the owners my friends. I started to drop in for dinner at night after work. After dinner, I would then head straight back upstairs to limit the stairs I had to climb.

Marta

Marta was captivating, the kind of woman who instantly commanded attention. Her jet-black hair fell in loose waves over her shoulders, framing a face that was both striking and unforgettable. Her eyes were a deep, alluring green, a rare shade that flickered with intensity and mischief, capable of conveying a thousand unspoken words with a single glance. She had the body of a goddess—toned yet curvaceous, with a natural grace in her every movement that seemed effortless. Marta's personality was as powerful as her appearance; she exuded a quiet confidence, a boldness that drew people in and dared them to come closer. Her laugh was rich and throaty, filled with the warmth of someone who lived passionately.

There was something raw and untamed about her

that made her all the more irresistible. She spoke almost no English or German. Italian and Spanish turned out to be our lingua franca. We met at a bar where I spoke Italian to her, and she responded in Spanish. She came to my apartment that night and—boom! Many of our trysts took place in the shower.

Making love was great, but outside the bedroom, we had little to say. Marta was full of resentment, an outcast and an exile from the third world. Our affair lasted about three weeks. She grew increasingly frustrated with me as time went on. I was, after all, an Israeli with believers of the strengths of the America. I was a symbol of the very capitalist world she was against. By the end, she was barely speaking to me at all.

Pazit

Pazit, whose father was in charge of El Al in Amsterdam, was the first Israeli beauty I had ever known. Pazit and I had taken the same course (for travel agents) at the Expert School for Travel Agents in Israel. I recognised her at once—she had something about her, an allure, an openness that was naturally attractive and automatically appealing.

At 1.61 metres, Pazit was slight and elegant, moving with a languid grace. Her short curly red hair was the colour of ripe cherries, contrasting with her pale smooth skin; her copper pendant earrings gave her face an artistic feyness. Her dark eyes were long and mysterious and promised adventure and mischief, her prominent cheekbones making her face exotic and pretty. She exuded a relaxed confident posture, and it was all pretty irresistible, especially since she was not pretentious. Her beauty was a gift—and then some. It was the ease, charm, and openness of her personality that stunned you. Indeed, when we first met, she was just riding her bike around in a helmet— and somehow made that look good, too.

Pazit, joined us and transferred to Frankfurt by herself. She asked only that I take her in, which I did, for six to eight months in my living room as a roommate. She promised to cook and clean instead of paying rent to which I agreed. We were never lovers, but we got along very well. She was fun to have around. She was my best roommate ever. Later, she moved to LA, where she married. I lost track of her then.

That year, my parents spent another sabbatical in Jülich, a small town near Cologne. I would visit them every other weekend. I loved those weekends. Jülich was quiet, with a quaint medieval flair, surrounded by green pastures and old stone buildings. It was a taste of the good life. It was a great time for me and my parents. We spent weekends together in Julich, and sometimes they would travel to Frankfurt to my place. They enjoyed their time in Germany mainly because they could be close to me again.

The office was working well, but at the time, El Al was in poor financial shape and did not want any local competition. Unfortunately, the combined pressure from El Al and the prevailing economic problems proved too much for Maof. The airline entered bankruptcy on November 9, 1984. At its closure, Maof owed around $10 million, with $4 million owed to the government and the rest to banks.

Mr Gadish, the owner, decided to restart the company from Frankfurt, so I was in the best place to help him relaunch the business. We stayed a team of five and restarted by selling flight tickets to Israel on different charter companies and creating land packages for Israel. It was a difficult winter season as sales went down, and we had to reduce staff to a minimum. In 1985, Mr Gadish closed the Frankfurt office as well and travelled to the United States.

And this was the end of Maof Airlines—such a shame.

CHAPTER 11
American Trade Show

Fortunately for me, one of the original partners of Maof had a new business enterprise—a trade show that would take place in Miami, Florida, in January 1986. He took over the office, making it the headquarters for European sales, and appointed me as sales manager for Europe.

Sales and Marketing

I created new business cards and started travelling around Europe to recruit as many exhibitors as possible for the trade show. I travelled to the Netherlands, Germany, Italy, Romania, the UK, and Switzerland. By the end of my tours, I had booked around 140 exhibitors for the trade show.

In Romania, it was my first visit since I had left, and I was anxious about going back as it was still under the Communist regime. It was 1985 when I arrived at the Intercontinental Hotel and got my room. I found two microphones in the air conditioning unit. Knowing this, I never spoke on the hotel telephone without running water and having constant noise in my room, like the radio or the TV. I travelled to Sinaia to visit my family friends, the Manea family, and then returned to the hotel. I finished my sales calls and immediately got on a plane back to Frankfurt. It was very frustrating to go back and feel followed.

Miami

Later that year, at the beginning of December, I travelled to Miami Beach, Florida, to take part in the exhibition. I was really upset that most of the exhibitors were the ones I had signed up for, and the rest were a bunch of Jewish entities from Miami Beach. When I asked how this happened, I was given a bunch of stories and excuses that just embarrassed me. I was put up in the Hotel Barcelona on Collins Avenue in Miami Beach for a month and a half and rented a car to move around easily.

Yael

While I was busy working to boost attendance at the exhibition and protect my reputation, my weekends were moments of respite, often spent by the pool or at the beach. There, I met an older Israeli couple who lived near my parents in Bat Yam; their daughter, Yael, lived in Miami Beach, they told me. "We should drive by and say hello to Yael," we agreed.

Yael was gorgeous: a 35-year-old blonde with an organic vibe and a smile that lit up the room. She was divorced and had an eight-year-old son, and she exuded a relaxed, easy elegance. I took her out to dinner, and then to dinners, and to other evenings in Miami, and then still other evenings in Miami but without any sex involved since her parents were around. She was drawn to me, but I think her projections were for something serious, perhaps even matrimonial, and mine were for nothing deeper than the evening. Not in Florida.

It was a limited relationship. She was not pushy, especially with her parents in earshot, and she preferred to keep things on the downlow. I spent a lot of money on it— a family vacation to Disney World and Universal Studios in Orlando were two key events. She never came through in the way that I had hoped. It felt like she wanted me in her life but did not give much back in exchange. I now see her as a person who knew how to use people. Oh well, water under the bridge.

Flashbacks From the Show

Back to the Trade Show, the year was already January 1985, and the exhibitors started arriving. I oversaw the Italian contingent and, of course, had to entertain them and ensure they had a great time. The Trade Show began, but there were no regular visitors and not enough professionals.

The exhibitors started getting angry, blaming me for the low traffic. I took a chance and called all the hotel managers in the Miami area to come, also inviting all the travel agencies in the Miami area, and, indeed, it started to get busier as they came.

One night, we all (the whole Italian delegation) went to see Gloria Estefan perform. We had a very nice dinner, but when we left, the maître d' came to us very agitated, asking if there was anything wrong with the service. It turned out we had forgotten to tip, and he said, "We do expect a 15% tip." The Italians, who never tip in Italy, had to add another $200 tip. For them, that was outrageous, and although I explained the tipping culture in the USA, they got mad at me again. Ever since, I've learned to always remember to give a tip.

When the trade show was about to end, all the exhibitors started packing their belongings at 11 am and left the hall. At that moment, I knew there would be no continuation for me with the organisation. However, I managed to obtain a paid vacation for five months, so I stayed in Miami and did some travelling.

Travels After the Show

First, I went to the Bahamas for the first time. I stayed on Paradise Island at the Holiday Inn, where I booked three nights. I enjoyed the beach and the pool and tried paragliding for the first time in my life. Soaring over the country's gorgeous islands and deep blue waters was an incredible experience. From the air, I could truly appreciate the beauty of the Bahamas with its calm blue seas and jaw-droppingly beautiful beaches. It's a great place to fly over the water, with so much to see everywhere you look.

Afterwards, I played table tennis at the hotel, outside on the pavement and barefoot. After a couple of ball exchanges, I made a leap for the ball and hurt my ankle so badly that I could not walk anymore.

After finishing my trip to the Bahamas, I took a plane to Boston, Massachusetts, to visit my friend, Nanu. He had recently finished his university studies, gotten married, and started working for Panasonic. He was living in a suburb of Boston. We explored the old town, where cobblestone streets met glass-enclosed shopping galleries. The Freedom Trail's historic landmarks stood beside trendy restaurants, and new high-tech campuses brushed shoulders with some of the USA's most prestigious universities. Boston has been a national leader in higher education and research, with Boston University and Northeastern University located within the city and Boston College in nearby Chestnut Hill. Two of the world's most prestigious and consistently highly ranked universities, Harvard University and the Massachusetts Institute of Technology (MIT), are in neighbouring Cambridge.

Nanu and I visited the Harvard and MIT campuses, marvelling at their historic and modern facilities. Afterwards, we went for dinner at a typical New England restaurant, where I tried clam chowder and fresh fish for the first time. It was a great time, and I left Boston with wonderful memories, flying back to Miami before returning to Frankfurt.

Back to Frankfurt

When I got back to Frankfurt, it was winter and cold. I returned to my apartment and started looking for a job, as I was now unemployed for the first time since I started working. Despite the trade show planning a second edition, I was determined not to be part of it. In March, I got a phone call from Mr Gadish, who told me to prepare myself to go to the States again as he had something in mind. That was the beginning of another long collaboration between us.

The night before I left was not without incident. My boxes were packed, the flat on Gutzkowstraße surrendered, and goodbyes were said to my Turkish friends and a few other neighbours I'd collected along the way. One of them was Inga, a divorced woman I'd known who lived down the hall, a headstrong firebrand who'd seen a lot of action and was equally determined to send me on my way in a manner neither of us would soon forget.

"Let's do this properly," Inga said. Whiskey, some filthy sex, and a few joints to take the edge off. The luxury of getting wasted, of taking an hour or even a day to say goodbye, she knew how to do it. No wonder it was such a goodbye. I can no longer remember how we laughed or who played what or what tiny secrets were whispered into whose ears, but we drank to excess. Booze, cigarettes, and weed enhanced everything—the touch and the kiss, the vibrations of the music, the dim light and the deep shadows, the soft energy in the room, and the promise of the night that seemed endless.

By sunrise, we drank in silence, toasted to each other and our memories, and uttered the last farewell to each other. By 2 pm, I was on my way to Tampa by plane, exiting one stage of my life and entering another, full of the unknown and a bit nervous about what might come, but also ready for what waited.

CHAPTER 12
A Beginning: the USA Adventures

Upon my arrival in Tampa, Mr Gadish was waiting for me. As we drove to our destination, he began explaining the new project. John Wallace, a pilot with Tower Air, had a side business involving camping for trailers and motor vehicles.

Inverness, Florida

He wanted to offer prospective clients a package deal to Israel, where the winner would pay for their spouse's full package. The goal was to create the best possible package with Tower Air, minimising our costs. John was eager to promote Tower Air products through this venture, making it a win-win situation for all.

John had rented an apartment for me in Inverness, a city and the county seat of Citrus County, Florida. It was a two-story house in a new development area, which I shared with a British colleague named Susan. She was an older woman, about 45/50 years old, pretty but very cold. We shared the house and drove to work together in her old Toyota Camry. Our workplace was a motor camp catering to a very low-income clientele.

During my time there, I took trips to Orlando, Clearwater, and Tampa, exploring the untouched outdoors that set this area apart from other destinations in Florida. I enjoyed unforgettable days on Charlotte Harbor, cruising, enjoying nature, and fishing with Susan.

I put together a package of travel for the purpose of advertising, and then, the very next day, Mr Gadish ended up fighting with John's wife, and the whole thing was dropped, and then I got the axe as well, as I had been considered a prop all along.

Susan and Heather

Luckily for me, Susan let me stay at home. When her English friend, Heather, came to visit, it was a whole new dynamic. She was much younger and hotter than Susan, and suddenly, I was living with two women. I was doing all the cooking and overseeing all the shopping. Mornings were for shopping and lying by the pool, reading, swimming, and Heather and I occasionally touching each other. The sex was just fantastic. Afternoons were dedicated to the World Cup in Mexico.

Dinner was barbecued fish or steaks, potatoes or rice, and three huge salads. Evenings were TV, movies, or just sitting on the porch looking at the lake, drinking gin and tonic, and smoking.

Sure enough, three months later, Susan had also argued with John's wife and was sacked. We got in the car to go to Miami. I drove Susan and Heather to the airport, and they decided to fly back to England. Susan handed her car keys to me. And just like that, I got a free car.

I stayed in Miami for a few more days before driving to New York. Mr Gadish had found another consulting job with CIT (Compagnia Italiana Turismo) and called me to join him there.

Driving to New Jersey

I packed up in Florida and went on a 1250-mile, three-day journey to New Jersey. I drove to Daytona Beach north to Cape Canaveral, passing by the Kennedy Space Center to inspect the rockets (and possibly get my car off the ground). I hit the road after a night's sleep.

The next day, I took to the road, sauntering around Jacksonville and Savannah, Georgia, in an effort to resist the steadily accelerating heat. My car didn't want to be slowed. Every 40 or 50 miles, it would get hot enough that I would have to reroute the air conditioning, roll down the windows, and pull off at every second gas station to cool the radiator. Picture me, head hung like a dog out of the window, frantic to escape the heat.

The comedy of errors had been 500 miles before I gave up and drove off to a motel. I woke up with a good meal at the neighbourhood diner and was ready for the last leg.

Day three followed suit: windows down, radiators, miles of Virginia highways. By the time I stowed myself into Atlantic City, I felt like I had crossed three deserts. But somehow, after what felt like a marathon, I was back in Bergen, New Jersey, completely run down but victorious, as if I'd completed a perverse endurance challenge.

CIT New York

I stayed a couple of nights at Mr Gadish's apartment before he took me to the heart of the action: New York City. We drove in to meet the general manager of CIT, Silvano Soldaini. Silvano was a textbook Italian—warm, animated, and a great host. His silver hair and his blue eyes made him look very good. He gave me the friendliest interview ever and hired me on the spot.

CIT was a powerhouse that promoted Italian tourism. Their mission was to put Italy on the map as a top destination while encouraging Italians to explore abroad. With backing from Italy's railways, Sicilian and Neapolitan banks, and ENIT (Italy's national tourist board), they'd built a network of agencies worldwide, setting the standard in travel marketing.

I started my new job right away and began hunting for an apartment; every evening was devoted to that cause. I lucked out when a former coworker, Isaac Stein, introduced me to an Israeli girl who had been subletting her apartment for a month. It was a room on 50th Street, near Lexington Avenue, with a tiny closet and bathroom but no kitchen. Still, it provided a roof over my head while I searched for something more permanent.

Work was intense from the start. I dove into the Italy-Israel project, crafting travel packages under the catchy name *On the Steps of Jesus.* But fitting in at CIT wasn't easy. With around 30 employees, most of whom weren't thrilled about an outsider from Israel joining the team, I had to work hard to prove myself.

CIT's office was on the seventh floor of 666 Fifth Avenue—a beautiful building despite its 'satanic' street number. Alitalia, Italy's national airline, had its office just across the hall, which felt almost too perfectly Italian. The building had a bookstore on the entrance floor and a subway stop right underneath, so it made commute, if necessary, very easy. And there I was, in the city that never sleeps, with a new job and a little room to call my own.

Sally

In the meantime, I kept looking for an apartment. One night, I met a girl at a bar who told me she was moving to Florida. Her name was Sally.

"Where do you live now?" I asked.

"On 47th Street, corner with Second Avenue," she replied.

"Do you own the apartment?" I inquired.

"No, it's rented, and I'm looking to sublet it," she said.

Those words were like music to me. "I'm interested. Is it fully furnished?"

"Yes, and the kitchen is fully equipped," she answered.

"I want to see it. What's the rent?" I asked.

"It's $1100 a month," she said.

After looking at the apartment, I said, "I'll take it."

Afterwards, we spent a pleasant evening together, consummating our sex needs before she left at the end of the month, one week before my current lease ended.

So, I sublet a studio apartment on 47th Street, near the UN quarters, off Second Avenue; the few blocks between my 'neighbourhood' and the storied East Side felt like I was in Manhattan, so I would walk south, feeling a tad starry-eyed. Sparks Steak House is a landmark steakhouse in New York City, 210 East 46th Street (Second to Third Avenue), where John Gotti had Castellani killed in 1985. It felt like a city full of energy and drama, and I was at its centre. I got to know two girls at the office, Alessandra and Janet, who became my best friends.

New programs

Terrorist attacks at the Rome and Vienna airports in December 1985 transformed airport security worldwide. They led to an entire overhaul of safety regulations, especially among airlines and ticket offices for large, politically charged companies such as El Al. Such incidents underlined the fragility of transnational travellers and the dramatic geopolitical circumstances of the period, which adversely affected travellers to North America in particular.

In response, I came up with reassuring taglines like *"Italy OK!"* and *"Europe OK*!" These were simple, catchy slogans designed to restore confidence in European travel. The taglines struck a chord, and I focused on promoting high-end packages to Italy, positioning it as a timelessly safe destination even amid rising security concerns. The campaign was an instant success: the cover featured a diverse group of Americans against iconic backdrops of Rome or Paris, all flashing the 'OK' sign, reinforcing the message of safety and enjoyment.

I developed straightforward, client-friendly packages; just like that, we were set for the next summer's offerings. This campaign was my breakthrough in the company, earning me newfound respect and recognition from my colleagues.

Jacky

One Sunday morning, I met Jacky, a stylish Seattle woman, at brunch on Lexington Avenue at the Loews Hotel. She was a 30-year-old tall, attractive woman in a smart, professional manner. She had a beautiful brown complexion, dazzling eyes, and a neat grey suit that emphasised her broad legs. She had an unsettled intensity in her eyes as if she were thinking elsewhere. We ate a leisurely brunch and then went for a walk in Central Park.

It was one of those New York autumn days when the trees were bright yellow and brown. It was filled with bicyclists, runners, volleyballers, and sunbathers, all seeking out the last ounces of heat. We walked together and kissed and enjoyed autumn's air and each other.

Jacky worked as a programmer for a Seattle-based hi-tech firm that was constantly meeting worldwide. Talented and enigmatic, she told me she had grown up in a commune and spent time in that freedom and all that it entails.

When I discovered she would be in New York a couple of days longer—and being a huge rock-and-roll lover—I suggested we catch Pink Floyd at Madison Square Garden on Monday night. She agreed, and I picked her up at 7 pm. The concert was mesmerising! Pink Floyd played all the songs they'd ever done, including *The Wall.* The lights, the music—it was all intoxicating. We arrived back at the hotel a little confused, almost lost in the music.

We then felt we deserved an elegant supper, so we took a trip up to her hotel room, where we spent the night, strengthening our bond; she was stoned out of her brain and felt horny. We fucked once, and then we fucked twice, and then we fucked again, and then I passed out. She was still turned on and taught me how to lick her like an ice cream. What a delicious dessert.

She said she wanted me to visit her in Seattle soon.

Three weeks later, on Halloween, I flew up to Seattle and saw Jacky for the first time since New York. Seattle was sombre and brooding in a good way: pointed mountains dotted the city, and green in every direction ensured the chilly, damp air that made it all the better to stay indoors.

Jacky was amazing, smart, sexy, and more than a little wild. We hung out for a couple of days in town and a few private nights to get to know each other. Raindrops fell on the windows, and our indoor nights gained another dimension of romantic interest when pine and new wet earth wafted everywhere. It was the perfect combination of fairytale backdrop and conviviality.

We went out to eat in seafood restaurants and rickety cafes, tasting local food and the homegrown cooking Seattle had become known for. The city was amazing, both slick and rustic, yet breathtaking in its natural beauty. At the end of my stay, I was all set to return to New York and the tourist business again, my heart racing from the glitz and glamour of the city. The trip to Seattle was an honour, a special place in my life to look back on. I was thankful for how it had turned out.

The day before New Year's Eve, Alessandra invited me to celebrate with her boyfriend, Paulo, at her apartment. They had a small apartment on 7th Avenue, just off 38th Street, and Alessandra promised me an Italian feast. I asked Jacky to come, and the two of us sat with them for New Year's Eve, eating all the Italian food Alessandra had ever made.

Just before midnight, a man came in, bearing huge plates of vitello tonnato and baked pasta. It turned out to be none other than Silvano Marchetto, the proprietor of 'Da Silvano' in lower Manhattan. His food was fabulous, and his personality was equally colourful. We left the party a bit drunk, going home to welcome the New Year in private—Jacky and I had what might have been the sexiest, best experiences of our lives.

The following two days, we spent most of our time in bed, with occasional trips to town for lunch or dinner. At the end of her visit, Jacky gave me a final souvenir I still treasure: Bruce Springsteen's five-disc *Live* collection. It was the perfect ending; I will always remember that winter fondly.

I fell in love with New York that year. I ice skated in Central Park, saw shows at Madison Square Garden

(Moody Blues, James Taylor, America), and even caught a Rangers hockey game.

I made new friends, including Alex, one of Ian's friends in Bucharest who had come to New York with his Romanian wife, Ina. Poor Alex was toiling away on his medical boards—it took him five years, but he made it with the grit. At the time, I was working as a tour operator in CIT and was arranging all kinds of trips to the peninsula, mostly pre-tours for trip leaders.

CHAPTER 13
New Starts

Livia

I got a call one day from a woman named Livia asking me to arrange a visit to Venice and Rome for a group of priests. She contacted me briefly by phone, and since she wanted to go on an inspection trip with her client, I set up complimentary accommodations for both of them in Venice and Rome—two nights each. She came back excited about the plan, so I grabbed the opportunity and said, "When you're back from Italy, and if it goes well, want to hang out with me?" She laughed and agreed. And that was where it all began.

We planned to meet at 6 pm at the NY Hilton bar across the street from my office. I was smartly dressed: brown double-breasted jacket, blue trousers, dark blue shirt, and brown loafers. Livia arrived, looking radiant as ever, wearing a beige raincoat with a beautiful green dress, a simple necklace, and white shoes. Her green eyes sparkled, and I was in awe.

"So, you have a headache?" I said after a couple of

drinks.

"Certainly," she said, smiling.

I decided to take charge and took her to a fondue restaurant on 56th Street. We took it very seriously: cheese fondue, meat fondue, and chocolate fondue for dessert. I got a bottle of red wine and a bottle of Perrier. She liked it—I felt like I was getting it right.

We talked about her group, about ourselves, and about our pasts. After dinner, she drove me home in her little Nissan. She reluctantly pulled up just a few cars from my building door, and we kissed good night. She had the weekend off before her group left for Italy and promised to call me. She was thrilled with the suite arrangements I'd put together for her.

By the time her group returned, it was summer, and we took a weekend to go to the Catskills. She had booked a motel, but when we arrived there, we discovered it was a dump. It was so bad that we took one look at it and then at each other and immediately decided to leave. We had underestimated how crowded the place would be with summer tourists. By the time we left, we could not find any other place to stay in. We drove around, looking for somewhere else, and at midnight, found a Russian restaurant.

"Let's stop here," I suggested. It was after midnight.

We ate the typical borscht, varenikes (dumplings), and jam-filled crepes for dessert. We took a couple of shots of vodka and ended up at a big, diner-style motel for the weekend. We sat there for hours, laughing and hanging out, feeling like we'd finally discovered some happiness.

We met once more the following weekend, and then I flew to Israel in October 1987 to attend my cousin Dani's wedding some distance from the city of Akko. I told my parents and Papi about Livia that night at the wedding. Their very first question was an old Jewish standby:

"Is she Jewish?"

"No, she's Christian," I replied.

"Do you love her?"

"I think so," I replied.

They exchanged glances and asked, "So, are you proposing to her?"

"I'm just trying to think about it, you know? I don't know. Maybe."

I decided to ask her to marry me, and, just as unaware as she was that I had to buy a ring (it had occurred to me only after seeing it in movies), I bought her a change purse and a necklace instead.

Back in New York, it was a matter of calling her from the airport, and the time I got home from the trip, she was there. *I'm too tired,* I told myself. By now, I knew much better than to do what I really wanted to do: drop to one knee in a restaurant over a rich or important meal, take her hand, and ask: "Will you marry me?"

Instead, I took her to a restaurant that was nearby and asked, "Will you marry me?"

She replied, "Yes, but you're an idiot."

So, that was a rocky beginning.

Meeting Livia's Family

Livia made a remark that I might not like her, but despite this bad omen, we started our lives together. First, we met her family—a meetup that Livia organised. It was a Sunday lunch. She had a big, caring family full of love. I met her mom, who had been divorced and was living in upper New York City with a friend/partner. I met her grandma, whom everyone called Grandma Livia, the matriarch of the family and the love of Livia's life.

Her brother, Joe, was still in university and was around s lot. All three were devoted to Grandma Livia. The family home was a three-story old-timer in the Bronx. The basement was used part-time by Tom and Lucille, who spent 5-6 months of the winter in Florida. Here, Raymond and his wife, Vicky, lived on the middle floor, while Grandma Livia dwelt alone on the top floor. Neither of the two brothers had any children and each married after the age of 50. Another of her brothers, Uncle Pete, and his wife, Connie, lived in the house next door.

The house itself was a standard turn-of-the-century, early-20th-century Bronx home, full of personality and memory. The three floors were linked by a straight staircase. The basement was homey with Tom and Lucille's stuff. The middle floor, where Raymond and Vicky lived, featured old-style streamlined furniture and décor. Grandma Livia's upstairs home was more old-fashioned and cluttered with the furniture and stuff of generations past since, in that family, she was the heart and soul.

The house was alive with quiet commotion. The aroma of Italian cooking filled the air: sauce bubbling on the stove, garlic bread baking in the oven, and strong coffee brewing, fresh and hot. The dining table had been covered with lasagna, meatballs, salad, roast beef, broccoli di rape, and a wonderful selection of antipasti. The walls were covered with family photos.

Livia's uncles and their wives were great, and how nice they were! Raymond and Vicky were quieter but very sweet. And Uncle Pete sat with his wife, Connie, alone on the poarch outside, drinking his rose wine.

Grandma was happy that her family welcomed me pretty much right away and admired my Italian—which was better than any of theirs. She enjoyed our conversations about Italy. She liked that I seemed to appreciate her culture and took pride in my roots. She liked me. She even liked that I was a Jew since the Jews were to make good husbands.

As evening crept in, we were in the living room together, chatting and catching up. Once again, her family couldn't praise us enough for the idea and were eager to hear about our plans and about our future together. Little by little, I felt closer to Livia's family.

The main thing I did then with the uncles afterwards was to watch football and baseball on TV before dinner.

Livia and I together

Livia and I grew closer, and I became part of her family, sharing meals and spending countless evenings with them. Their warmth and acceptance made it feel like home, and they appreciated how I brought a little extra spark into Livia's life (maybe even some entertainment, as they always laughed at my jokes).

Not long after, she took solo trips to India and Vietnam—her favorite places. She fell in love with Southeast Asia and made a point to go back whenever she could. From the start, our lives were woven together in every direction. Eventually, she moved in with me in my tiny studio, which we filled with love—and a few arguments over closet space.

Livia was cultured and stylish, with a hint of wildness that made her both exciting and mysterious— enigmatic, even, in the way of a serious young lady who had true grime under her nails. She was theatrical and engaging, possessing that rarest of gifts: a touch of rebellion that was illicit and alluring.

She had the ability to turn the bleakest situation into

an attractive proposition. An engagement with her could range from the mundane to the sublime. Her thoughts would seamlessly transition from the sober criticism of an obscure piece of pottery to the whimsical construction of a faraway fairy castle. Within the same breath, she might chide the fickleness of a recent bouquet of wildflowers and dive into a soul-searching analysis of the religious practices of an extremely obscure sect.

Livia had an eventful past. She travelled with a band of itinerant artists, drifting from one forgotten museum to the next and living in bucolic communes that seemed lost to time. These trips prepared her for the world to come, each experience adding a new layer to her rich tapestry of stories. She continued to weave her adventures with canvas-skinned gypsies into a narrative of travel and love.

Yet, despite her wanderlust, Livia held her family close to her heart. Her attachment to them was absolute, giving her life a sense of direction and anchorage. She always returned from her escapades with the same determination to share her good fortune and success.

In essence, Livia was a whirlwind of fascinating stories and experiences, yet she maintained a core of loyalty and love that made her truly unforgettable. Her ability to remain authentically herself in every situation cemented her as a person of great interest and admiration.

Christmas and New Year 87'

Ian and his wife (Pitty) visited on holiday to New York during that time. We all stayed together in our L-shaped studio, which meant we could convert the living space into a bedroom with an opening couch. In a small apartment, this was a practical arrangement, and we had a lot of fun, though Ian did not get along with Livia. They were both bossy, and it was not easy to keep them both happy.

One day, she got tickets for the ballet, *The Nutcracker*. Ian didn't like it, but I was so proud of myself for having planned something to do in New York City after all. We then went to the Blue Note and listened to some jazz. Ian liked it. It was a good evening.

And yes, Christmas night was another one of those fun times. Livia wanted to go to Grandma's at dinner, and Ian wanted to go to Lake Placid to visit some friends from Romania. Stuck in the middle, you know what I agreed to? I had to please them both, so I decided we would be going to Grandma's for dinner and then driving to Lake Placid at 8:30 at night.

We arrived, and Ian's friends encouraged us to join them for dinner, which we already had. It was all Romanian food, which was quite fine. Then we had another dinner where typical romanian foods were served. There was an awkward phase when it came to opening presents, an even worse one when they assigned sleeping accommodations. On the floor with other friends and sharing a sleeping bag was uncomfortable for both of us, but Livia was more agitated. It was decided we would leave early the next morning, and we did.

A few days after Ian came back, I decided to throw a New Year's Eve party in my studio apartment. There were 40-50 people there, and it was a mess but fun—how Ian and I liked it. It was his stay here.

Work in the USA

January was a very slow month for the travel business, so I restarted from scratch, taking some time off from making travel requests to join a new venture that involved Italians travelling in the States. CIT—the company I worked for—was a government agency in charge of selling the ItalianRail and managing the land program for Italian ministers and big VIPs in the US and Canada.

I had to deal mainly with Italian VIPs. They usually travelled with a lot of money and expected the best. I used to arrange delegations of members of Congress, each one coming with his or her guide named Victor. Victor was a Russian émigré living in New York who spoke perfect Italian and knew everything about these people, their habits, their needs, etc. He understood what they would want, including from hotels, porn movies, prostitutes, alcohol of every type, and even cocaine—something of which, at that time, I had no idea because I was an organiser. But as they had the money for all these things, we were able to fulfil their requests. We had two or three delegations a month; we were working constantly. I searched for hotels, limousines or minivans, and entrance tickets to the various shows.

Later that month, I had a business trip to Venice and asked Livia to come down for the weekend. She flew in on Friday and stayed for the weekend, and we spent a romantic weekend together in Venice. It was still very cold in Venice in January, but the walks were so romantic. During the foggiest evenings, the canals, the Grand Canal, and even the Doge's Palace were floating in the blue and the silver mist.

We walked one night in the city under the midnight bells of St Mark's Campanile, and the only thing we could see was the fog over the Grand Canal. It was beautiful, like that film, *Don't Look Now*, with Donald Sutherland and Julie Christie. The hotel was nice, just off St Mark's Square, and the food was great. We ate fish, which they catch and cooked just right, and the wine to go with your dinner was just sublime.

It was breathtakingly romantic, a wonderful weekend in Venice that some might resist describing as work; the experience was too exciting, making us feel more connected to each other and adding another rich, colourful page to our story.

Wedding

We decided to have our wedding on the 6th of

March 1988. The venue was the Omni Park Central on 7th Avenue. I managed the hotel arrangements, menus, DJ (for once, not DJing my own event), and the photographer. Livia took care of the flowers. The total cost came to about $6500, which her mother paid.

We went wedding dress shopping with her mother, and Livia found a beautiful dress at Bloomingdale's for a very reasonable price. My best man, Alex, and her maid of honour, Elaine, were ready for the big day. Livia was the old type of person in that matter, so she had to ensure we were officially married before my parents arrived, so we had a small ceremony at City Hall. My parents were delighted to meet Livia when they arrived at the airport.

In preparation for the wedding, we bought rings and a tuxedo for me. One evening, we went out with Livia's father, Joseph, and her brother, Joe, along with my parents. Her father, a known womaniser, brought a bimbo to the dinner. After a drunken evening, Livia and Joe asked their father not to bring that woman to the wedding.

The day before the wedding, we stayed at the Omni Berkshire Place Hotel, a luxury 5-star hotel, to have some time alone. Thanks to my work connections, we received significant discounts and complimentary rooms. That night, we dined at the fondue place where we had our first date, adding a nostalgic touch to our wedding eve.

Our wedding was a simple yet beautiful affair, reflecting our love and commitment without extravagance. The guest list included about 75 people: 50 from Livia's side and 25 from mine, mostly family and just a couple of friends . Livia wore a simple, elegant beige dress with delicate lace detailing, while I donned a classic Tuxedo with a bow tie.

Her bouquet of white roses matched the rose in my lapel perfectly.

The ceremony was brief but heartfelt. We exchanged vows we had written ourselves, filled with personal promises and expressions of our love. The officiant, a kind elderly non-religiously attached minister, led us through the traditional rites with warmth and sincerity. As we said, "I do," and exchanged rings, there wasn't a dry eye in the room.

After the ceremony, we gathered in the main hall for a modest reception. The tables were set with white linens and simple floral centerpieces. We served a choice of finger foods, followed by a full dinner with pasta as the first course, and beef fillet as a main with roasted potatoes, fresh fruit, and a selection of pastries. A big cake, decorated with white frosting and fresh flowers, was the centrepiece of the dessert table.

Guests enjoyed champagne and different other liquors as they toasted to our happiness and future together.

Livia and I took a moment to step away from the

crowd and walk through a small courtyard attached to the venue. The setting sun cast a golden glow over everything, and we felt truly blessed to be surrounded by so much love. We returned to the reception to cut the cake, sharing a sweet moment as we fed each other the first slice.

The evening ended with heartfelt speeches from our closest friends and family. Livia's grandmother shared stories of Livia's childhood, while my father spoke about the joy of seeing his son find true love. The speeches were filled with laughter and a few tears, making the day even more memorable.

As the night ended, we hugged our guests and thanked them for being part of our special day. Livia and I left the venue hand in hand, ready to start our new life together. Our simple wedding was a perfect reflection of our love—pure, genuine, and surrounded by the people who mattered most to us. Some friends came to our hotel afterwards to have more drinks, and then Livia and I went on to enjoy our wedding night with all the excitement and intimacy it entailed.

CHAPTER 14
Starting a Life Together

Back from the wedding, I learnt that Gloria, Livia's mother, was really broke. She started a garage sale and sold everything she owned in that garage sale. The truth was that those two ladies—Gloria and her friend—were broke financially. They had had a bad year in the New York real estate market buying apartments, and they lost all of them. So, they both decided to leave for an apartment in Atlantic City. They sold everything to strangers except for some paintings and sculptures. It was a terrible atmosphere. Gloria gave us some pots and dishes. She had also sold her own house in Yorktown, NY.

I reminisce about the weekend when Livia, her brother, Joe, and I cleaned her house before the sale. That was a very hard day for all three of us. We had to go through the whole house, cleaning every room out and getting rid of most of the stuff in the house. We had pizza for lunch, and in the evening, we went to a local joint where they would go for dinner as children. After a long weekend of shared happy and sad memories, we came back to the city.

Apartment in Riverdale

Livia asked her mom about the apartment we found in Riverdale.

Her mom said: "Take it now; it's a great apartment. You should do it right away."

We didn't know any better, so we went and bought the apartment on a balloon mortgage. The payment was quite high, but it included maintenance of the apartment (which had a door attendant 24/7), a pool, and an underground garage. It was a two-bedroom apartment with a living room, dining room, kitchen, bathroom, and plenty of closet space, all for $10,000 USD—with a monthly payment of 1500. We were so excited that we started to move in right away.

One afternoon, we made an appointment at the Manhattan apartment. Livia was taking her Judaism lessons, and I was at work. After finishing my work, I went to the Manhattan apartment, and eventually, I fell asleep. I never heard Livia or the door attendant; I did not hear anything. When I woke up at 8 in the evening, Livia wasn't there. I ran downstairs, and the door attendant told me that Livia had come to the apartment and left since no one had answered. I called Livia, and she started screaming that I fucked everything up. I took a taxi and got back to our apartment in Riverdale.

That spring, I flew to Atlanta in May to attend the annual Pow Wow, a domestic travel show. 'Pow Wow' is a Native American term for 'Let's get together.' It is a trade show where domestic exhibitors (tour operators, bus companies, hotels, etc.) meet domestic buyers and where international buyers can meet the suppliers. The show is still held. We exhibited at the Pow Wow with a California company.

Janet and I went to Atlanta, representing CIT. We were very busy and had back-to-back meetings during the day. Then, at night, in addition to the city's organised events, we went out with two of our booth partners to check out the best nightclubs. We had a great time networking as well as going out.

As Livia and I had not had our honeymoon yet, I planned a special trip to Italy for us in May. For both of us, the desire to travel was always there, and it became a significant part of our marriage.

Our shared love for exploration led us to countless adventures around the world, enriching our lives with unforgettable experiences. In the following chapters, I have detailed only a small part of our most memorable trips. I hope these stories provide a glimpse into our journey together and do not bore you too much. This is the way we wanted our life to unfold, filled with travel, discovery, and cherished memories.

The Honeymoon

Thanks to our travel-industry perks, we scored a five-star honeymoon at a discount and took off to Italy. We flew into Milan, picked up a rental car, and headed straight to Stresa on Lake Maggiore. Livia, with her charm, had managed to get us an upgraded room with a view of the luxurious Les Iles Borromees hotel. We didn't waste time—we dropped our bags and headed straight to dinner, as any sensible honeymooner would!

On day two, we visited Isola Bella and explored the grand Borromeo Palace, full of chandeliers, frescoes, and furniture so antique. The palace gardens were a story in themselves, with exotic plants, statues, fountains, and views that looked like they belonged on a postcard. We strolled around, stopping at cafés for Italian pastries and coffee.

Naturally, the weather had other plans, and we ended up drenched from a surprise downpour. Back at the hotel, we warmed up with some hot chocolate before heading out for dinner. We hit it off so well with the restaurant owner that he actually drove us back to the hotel—I guess he wasn't ready to let us loose on the Italian roads again!

The next day, we ventured to Santa Margherita Ligure and Portofino, both full of lively cafés, boutiques, and cosy restaurants. We had a seafood feast, sampling the daily catch prepared in true Ligurian style. On our way back, we stopped at a local restaurant for dinner (because apparently, we had never met a meal we didn't like).

The following morning, we took the funicular up Mount Mottarone, where we were treated to stunning

360-degree views of Lake Orta, Lake Maggiore, and the Alps. After strolling around Stresa in the afternoon, our friends from Milan, Silvian and his girlfriend, Monica, joined us for dinner, where we indulged in more Italian cuisine (we were practically honorary Italians by then).

Next, we decided to head to Switzerland, driving from Como to Campione d'Italia and then into Lugano. We stayed at the Splendide Royal, sampled Swiss chocolate, and admired watches we could never afford, then wrapped up with dinner by the lake.

The following day was a bit of an adventure—I took the mountain road around Lake Lugano, convinced we'd have enough fuel for at least 25 kilometers. Spoiler alert: we didn't. Luckily, we found gas in Losallo, though it was touch and go. At the border checkpoint at Pizzo Paglia, the patrol had never seen an Israeli passport before, so we enjoyed an unexpected two-hour 'rest stop' while they sorted that out. We then drove on to Sondrio for lunch, a place only the truck drivers seemed to know about—Bresaola with arugula and Parmesan—followed by a dessert stop in Madonna di Campiglio, and finally, we made our way to our hotel in Limone sul Garda, where grappa was waiting.

We spent the next day exploring Riva del Garda, stopping for lunch in Desenzano del Garda, and finished up at our final destination, Milan, checking into the newly opened Four Seasons.

Time in Milan was spent in style: dinner at an ultramodern restaurant, followed by a night out clubbing. The next day, I showed Livia my old haunts around the city. We visited the cathedral (Duomo), the Galleria Vittorio Emanuele II, and the convent of Santa Maria delle Grazie to see da Vinci's *Last Supper.* To top it all off, we had a home-cooked meal at my friend Sorin's place.

And that was the end of our honeymoon—a blend of adventure, food, and enough fond memories (and calories) to last a lifetime!

Furnishing the Apartment

After returning, we started to look for the furniture for the apartment. We found a beautiful white L-shaped sofa for the living room. We bought a small glass table for the living room. We also bought a dining room table and chairs. For the bedroom, we bought a set: a bed with a double mattress and a matching dresser with a huge mirror. The set was black, shiny, and impressive. Also, we bought an air conditioner for the bedroom and another one for the living room. In the second bedroom, we put the couch we brought from our apartment in Manhattan. We also installed a TV. We also bought a Nissan Maxima for Livia and sold her old car.

Then, after having the apartment furnished, we returned to our routines: me to the city job and Livia to her travel agency. It was the busiest time of the year at work when many Italians came to the States. I started organising groups for tours: first in the East, then the West, and later a grand tour of the USA.

For someone so industrious, Livia's position at a travel agency offered a palatable quid pro quo: she was paid just shy of minimum wage, but almost all her weekends were free to travel. Every three weeks, she left on agency-sponsored trips to choose her own destinations—Paris, Naples, London, Indonesia, or Bali.

Isreal Visit

That fall, I brought Livia to Israel—not for the first time, but definitely her first time meeting the *whole* clan. We kicked things off with lunch in Haifa, where we managed to gather my grandfather, Papi, Miricel and Matei, Ariel and his girlfriend, Rina, Dani and his wife, Heidi, along with half my parents' friends, Ian and his wife, Pitty. It was like a family reunion on steroids.

To really set the scene, my parents hosted a Rosh Hashanah dinner with about 20 people, including Papi. We were staying in my parents' apartment, which sounded cozy in theory, but let's just say air conditioning was still a dream there. Livia—who was melting in the Israeli heat and humidity—managed to gently 'suggest' they buy one, and they eventually caved. It became the fastest appliance purchase in family history.

Our sleeping arrangements were another adventure. We were in my parents' old apartment, where my grandmother used to stay, on a mattress so uncomfortable it might as well have been a wooden plank.

One morning, I found Livia on the living room floor, where she'd opted for a change of scenery (and possibly better sleep). By the end of the trip, I think she was considering pitching a tent on the balcony.

Every night, after dinner with my parents, we'd dutifully trek over to Ian's place for a visit. Between the family gatherings, the mattress-from-hell, and a schedule that would put an endurance athlete to shame, it was a *very* long 10 days. But we survived, and she left with a true initiation into my family's world.

Alex, Mike & Irene Poker Nights

At home, we began playing poker on Saturday evenings with Alex, Mike, and Irine, who lived in their own flat in the same building as Alex. We'd play after Saturday night dinner, which consisted either of us going there for a meal or them coming for a meal at our place, depending on who might be working or travelling. They'd always grill meats and make a salad. Livia would make chili con carne or a range of pasta with different sauces and toppings.

Sunday Suppers in Family

Every other Sunday night, we'd go up to the Bronx for an entire family dinner—it was customary. The feast was a food-bomb of epic proportions. We began with antipasti: prosciutto, salami, and a bunch of cheeses. And then, a mountain of meatball pasta and gravy. Just when you thought you were done, up comes the prosciutto and melon, a sort of 'stopover' before the main course: roast beef with yellow potatoes, green beans, and broccoli di rape. The salad came with an iceberg salad and olive oil and vinegar, in case anybody felt they missed out on a veggie.

And then came the dessert: cannoli, fresh fruit, and, for the daring, a coffee shot of anisette. It was a whole experience. It was actually pretty easy for me, mostly sticking to the pasta, antipasti, and desserts and skipping the meatballs and the sides. The meal was approximately four hours long, with time to take breaks to watch football (because it wouldn't really be a family reunion without a little sport!).

Thanksgiving

Thanksgiving was always important to Livia, and she enjoyed spending it with her brother, Joe. He, however, always looked forward to enjoying it with his friends. The same year, we all met at The Mark Hotel on Madison Avenue in a suite overlooking the busy street. The Thanksgiving dinner was exquisite, with all the familiar side dishes and the perfect dessert to round out the meal. It was delicious, and it was nice to start the holiday with that big city view.

We toured the city the next day, including visiting the Metropolitan Museum of Art (a real-time culture tour). Beginning with the colossal front door on Fifth Avenue, the towering façade presented a forest of illusions. Inside, we meandered among endless halls, from ancient Egyptian treasures to classical Greek sculpturing, Renaissance paintings, and modern art. We marvelled at the Temple of Dendur, sat in awe of Van Gogh's Starry Night, and lost ourselves in the gorgeous period rooms where we felt like we'd entered other worlds. Later, we drove back home.

New Year

It was New Year's that we celebrated with our new Italian collaborators. Our group assembled at a Greek restaurant and, for the first time, tried pigeon, which was surprisingly delicious. Then we toured a retro club with a twist: the tables were placed inside vintage cars, with velvet seats making it uncomfortably comfortable. The music was excellent, and we couldn't get enough of dancing, laughing, and toasting the new year. I drove our friends to their hotel and back home at the end of the night, finishing off a great New York evening.

Extravagant Start of a Year

We had a sort of supernova year, a big year all over the world without knowing. January doesn't get people travelling, so we booked our vacation for February in the Caribbean. Livia set it up. She was there in November on an educational tour of hotels, and she got angry with the people from the tour group because they went to only four or five hotels, which was not enough.

Therefore, she took an overnight boat to St Barts with a guy from St Martin, which pissed me off, too. Jealousy was my second last name, and I was just angry even though Livia told me that nothing happened.

So, we went together to the best hotel in St Barts. We flew from New York to St Martin and from there to St Barts in a nine-seat plane. We rented a tiny jeep at the airport and drove it to the hotel. We stayed three nights at Hotel Guanahani & Spa, one of the best in St Barts. It sat on a peninsula, surrounded by two white-sand beaches, with French joie de vivre and a Caribbean informality. The spa was world-class, with many restaurants, tennis, and every kind of water sport available. The villas and cottages were bright, spacious, and private. It was a dream. Then we flew back to St Martin and on to Anguilla, a British overseas territory in the Eastern Caribbean, renowned for its white sand beaches, slow-paced lifestyle, and luxury resorts. We stayed at Malliouhana Hotel, one of the most luxurious luxury hotels on the island. It was super chic and very luxurious, with impeccable service, a secluded and calm atmosphere, a gourmet restaurant, and access to one of the most beautiful beaches on the island. Our suite was right on the beach, and I complained about the long walk to the room (never realising the beauty of nature and surroundings).

I almost drowned one day because the waves were too strong and high. I discovered the conch and had it at every meal. There was a near-shore island that you could take a boat to from a restaurant where we went for lunch, and then you took the boat back to the hotel. We walked for miles and miles along the beaches. In the evening, we went to a restaurant at the Cap Juluca Hotel on Maundays Bay for Caribbean food. By the third day, we flew back to St Martin and then on to New York.

Passover in the Apartment

We worked up until Passover, and then we did it all over again. Every year, in early April, Livia cooked for whichever friends and family happened to be around at the time. She cooked everything, and she had enough Haggadahs so that everyone could read. She bought a seder dish to be in the centre of the table. She did all the traditional foods and invited Joe, Alex, Grandma, her mother, and her friend from Atlantic City. It was a riotous dinner of laughing, singing, and eating.

Las Vegas and the Trip That Followed

The International Pow Wow (or IPW), held in Las Vegas, Nevada, in May, is an annual travel trade show that brings together thousands of international and domestic travel buyers and media to conduct pre-scheduled business appointments with US travel exhibitors to promote travel to the United States, negotiate future business, and network with industry professionals. The Las Vegas Hilton played host—a busy hub of activity, a microcosm of Las Vegas itself: luxury, hospitality, and world-class entertainment. I flew to Vegas with Janet; we wrapped up our meetings and enjoyed an evening with Wayne Newton, Mr Las Vegas himself.

On the weekend, Livia flew in, and I kicked off our spring getaway in Las Vegas, where we spent a couple of nights before taking a scenic flight to the Grand Canyon. We soared over Hoover Dam, Lake Mead, and the Colorado River before landing for a guided tour, hitting all the best lookouts. Back in Vegas, we caught the Pointer Sisters live, then ended up ditching a subpar Italian restaurant for a burger across the street—a much better choice!

Next, we picked up a car and hit Zion National Park, Bryce Canyon, and finally, Lake Powell, where we stayed at Wahweap Lodge. We took a boat ride to Rainbow Bridge, winding through stunning, secluded canyons. Another day, we cruised from Glen Canyon Dam to Horseshoe Bend and Lees Ferry, taking in the Colorado River from a whole new angle.

From there, we headed to Sedona, with a quick stop in Flagstaff, for a country lunch. Sedona's red rocks were unforgettable, and despite the hotel's no-smoking policy (my cigar dreams dashed), we enjoyed the views. The next morning brought an unexpected question from Livia: "Have you ever ridden a horse?"

"No," I replied, already a bit wary.

"Well, today's your lucky day!" she laughed.

Minutes later, I was up on a horse, only to realise I

hadn't quite positioned myself properly. (My discomfort was…memorable.) We spent the afternoon eating at L'Auberge de Sedona, enjoying a relaxing meal, and ending our stay with some poolside lounging.

We wrapped up in Phoenix at the Ritz-Carlton, staying cool by the pool and exploring Scottsdale's Old Town with its Western-themed shops and art galleries. After a Southwestern feast and a hike up Camelback Mountain, we topped off our adventure with drinks at the Rusty Spur Saloon. It was the perfect mix of wild landscapes, city lights, and memorable mishaps.

Los Angeles Work Trip

Business had to resume, and we went back to the office. It felt strange, a lot of telex correspondence with our main office in Rome. They were concerned about the LA office and how we were doing. I was asked to go to the LA office and 'check it out' and spend some time there.

So, I flew to LA for one month and stayed at the Mondrian Hotel, Los Angeles, known for its minimalist and futuristic design aesthetic. They wanted a design with minimalist detail and wanted it not to look worked on too much. The overall effect is not so much modern as clean-cut and minimalist. Designers, artists, and celebrities followed trends; this was a crowd this hotel wanted to attract.

I had a large room on the 10th floor with a great view of the valley. I hired a car to drive to the office that's near the airport. I worked in the office from morning to night, checking the work and dealing with my regular job in New York. It was very stressful there. Everybody else in the office was very insecure. They were sometimes afraid to be fired. After a month of working, mostly working at my New York job, I didn't think anything was wrong, and I came back.

My Father's Accident

That time, my parents came for a visit. We had them stay in our apartment. Then the schedule was the same—the only difference was that, after work, sometimes, we met in the city for dinner and then went back to the apartment.

One day, when my parents were in town, the worst thing that could have ever happened to my father occurred. He was on his way to meet my mom when he tried to cross the street. At the corner of 60th Street with Lexington Avenue at the green light, a delivery bike rode a light and hit him. He fell and was in so much pain that I had to come and pick him up. As soon as I could, I got to him and called a taxi, then took him home. I asked if he wanted to go to the hospital, and he said no. He was too stubborn like me. So, we got home, and he went to his room and went to sleep.

The next day, he asked us to take him to the hospital. Well, we drove to the hospital. Susan, Livia's partner in the travel agency, was married to Neal, the head of Gynecology at Lawrence Hospital in Bronxville.

Livia called Susan, and she gave me directions. We took my father there.

Neal did a radiography, and they saw that my father's hip was broken. My dad underwent surgery to replace his hip. Poor him. It was very painful. He stayed at the hospital for 10 days, but I got him ready so that his insurance covered it, and then I arranged a TWA first-class flight home. And that's it—the end of the trip. I was worried, but my mom assured me that everything was ok. He eventually went to physiotherapy and exercises and felt much better.

Holidays

Rosh Hashana, the Jewish New Year, rolled around once more, and Livia outdid herself with a magnificent dinner. She served all the traditional dishes, plus a hearty baked pasta she said the Italians insisted on adding to any festive meal. The table was packed, filled with the warmth and laughter of family and friends: Joe, Alex, Mike, Irine, and Grandma, all gathered around for the celebration.

The evening had that perfect blend of formality and humor. Each person shared a story or two, some recalling past celebrations, others poking fun at family quirks. Grandma was in rare form, mixing heartfelt blessings with her signature wit, while Joe and Alex couldn't resist cracking jokes over the baked pasta that had mysteriously found its way into the Rosh Hashana feast.

With great food, lively company, and just the right touch of Italian flavour, it was an evening that truly captured the spirit of both New Year's and family traditions.

LA Again

Despite an insipid holiday break, I was abruptly called back to Los Angeles—not for sunshine, but for something far less grand: managing the reduction of our North American operations. Two of our offices, in Chicago and LA, were closing. The LA office needed a full sweep, except for the room occupied by our most valuable partner, the Italian rail office. It was a bittersweet return, punctuated by an extended stay at the Regent Beverly Wilshire Hotel, where rooms were spacious, the service impeccable, and the rooftop pool ideal for an after-hours swim.

This time, I had a silver lining—Livia came along. Weekends became our mini escape as we strolled Rodeo Drive, a fantasy lane of posh boutiques and designer shops where the clothes have better bank accounts than most people. Our culinary adventures were equally indulgent; we dined at Spago, Wolfgang Puck's famed restaurant, and several Italian spots, including Il Cielo—considered one of LA's most romantic restaurants, which I can neither confirm nor deny. Madeo was a particular treat, an intimate, family-owned restaurant with authentic Italian charm.

One night, as we savoured a plate of pasta, I glanced

over and spotted Actor George Segal dining nearby.

One morning, we were in the hotel, watching the news, when something of important significance occurred: the Berlin Wall fell. The old frontier that had kept East and West Germany apart for decades no longer existed. We stood bowed—as if we were watching history unfold—and then got on with our lives. The anticipation was tangible, although I had no idea what else was in store for me back in New York.

When I went back to the office in New York, I was confronted by something less than a welcome sight: a procession of British accountants had marched down on us in sombre suits and even more grim faces. They told me, over a blanket of wintery warmth, that they had to make some decisions about the future of the company. They checked the files and the paperwork of the office, the accountancy, and the money situation. For three weeks, they'd wander in and out of town, performing their enigmatic accounting. Finally, on a Thursday, they took me to the Berkshire Hotel and blew the whistle: I was going to lead the whole company's North American business. With our inbound tourism branch and rail activities being all that remained, I'd run everything. They requested that I pick two team members to contribute, so I picked Alessandra and Serena, a woman who also worked for ItalianRail.

Then came the real shocker. They wanted me to call them that evening and show up at the office at 7 am without specifying why. I signed a contract, knowing that now that I was the president of CIT NYC. The next morning, I arrived at the office with the air of a new leader to see private security and locked gates. All employees had been laid off in an instant, with a severance pay packet to cushion the blow. Each individual was permitted into the room, briefly monitored, to get his possessions. It was surreal—one minute, I was their friend, and the next, their executioner. I looked like a dumb gatekeeper, staring at friends and colleagues, even at the one guy who always brought panettone before Christmas.

My presidency, it turned out, was about as illusory as a New Year's resolution. A week later, I was invited to London to 'examine the company's future.'

I asked if I'd have any real power, and they shrugged: "Obligations? Yes. Powers? No, absolutely not."

They clearly needed a puppet, not a president. I chose sanity over corporate manipulation and passed the baton to Alessandra, walking away with the same severance package as everyone else. I lost my rule before I'd even picked out a cup.

And like this, I ended 1989 with a few new adversaries but no corporate pressure. Livia and I went to her family's Christmas, and we had a simple, intimate dinner in the city for New Year's Eve, toasting to another decade.

CHAPTER 15—Pt 1
The Years Following

Central Holidays and USA Travel, 1990

Ah, 1990—a year of career roller coasters. One month, I was the 'president' of the company, and the next— well, let's just say I was looking for a new position. As luck would have it, this was also the year I met my future boss, Joseph Berardo, the brains behind Central Holidays, a big-name tour operator to Italy. Central Holidays started out in Moonachie, NJ, and eventually moved to Jersey City. They were the largest player bringing Italian tourists over to the States, and I was ready to help them make the magic happen.

Joining me was Aldo Sciarinno, an Italian gentleman with deep connections and a flair for business. Our goal? Launch a brand called *USA Travel* to entice Italians to experience America. I even saw potential in bringing in Israeli tourists, so the plan had scope.

BIT Milan

Our strategy was to be innovative, so we quickly

booked a table at the BIT Milan (Borsa Internazionale del Turismo), the biggest tourism fair in Italy. We left Antonella, Aldo's 'adopted daughter' in charge, back at the office. Antonella was strong-willed and sharp, handling things like a pro.

At the Grand Hotel Fiera Milan, across from the fairground, we checked into comfortable rooms with all the modern perks. Then came dinner. An Italian dinner with Aldo is an experience—he ordered for everyone and sometimes even 'supervised' the chefs in the kitchen. Every meal was a feast, and with Aldo's social energy, it felt like a party. When the fair opened, we split up to meet clients, some within and others outside the trade show, picking up a few new partnerships before heading back to New York.

Family Matters and Hospital Visits

Back home, Livia's grandmother's health started to decline, and the hospital became her second home. Throat cancer had left her needing a device to speak, making her condition all the more difficult. Livia was there for her as much as possible, juggling work and family. Her trips became rarer, and she'd often come home late, yet we still made time for shows like *Phantom of the Opera* and *A Chorus Line.*

Livia also introduced me to the New York City Opera, a treat that soon led to dates at the MET. Evenings together became precious as we enjoyed movies, dinners, and a lot of laughter to keep our spirits up.

Pow Wow and Ritz-Carlton, Naples

In 1990, the International Pow Wow was held in Orlando, Florida. Aldo and I attended, staying at the Peabody Hotel, and made contacts from around the globe. When it was over, Livia joined me for a weekend at the Ritz-Carlton in Naples. This beachside resort is a paradise of luxury with two outdoor pools (the adults-only one was our sanctuary) and great views of the Gulf. We had lunches poolside, basking in the sun, and enjoyed sunsets with dinners at The Grill—known for its steak and seafood, or Terrazza, with its Italian menu. It was a blissful break from doing absolutely nothing.

Afterward, I took a quick trip to Israel to check on my father, who was adjusting to a new hip. We visited family and friends as usual, catching up with cousins, old friends, and my grandfather.

Returning to New York to Livia's Grandmother

Ten days later, we returned to New York, where Livia's grandmother's health had worsened, prompting a move to hospice. This top-tier facility was funded by her son, John, a successful innovator in 'safer' cigarettes, who covered her care costs. Livia visited her every day, while I joined on weekends. Despite her condition, Grandma Livia always lit up when we arrived.

Rosh Hashana: Dinner and Shenanigans

Amid all the stress, Livia somehow managed to cook a fabulous Rosh Hashana dinner, inviting our friends Alex, Joe, and Terry. After dinner, the Grappa came out, and one bottle led to another. Livia convinced Terry and Alex to stay over since we'd all had a bit too much to drink. She set Terry up in the spare room and Alex on the couch. Little did we know, they'd polished off the second bottle of Grappa and, well...spent the night together on the sofa. The morning scene was priceless!

Thanksgiving Turkey Troubles

When Thanksgiving rolled around, we hosted Alex, Mike, and Irene. I attempted to carve the turkey but ended up practically hacking it to bits. Livia, horrified, took over. We stuck close to home for New Year's, spending it with the same crew, ringing in 1991 with a cosy evening together.

This year was packed with travel, family milestones, unexpected career twists, and a few laugh-out-loud moments. The ups and downs of work, the closeness of family, and the antics of friends made 1990 a year to remember.

1991: A Year of Travels, Family, and Unexpected Events

The year kicked off with big global news: the Gulf War or Operation Desert Storm. In August 1990,

Saddam Hussein invaded Kuwait, leading to a US-led coalition to push Iraqi forces out in January 1991. This hit close to home for me, especially when missile attacks targeted Israel. I called my parents daily, feeling the anxiety thousands of miles away.

Meeting Bruno: New Business on the Horizon

Early in the year, I embarked on a sales trip to Germany and the Netherlands. After flying into Amsterdam, I took the train to Frankfurt, where I met with Bruno, an Italian client who had set up an incentive company in Germany. He had big plans: he was organising a US launch for Warsteiner beer and needed someone to manage the New York side of the trip, while his friend Jim in Phoenix handled the West Coast. I gladly accepted—this was going to be a huge account for us!

Back in New York, I wrapped up the 64-page summer brochure for escorted tours and fly-and-drive packages. This was no small feat in the pre-internet era, believe me! Meanwhile, Livia balanced trips to her grandmother's side and the occasional weekend getaway.

Denver and Aspen: A Business Trip With a Side of Adventure

The International Pow Wow event in Denver, Colorado, arrived, and this time, we brought our wives along. Livia and Nina (Aldo's wife) joined us, and we stayed at the luxurious Lowe's Denver Hotel, where the food was impressive. Aldo, true to form, went into the hotel kitchen the first night to make pasta *cacio e pepe* himself.

While we attended the trade show each day, the ladies explored Colorado's sights, visiting Vail and Breckenridge. One evening, we saw a John Denver concert in a local park—yes, we watched Denver in Denver. The weekend took us to Aspen's Little Nell Hotel, famous for its top-notch service and luxury. Despite it being 'mud season,' we enjoyed the quiet charm of Aspen, strolled the streets, and even had a lighthearted encounter with a policeman in summer attire. The drive back, full of mountain views and laughs, was a fitting end to our Colorado adventure.

Livia's Father's Illness

Returning to New York, we were hit with tough news—Livia's father was diagnosed with cancer. I took a quick trip to LA for work, then met Livia and her brother, Joe, to drive down to San Diego to see him. Despite his illness, he threw a lively party for family and friends, complete with beer and scotch. It was a chaotic evening, but we soon learned his prognosis was terminal. The family gathered for one last lunch, and then we returned to LA, where I had to conclude business matters by letting an office manager go.

Saying Goodbye to Grandmother Livia

Back in New York, Livia's grandmother's health

took a turn for the worse, and she passed away on October 18. Livia was heartbroken. At the funeral home, she refused to go inside and see her grandmother in the 'glamorous' Italian American tradition of open caskets. We stayed outside, greeting mourners as they arrived. Livia also chose not to be near the grave at the funeral, following her own quiet way of saying goodbye. As per tradition, we had a large meal afterward—only in Italian culture does grief come with pasta.

A Visit to Livia's Father and a Tucson Getaway

Just a few weeks later, more news came: Livia's father's condition worsened, so we flew to Phoenix, where he was temporarily living with his sister in Prescott, AZ. We stayed at the Holiday Inn in Prescott, which had a beautiful backyard and pool. Livia cooked for her father, with dinners at 5 pm sharp, leaving me ravenous by 8. We'd sneak out afterward to a local Western bar for burgers and steaks to top off the night. After five days, we took a detour to Tucson for some downtime at Loews Ventana Canyon Resort.

In Tucson, we soaked in the resort's luxury and enjoyed the scenic desert. A trip to Saguaro National Park introduced us to a friendly Jewish cowboy named Cooper, who took us horseback riding through the cacti-strewn landscape. We also visited Biosphere 2, an intriguing experiment in closed ecological systems, and learned about survival in isolated environments. The desert setting made the visit both educational and surreal. We also explored Old Tucson Studios, a movie set and theme park, capping off our 'escape' with a mix of relaxation and a taste of the Old West.

December and a Final Goodbye

In December, we flew to Israel to visit my family. Then, on December 9, we received the news that Livia's father had passed away—just one day before Joe's birthday. Although we considered returning to the States, Joe insisted we stay in Israel, reassuring us that it was ok.

A Year of Change and Adventure: 1992 Careers on the Rise

By January, both Livia and I were thriving in our travel careers. I worked in Jersey City, coordinating travel packages from Italy and Israel to the US, while Livia managed high-end travel for VIP clients in White Plains. Our long commutes were worth it—we loved our jobs.

After a tough 1991, with the loss of Livia's grandmother and father, we were ready to refocus on work and move forward.

Bruno's Warsteiner Beer Inspection Trip

In January, one of our biggest clients, Bruno, from Germany, came to New York to finalise plans for an incentive trip. He had high standards—nothing was too small to overlook. For the event, Bruno's company had organised an exclusive New York trip for clients to promote Warsteiner beer in the US.

The planning was a marathon. We inspected hotels, booked buses, and met with guides. Bruno wanted every hotel, restaurant, and entertainment spot ready to serve Warsteiner at all times. This meant booking top venues, ensuring each stop had the right beer on hand, and even training staff to talk up the brand. Bruno wanted to personally meet every guide and insisted on selecting the manager for each restaurant, all with Warsteiner on tap.

February: BIT Milan and a Hernia Surgery

February started with my annual BIT fair in Milan, where I caught up with clients and worked on our summer brochure. When I returned, I went straight into hernia surgery. Recovery wasn't easy—I was practically immobilised. Livia, thinking I'd be fine, went to the opera that night, leaving me alone to 'rest.'

Livia's Journey into Judaism

During this time, we began learning about Judaism at a synagogue in New York. One of the main teachings emphasised was to let go of celebrating Christmas, a key holiday in Christianity. This was a significant shift for Livia—not because of any religious attachment to Christmas, but because it held a special place in her heart for family gatherings and traditions.

Livia was eager to connect more deeply with Jewish

culture and understand its values. She read numerous books on the subject, aiming to integrate it into her life. Although she didn't wish to become orthodox, the reform movement seemed appealing to her as a more flexible approach. Her curiosity about religion wasn't limited to Judaism; she also held a deep interest in Hinduism and Buddhism, immersing herself in their teachings and philosophies.

Weekends With Friends

Weekends offered a break, and we often visited friends like Raymond and Vicky, who had just moved to a spacious new retirement community in Yorktown. Our place also became a popular stop for Israeli friends, including Daniela, her husband, and Sorin, who often dropped by without much notice.

Pow Wow in San Francisco and Lake Tahoe Road Trip

In spring, we attended the Pow Wow in San Francisco. The convention went well, and I secured a big account with Boaz Waksman from Ophir Tours Israel, a major win for our business. After the show, I picked up Livia, rented a Mustang convertible, and we set off for Lake Tahoe. We stopped at Donner Pass, stayed at the historic Cal Neva Lodge, and explored the lake before detouring through Reno and heading to Yosemite for a few scenic hikes and a horseback ride.

From there, we continued to Carmel, stayed at the

Mission Ranch Hotel, and drove the famous 17-Mile Drive. We capped off our trip back in San Francisco with a memorable waterfront dinner in Sausalito.

Bruno's Warsteiner Event in Full Swing

As September approached, the Warsteiner event was ready to start, and Bruno returned to New York with two of his team members for final prep. He had a long list of demands, ensuring everything would run like clockwork. First, he required me to stay at the Hyatt New York throughout the event, available 24/7 for any need. Then, he requested eight cell phones—luxuries at the time—to keep his team and guides constantly connected.

The logistics were intense: we had three groups of 150-170 guests, requiring seven German-speaking guides and six buses per group. Every day, Bruno met with the guides at 7 am to go over the day's schedule, and he expected me to be one hour early at every venue to confirm every last detail—including making sure each stop had Warsteiner beer on top, front, and centre.

Despite the pressure, the event went flawlessly. Bruno was thrilled, as were the guests, and I knew it had been worth it. For my efforts, the event generated $70,000 for the company and netted me a personal bonus of $10,000. Joe Berardo was pleased, and I was proud of what we'd pulled off.

Thanksgiving Celebration and Il Postino Indulgence

With my bonus in hand, I treated Livia to a luxurious Thanksgiving getaway at the Loews Regency New York. We enjoyed a sumptuous Thanksgiving dinner, explored the Guggenheim Museum, and had an indulgent Italian meal at Il Postino, where the Branzino in Salt Crust paired with Gavi di Gavi wine made it a meal to remember. We capped off the night with a quiet walk in Central Park and a Manhattan nightcap at the Pierre Hotel bar.

Christmas and Big News

Christmas brought family time, and with it, a surprise: Livia's mother announced that she and her friend, Elizabeth, were moving to Puerto Rico, leaving Atlantic City behind. We never got a full explanation, but they were set on it. As New Year's Eve passed, we looked forward to 1993 and the adventures it might bring.

CHAPTER 15—Pt 2

1993

A Year of Changes, Health Scares, and Big Decisions

The year kicked off with an unpleasant surprise from our mortgage company. Despite making payments like clockwork, we found out we'd only been covering the interest and still owed a huge chunk of the principal. By April, they were demanding 85% of the mortgage. Stunned and frustrated, Livia and I realised we'd been living in mortgage-land naivety. And all that due to the advice we received from her mom.

Heart Troubles Resurface

Shortly after, my health took a downturn. I began experiencing circulation issues tied to a congenital heart defect—ventricular septal defect (VSD). This birth defect had caused problems over the years, even leading to a brain abscess. I spent a rough six weeks in and out of Lawrence Hospital, dealing with bacterial and fungal infections, on a heavy round of IV antibiotics.

Working from home with my IV pump wasn't ideal, but Joe and Aldo were understanding. It was also the first year I missed the BIT fair in Milan.

Considering a Move: Where to Next?

By April, with health and mortgage woes, Livia and I started contemplating a fresh start somewhere new. California, Arizona, and Florida all came up as possibilities, but nothing clicked. Then, on a whim, I suggested, "How about Israel?" Livia thought it was a bit wild, but the idea grew on us, especially when she began conversion classes to become Jewish.

Pow Wow and an Offer from Boaz

In May, I attended the Pow Wow convention in New Orleans with Aldo. I reconnected with Boaz from Ophir Tours, who had always hoped I'd join his company. We talked about possible roles in Israel, and his interest gave me a boost of confidence for our next steps. Other companies were also keen, so I felt like there were options waiting in Israel.

The Israel Exploration Trip

In July, Livia and I flew to Israel to see what life might be like there. I interviewed with several companies but held off on any commitments until we made the move. Livia, always practical, compared grocery prices, and we toured different towns to figure out where we'd want to live. We spent two weeks with my parents, soaking in as much information as we could. Back home, Livia dove into intensive conversion studies, determined to complete them before our move.

Surgery on the Horizon

As I settled back into work, my surgeon set the date for a major heart operation in October. Livia and I also managed our usual commitments with friends—visits with Raymond and Vicky, family gatherings, and helping our friend, Terri, who was expecting twins. In September, Terri's twins arrived, and we attended their christening before I prepped for surgery.

The Big Surgery

Livia was nearing the end of her conversion studies, and her final mikveh ceremony was scheduled for just after my surgery. So, on October 6, I was admitted to Presbyterian Hospital in New York for an intense procedure to repair my congenital heart defect. The surgeon used the pericardial sac from my own heart to patch up the ventricular defect and fix both my mitral and aortic valves—no metal or artificial parts, just 100% me. If there was a 'farm-to-table' version of heart surgery, this was it.

The six-hour operation was followed by three days in the ICU, surrounded by monitors, IVs, and a ventilator. On the first night, I convinced a nurse to let me watch the *World Series*, promising I'd drift off eventually. By day two, I was off the ventilator and moved to a regular room.

Hospital days were long and, honestly, pretty dull. Livia visited every evening after work, often with my parents, who were dedicated visitors but not exactly a comedic duo.

The day after my surgery, Livia completed her conversion, officiated by an Orthodox rabbi. Once I started feeling stronger, I spent time reading and walking the hospital halls to regain strength. Nine days later, I was discharged and ready to start a steady routine of exercise and rest at home.

Getting Ready to Move to Israel

As my health improved, we shifted focus to our big move. We scoured Canal Street for 220v appliances, knowing our American gadgets wouldn't work in Israel. We then coordinated with a shipping service to pack everything into a container. The flight to Israel was set for November 22, giving me time for two final check-ups at Presbyterian Hospital and to recover enough to handle the long trip.

By early November, Livia left her job at the travel agency and threw herself into packing, running errands, selling her car, and filling out immigration forms. She was like liquid mercury—moving constantly, doing everything from cooking and hosting friends to managing the whole transition.

Final Goodbyes

True to her warm nature, Livia organised a series of

farewell dinners with our friends and family. Aldo and Nina came one night, Alessandra and Paolo another, then Alex, Mike, Irene, and Joe.

Our last big goodbye was with Raymond and Vicky. By November 19, after packing most of our essentials, we held a yard sale for the rest. Friends like Mike, Irene, Alex, and Joe came over the next day to help us finish up the packing.

Getting Married (Again), Jewish Style

With two hours left before the movers arrived, we squeezed in a third wedding—this time, a Jewish ceremony at the synagogue. Joined by friends Susan, Neal, Mike, and Irene, it was a short but meaningful event. When we returned to the apartment, everything had been cleared out.

That night, we splurged on a stay at the Four Seasons, enjoying a last bit of New York luxury. The next day, a limo took us to the airport for our one-way flight to Israel. Planning it all while recovering from surgery was no small feat, but Livia had made it look almost effortless.

Arrival in Israel

After landing, we drove to our new rental apartment—a place with wildly colourful walls in shades of pink and blue. It was winter, damp and chilly, and Israeli apartments aren't exactly known for their insulation. My parents were eager to help us settle in, so much so that we barely had a moment alone.

The next morning, after a quick job search, I returned to find Livia curled up in bed, wrapped in three blankets and feeling homesick—it was Thanksgiving, her first away from family. We decided right then to find a new place.

New Beginnings and Old Friends

Over the next few days, friends like Ian and Pitty and Gerard (now Gadi) and his wife, Adina, visited, which made the transition easier. On November 29, I officially began working for Boaz at Ophir Tours. My new office setup was...minimalist. I had a desk, a chair, and a phone—no computer, no extras, just the basics. It wasn't glamorous, but it was a start, and I was ready to dive in and make things happen.

We focused on finding an apartment near Tel Aviv, where my job was located. With no car, central living was key. Soon, we found a beautiful place downtown, right by the city hall. It was spacious, with two bedrooms, a large living room, a dining room, a kitchen, and two terraces. We kept some of the apartment's furnishings, bringing only our own living room and bedroom sets. By Christmas 1993, we were officially moved in.

New Year's Celebration

For New Year's Eve, we dined at an exclusive Tel Aviv restaurant with Ian and Pitty. The spot was renowned for its gourmet dishes and upscale ambiance—the perfect way to celebrate our fresh start in Israel.

CHAPTER 16
A New Life in 1994-1999

As the new year began, I reflected on the events as they unfolded. Livia had started taking Hebrew lessons at an ulpan in Tel Aviv, where she met two women: Angelica, a German girl, and Terri, an American woman who had recently divorced and moved to Israel to be with her old flame, Avi.

Livia's Ulpan, Roxy, Work

Around this time, we adopted a labrador puppy. We named her Roxy; she was so small that I could fit her in the jacket pocket of my winter coat. But she grew quickly, eventually becoming large enough to chew the legs of our dining room table and the edges of the walls in the lounge. Livia loved having a purpose, taking the dog to the park and the vet.

Initially, there was no specific role for me at Ophir Tours, so I spent my days meeting with Boaz to brainstorm ideas and set goals for future projects. We were constantly looking ahead, shaping new strategies and challenges. That year, I attended the BIT trade show in Milan, where I learned about Valtur, an Italian company similar to Club Med, with resorts across Italy and abroad. I managed to secure exclusive rights for Ophir Tours to represent Valtur in Israel, a significant deal at the time since every tour operator was competing for exclusive agreements to gain an edge before the days of online booking platforms.

In April, Boaz fired the manager of the Holiday Division and asked me to take over. It was the start of the busy summer season, so I quickly restructured the team, letting go of two employees from the previous management and hiring fresh staff to help us handle the workload.

I spent two weeks in Greece, meeting agents and partners in Rhodes, Mykonos, and Crete. Our Turkish agent, Abdullah Nayman, joined me in Antalya and Istanbul, where we finalised contracts. I also arranged two charter flights for the summer season: one to Mykonos with Arkia Airlines and another to Munich for Austrian holiday packages based in Tyrol.

Concerts, Meeting Old Friends, and Livia's New Group

That summer, we attended outdoor concerts by Peter Gabriel, Lou Reed (who opened for Peter Gabriel), and Kiss with Angelica. We spent evenings with Ian and Pitty, going to movies or having impromptu dinners on Friday nights. We also regularly dined with Terri and Avi.

Livia and Terri joined a group of American women who called themselves 'the Mahjong Marvels.' They met every Thursday evening, rotating houses for food and drinks before playing.

One evening, I came home from work to find Livia in a rage because some guy had flashed her while she was walking in the park with our dog, Roxy. I calmed her down, and we went out for dinner.

Burglary

Then, one day, Livia returned home from ulpan (her Hebrew class) to a shock: we'd been burglarised. The front door was wide open, and Roxy was unscathed—she had not awakened or yawned, let alone attempted to scare the thieves. She had apparently napped the entire time the burglars were there, likely imagining that she'd sell them a coffee rather than chase them away.

We reported it to the police, although, alas, their insurance covered the theft of a costly bracelet I'd given Livia for one of her birthdays. She wept and was devastated because, for Livia, the memories attached to it were so vivid for her. However, we were relieved that Roxy had not been injured.

Papi

At the same period, we were also in close contact with relatives, particularly my parents. My grandfather, Papi, died at the age of 94. We attended his funeral in

Haifa with the extended family. Papi was a lovely man, always so calm and careful; he was a witty guy. He was a man everybody adored, a constant figure of kindness and wit. It was painful for all of us to lose him, but even his memory served as a source of comfort.

In the meantime, Livia visited Cyprus a few times with her friend, Angelica. She would always return with a smile on her face, telling me of the hospitality and gentility of the Cypriots. Each visit was a breath of fresh air that was a welcome reprieve from our everyday struggles in Israel.

One day, Livia came home with Terri and casually announced, "I got a new car."

"A brand-new Toyota Corolla," Livia said again nonchalantly.

That week, just before starting her work, she and Terri decided to go to the Carmel Market, and just like that, they found themselves in the middle of the market (which is a pedestrian zone only). I do not know how they came out alive. Terri had also bought herself a new Honda Civic. They were both proud of themselves.

I helped Livia in applying for a position as a travel agent. She soon started working as an inside agent for Motorola at Ophir Tours and was shortly thereafter appointed manager of the Travel Department of the Association of Americans and Canadians in Israel (AACI). This became her main job at Ophir Tours as the years went by.

Istanbul Weekend

Travelling was, as usual, one of our main enjoyable moments in life, and every trip, long or short, was a memorable experience for both of us. We travelled that year to Istanbul for a weekend with Ian and Pitty. It was just a great way to experience the vibrant city and the nightlife.

Thailand Adventure

Bangkok: We kicked off our trip in Bangkok, exploring iconic sites like the Grand Palace and Wat Phra Kaew, home to the revered Emerald Buddha. At Wat Pho, we admired the massive Reclining Buddha. A scenic boat ride along the Chao Phraya River took us to Wat Arun, the stunning Temple of Dawn. Evenings were spent savouring local Thai dishes at the Regent Hotel and other authentic spots.

We toured the Jim Thompson House, learning about the man who revived Thailand's silk industry and browsed vibrant local markets. One day, we ventured to the Damnoen Saduak Floating Market, where vendors sold colourful produce and crafts from their wooden boats.

Chiang Mai: After a few days in Bangkok, we flew to Chiang Mai. We climbed the Naga staircase at Doi Suthep and enjoyed breathtaking views. We explored the handicraft villages of Bo Sang and San Kamphaeng and strolled through the bustling Chiang Mai Night Bazaar.

Chiang Rai: From Chiang Mai, we drove to Chiang Rai to see the White Temple, the Blue Temple, and the Golden Triangle, where Thailand, Laos, and Myanmar meet. A visit to the Hall of Opium Museum added depth to our experience. We returned to Chiang Mai for a quiet evening, reflecting on our journey.

Phuket: Next, we headed to Phuket, where we relaxed at Deevana Patong Resort & Spa, enjoying the tropical gardens, pool, and beautiful beachfront setting.

Hong Kong: After our time in Thailand, we flew to Hong Kong for a two-day experience, exploring the vibrant city and all it had to offer.

Back to the Office

1995 was a year of growth—and some serious hustle—in my office. Our team expanded from seven to eleven as the number of flights and agreements with charter airlines and international hotels skyrocketed. The operation was still delightfully old-school: Victor handwrote tickets; Galit, Yulia, and Eti managed yield management of the flights; Maya, Hadar, Evi, Limor, and Orly handled hotel bookings; and Osnat, my new secretary, kept everything running smoothly. I was often at the office until 8 pm, fueled by endless coffee and late-night pizza runs. In that period, I travelled quite a lot to Rome, Milan, the Greek Islands of Crete and Rhodes, Athens, and Cyprus—all for short one-or-two-day trips all for business.

Herzliya

Herzliya, a coastal gem just north of Tel Aviv and named after Theodor Herzl—the visionary behind the Zionist movement and the state of Israel—offered a unique blend of small-town charm and emerging luxury. The Mediterranean breeze carried a salty, refreshing scent, mingling with hints of blooming bougainvillea in vibrant purples, reds, and pinks that lined the streets and adorned the houses. The town had a relaxed, sunlit vibe, with wide, sandy beaches stretching along the coast and crystal-blue waters sparkling under the sunlight.

Herzliya's marina was lively, bustling with sleek yachts, fishing boats, and cosy cafés. The aroma of freshly baked pita and grilled fish wafted from nearby restaurants, inviting visitors to savour the local flavours. On market days, the air came alive with the earthy smell of fresh produce, olives, spices, and the sweet fragrance of oranges from nearby groves.

Herzliya Pituach, with its upscale villas and lush greenery, contrasted with the quieter, more traditional neighbourhoods that still held onto their roots. By evening, the town settled into a gentle, warm glow as the sun cast pink and orange hues over the sea, creating a peaceful coastal retreat just steps away from the energetic pulse of Tel Aviv.

A New Home by the Sea

That fall, Livia and I moved into our new apartment

in Herzliya, right on the Mediterranean. It was a dream spotlight, airy, with a stairway to the roof and a huge 78-square-metre terrace overlooking the sea. We filled it with furniture that we brought from the States, installed ceiling fans, and even rearranged the kitchen for maximum storage (because there's never enough!). It was warm, cosy, and perfect for us. It was ours!

A Nation in Mourning

On November 4, Prime Minister Yitzhak Rabin was assassinated by Yigal Amir, a far-right extremist who opposed Rabin's peace efforts, particularly the Oslo Accords that aimed to bring about a lasting resolution with the Palestinians. The assassination happened just moments after Rabin delivered a speech at a peace rally in Tel Aviv—a rally filled with hope and support for the ongoing peace process.

The shock of Rabin's death was immediate and overwhelming. It felt as though the entire country was plunged into grief and disbelief. Everyone around me was visibly affected; people I'd never seen display emotion were openly crying. Rabin had been a symbol of courage and vision, especially for those who hoped for a peaceful future. His assassination was more than a personal loss; it was a blow to the national spirit and to the idea of peace that he had championed.

The days following were sombre, with public gatherings, memorials, and candle-lit vigils everywhere. Conversations took on a heavy tone, reflecting the deep sadness and uncertainty that gripped the country. Rabin's assassination left a lasting scar, marking a pivotal moment in Israel's history and a personal reminder of the fragile nature of hope in the face of violence.

A Christmas in Kitzbühel and a Ski Mishap

To lift our spirits, Livia and I decided to spend Christmas in Kitzbühel, Austria. She knew I'd love the Tyrolean Christmas charm, so she picked Hotel Erika, a beautiful blend of traditional and modern Tyrolean styles with excellent skiing facilities. The moment we arrived, I was eager to hit the slopes. Borrowing a friend's ski gear, I signed up for a half-day lesson, and by day three, I felt ready to conquer the bigger slopes.

Then came the infamous fall. While attempting a small jump on a blue slope, I wiped out and injured my knee. Meanwhile, Livia was enjoying hot chocolate at the cable car station. Her reaction when I limped over was like: "That's what you get for going skiing when I was waiting!"

Still, she suggested we go for lunch at a nearby mountain refuge before heading to the hospital.

Hobbling along, I enjoyed a fantastic meal before a surgeon drained my knee and cheerfully sent me on my way with a "Have a nice vacation!"

The next morning, knee and all, we went sledding through the snow-covered town, which looked like a

Christmas postcard come to life. Snowflakes fell as we enjoyed a horse-drawn carriage ride—a magical moment that made me forget about the knee entirely. Christmas Day was spent touring nearby alpine towns, like St. Johann and Going am Wilden Kaiser, each with stunning mountain views. We wrapped up the trip with a night at the new Kempinski Hotel at Munich Airport and flew home the next day.

Knee Surgery and a Busy Year for Business

Back in Israel, I scheduled knee surgery for early 1996. Recovery meant lots of physiotherapy, limited movement, and not being able to drive for a couple of months. Despite my recovery limitations, the business kept us busy: we hired new staff, and our operations expanded to include flights to Greece, Verona, Rome, and more. I was frequently travelling, arranging hotel and ground logistics for our growing operations.

In July, Ophir Tours went public, so it was on the Tel Aviv Stock Exchange. Livia was also on a roll, securing exclusive kosher escorted tours in partnership with AACI and launching a successful kosher Mediterranean cruise in September.

Valtur Dalman

In June, I struck a deal with Valtur to use their club in Dalman, Türkiye, during the Jewish holidays—a 10-day event in early October. I planned to fill the place with five hundred guests per week, offering packages of 3, 4, 5, and 7 nights. Coordinating this was no small feat;

I managed sales, marketing, and charter flights and even brought in an Israeli team to manage the on-ground operation. We had six staff members from Israel and two from Istanbul to organise daily excursions for our guests, sold directly on-site. It was a whirlwind project that had me juggling planning like a circus act, but the recognition—and satisfaction—was worth every late-night call.

WTM and the Alava Discovery

At the WTM in London, I stumbled upon two representatives from the Alava Tourism Association in Spain's Basque region. We quickly set a common goal: to establish a new flight to the Basque Country. Diving into research, I realised the immense potential for Ophir Tours. Boaz backed the project, pending the budget the Alava team could commit. The idea made a lot of sense and perspective for the future.

Livia's Mom: Thanksgiving in Puerto Rico

Our annual Thanksgiving (or Christmas) tradition involved visiting Livia's mom, now settled in Palmas del Mar, Puerto Rico. Their house was in a stunning resort community where we would unwind, feast on traditional Puerto Rican cuisine, and explore. A yearly highlight was visiting Old San Juan, where the vibrant Caribbean life blended history and culture into a colourful experience. Livia's mom and her partner were avid casino-goers and had even started a catering business in the resort, delivering meals by golf cart—

nothing short of an adventure in itself!

New York Christmas With Joe and Catherine

After Puerto Rico, we would hop on a flight to New York, usually staying with Joe or at a nearby hotel. Their townhouse near Broadway, with three floors and a prime location, was a perfect location for us to wander in the city. This year, we met Joe's girlfriend, Catherine, a lovely Jewish girl. Catherine invited us to Sunday brunch at her parents' spacious apartment on Park Avenue. New York City at Christmas is like stepping into a magical snow globe, with holiday spirit everywhere. In the evenings, we would take cosy horse-drawn carriage rides in Central Park, snuggled under warm blankets, the city lights twinkling against a backdrop of softly falling snow. It was holiday magic—a perfect blend of New York's hustle and festive charm.

We also caught up with Raymond and Vicky in Yorktown and had drinks with Terri, savouring the city's Christmas glow, with store windows decked out in cheerful, over-the-top decorations. Spending a week in New York, surrounded by holiday cheer, was the ultimate way to end the year.

The Second Meeting With Alava Representatives and a Visit to Vitoria

My year began with a trip to FITUR, the Spanish trade show, followed by a visit to Vitoria, Spain, to meet with the City Council and the Alava representatives who were supporting our initiative. As promised, they invited me to explore the city. Walking through Vitoria was like stepping into the past; its narrow, cobbled streets and well-preserved medieval architecture told stories of another era. I explored the Old Town, a UNESCO World Heritage Site, with its grand Gothic cathedral and charming plazas. The pintxos were the best I had ever tasted, and I made it a mission to sample something unique in every little tavern. Even in winter, the warmth of the people and the rich Basque culture added to the city's charm.

The City Hall officials committed substantial support for the flights, offering Ophir Tours cash grants and free airport services to cover at least twenty-five percent of the expenses. However, there was a logistical challenge: Vitoria did not have an available aircraft, so I arranged to source a plane from Palma and collaborated with a Spanish tour operator to sell seats on the Vitoria- Palma-Vitoria leg.

During my trip, I also secured hotel deals in Vitoria, Bilbao, San Sebastián, and Pamplona. In Bilbao, the Guggenheim Museum captivated me with its reflective titanium curves that seamlessly blend the city's industrial past with modern artistry. San Sebastián offered stunning views of La Concha Beach, a vibrant Old Town with buzzing pintxo bars and the finest gourmet bites in the Basque Country. In Pamplona, I traced the famous path of the Running of the Bulls, which was thankfully quiet this time of year, allowing me to fully appreciate the city's medieval atmosphere. Each location left a strong impression and helped me finalise hotel partnerships for our tours.

Marketing and Promoting the New Destination

Back in Israel, I drafted itineraries for escorted tours and fly-drive hotel packages, followed by producing a TV feature to introduce the Basque Country to Israeli tourists who have always been interested in new destinations. In early April, I returned to Spain with a TV crew—a reporter, a cinematographer, and a sound technician—to film footage for an upcoming broadcast that would air before flights launched in July.

Soon after, a Basque delegation visited Israel to promote the destination. We hosted two dinners at Spanish restaurants—one for journalists and one for travel agents—sponsored by the Basque region to generate excitement and media coverage for the flights.

Finally, I had the honour of being the first Israeli passenger on the inaugural flight from Tel Aviv to Vitoria, a memorable journey marking the start of this new venture.

Trieste Flights and Winter Destinations

While attending the BIT show in Milan that February, I met Andrea Sarto, the acting marketing manager of Trieste Airport. We were arranging Ophir Tours' second flight to Trieste for that summer, and with a generous marketing budget from Ophir, I had the green light to promote the flight and reduce any risks. Booking this summer flight was straightforward, but I was already eyeing a new challenge: winter flights to Trieste for the 97/98 season.

Just before launching the Vitoria route, I headed to Trieste with my boss, Kobi, to scout potential winter destinations. We ventured to Tarvisio, a charming town nestled in the Julian Alps near the Austrian and Slovenian borders. Tarvisio is a year-round paradise for nature lovers, offering winter ski trails and summer hiking and cycling, especially around the scenic Fusine Lakes. It had winter magic written all over it.

Then we visited Piancavallo, perched on the foothills of the Dolomites. With its laid-back vibe and fresh runs, Piancavallo offers an easy ski or snowboard ride for beginners and a challenge for advanced skiers and snowboarders alike. Pine forests frame the town, some preserved as hay and pasture for centuries, adding to its rural feel.

We scoped out accommodations and found Hotel Antares, the only 4-star spot in Piancavallo. With spacious rooms and stunning mountain views, the hotel offered just the right mix of luxury and comfort. It even had an on-site wellness center, complete with a sauna and hot tub—a must for unwinding after a day on the slopes.

Weekend Expedition in the Golan Heights

That year as well, we went to the Golan Heights with Avi, Terri, and Roxy. We did an overnight stay at a hotel there and had an excellent dinner. The next day, we were to go to Banias, a nature reserve. It was nice because, obviously, Roxy was there with us for the first time. It was her first trip, and she had such a great time.

New Places and New Ideas

The following year kicked off with our charter flights to Venice, which replaced Trieste—and let me tell you, our customers coming off the plane from Piancavallo were positively ecstatic. You'd think they'd just skied straight through heaven; they were so thrilled. Buoyed by this success, I was ready for the BIT show in Milan, where I was a guest of the Italian Chamber of Commerce.

And that's where I met Emanuela Zago—my future partner in both business and brilliant ideas. Emanuela was an incredibly sharp and funny Italian lady who had the kind of wit that could keep anyone on their toes. We hit it off immediately, bonding over dinners that included top-notch Italian wines, as all good business meetings should. We threw around ideas like we were solving the world's problems, brainstorming ways to bring our grand plans to life.

Our partnership turned into a lasting friendship, one that only got better with each year. It was a perfect mix of laughs, business savvy, and the occasional glass of something Italian and delicious to keep things inspired.

Celebrating 10 Years in Paris

March 1998 marked our 10th wedding anniversary, so naturally, we celebrated in Paris. We checked into the glamorous Hotel de Berri near the Champs-Élysées and wasted no time. Our first stop? A charming brasserie, where we devoured steak tartare, a fresh green salad, and a bottle of wine—a perfect 'bonjour' to Paris.

The next day was dedicated to the Louvre. The sheer grandeur of the palace and Pei's glass pyramid were stunning. We joined the crowd around the Mona Lisa, where her mysterious smile led to endless speculation between us. Moving through galleries, we admired everything from Vermeer's delicate brushstrokes to the timeless beauty of the Venus de Milo. By sunset, we strolled along the Seine, the Louvre's glass reflecting the golden glow of Paris.

Then we took on Montmartre, wandering its cobblestone streets and capturing Sacré-Cœur's views over the city. We paid homage to Jim Morrison at Père Lachaise, a quiet, spooky place with ornate tombs and shady paths. Later, we browsed a lively Parisian market, buying artisanal cheeses and fresh baguettes for a classic French picnic.

Our fourth day was all about Notre Dame and a little shopping. The cathedral's Gothic facade and majestic towers left us in awe while its bells filled the air. We then hit Galleries Lafayette, admiring the beautiful glass dome before picking up some Parisian treasures. That evening, we indulged in absinthe cocktails at Café de l'Absinthe, an experience that felt straight out of the Belle Époque. With retro decor, vintage bottles, and herbs floating in a glass, the ritual was almost hypnotic. We savored duck confit, drank more absinthe cocktails than I'd admit, and ended with a perfect tarte tatin.

The Musée d'Orsay awaited us the following day. Housed in a grand Belle Époque railway station, it felt like stepping into an art lover's paradise. We explored impressionist works by Monet, Renoir, and Degas, soaking in the vibrant colours and unique brushwork. We spent ages marvelling at Van Gogh's sunflowers, Gauguin's Breton women, and Seurat's pointillist perfection. From the giant clock-face window, we watched Paris go by below, adding to the magic of the day.

On our last morning, we savored one final Parisian breakfast at a sidewalk café, reflecting on our adventures. Leaving Paris, our hearts were full—10 years of love celebrated in the City of Love.

New destinations

In April 1998, I had to open a new destination to Madeira, where I stayed at the Savoy Hotel and enjoyed the island's natural beauty. In Lisbon, I explored historic districts and cultural landmarks. I completed the agreements for hotel and land arrangements.

At the end of the summer, we had another new destination to open—Seychelles, one of the most famous archipelagos in the Indian Ocean. From Rome, I flew to Mahé with Air Seychelles, the national airline. When I arrived, I met the local agents' who were very cordial and informative. I looked at the rooms and other facilities like a restaurant, a pub, a dance hall, and a bar for the foreign teachers.

I travelled to a few different islands and looked at several different hotels. In Mahé, I stayed at the Berjaya Beau Vallon Bay, the intimate La Roussette, the Hilton Resort and Spa, and the beautiful Four Seasons Hotel. I checked out the rooms, dining options, and recreational facilities. After that, I flew by a two-engine propellor aircraft to Praslin Island, where I drove out to Constance Lémuria, Raffles Seychelles, and Club Vacanze—three of the most luxurious hotels in the world, each one with superb room quality and service.

After Praslin, I went to La Digue. This island, considered one of the prettiest and most peaceful in the group—where the only vehicles are bicycles—was chilled out. I stayed for the day and returned back to Mahe in the evening. I went there just to see a couple of hotels, and being an Israeli tourist, I did not finalise anything since it was too far and without any entertainment. As soon as I arrived and had time to re-evaluate the properties, I visited them to select which ones to feature in the brochure. This seemed like my first thorough tour of the new destination and its offerings.

Valtur Pollina

In April, I met with the owners and marketing team of JR Duty-Free, who were interested in offering a special vacation package for their clients—a 4-day paid trip to Sicily in the fall, staying at Club Valtur. This resort, located on Sicily's northern coast near Cefalu and within reach of Palermo, was perfect for the plan. The idea of taking over a part of the club in the low season appealed very much to the owners of Valtur. And I got a very good deal price-wise.

The concept was simple: three groups of 100 people would enjoy an exclusive experience at Pollina, one of Valtur's clubs. The entire operation turned out to be a huge success. Livia joined me for the final eight days, and we had an amazing time exploring Sicily together, making the business trip even more memorable.

Winter 98/99

We started selling the winter resorts for next season, 1998/99. We were selling the ski destinations based on charter flights to Venice and Torino. Venice was for the Piancavallo and Valtur Marilleva, and Torino was for Valtur Sestriere. Meanwhile, we developed other Valtur pursuits, investing in a major TV ad campaign that grew our roster of resorts and eventually promoting winter resorts, with reps visiting each area and sending representatives to cater to the Israeli guests, with daily activities translated into Hebrew and timely transfers, given that while many of Valtur staff didn't speak English, all our reps did.

Everyday Activities

Livia was fully occupied with the AACI program and took over running one of Ophir Tours' offices on Yarkon Street. Despite my frequent business trips, our personal lives were wonderful.

We enjoyed movie nights with Ian and Pitty, dinners with Terri and Avi, Livia's Thursday evening Mahjong games, and visits to or from my parents every Saturday. During the summer, we would have lunch outside, grilling meats, fish, and shrimp. Livia always prepared her famous Caesar salad and grilled potatoes.

London and Meeting With the Vitoria Gals

I travelled to London for the WTM once again, and while there, I took the opportunity to reconnect with the ladies from Vitoria to thank them for a fantastic and successful season. I invited them to an elegant dinner in town, and the evening turned out to be both enjoyable and productive. They promised to continue supporting our flights in the coming years—a very promising outcome for future collaborations.

Puerto Rico and New York Trip Again

We looked forward to going to New York and Puerto Rico for the winter. We had a great reunion with Livia's old friend, Terri, now divorced, and her twin daughters, Deanna and Tessa, aged 10. We stayed with

Joe and Catherine on the Upper West Side. The city was in a high celebration mood before the holidays. We had a large family gathering at Raymond and Vicky's.

Seychelles

In 1999, the week before the BIT travel fair, I escorted Livia to the Seychelles. All costs were complimentary of either Air Seychelles or Club Vacanze, who provided seven nights of free accommodation at Club Vacanze. This way, I was sure to be back in time for the BIT. We stayed there for one week.

What a holiday. The resort was a perfectly sculpted place of charm: traditional Seychellois architecture merged with indigenous palm trees and pristine white sand beaches overlooking the azure of the Indian Ocean. The first sight of the sea—ever-changing, light dancing over its surface, and so clear that, even in deeper water, we could see the bottom as clear as air—set the scene for a week of rejuvenation and discovery. The sea was so clear it was possible to see the bottom, even in deeper waters.

We stayed in waterfront cabins resembling the 'trulli' of Puglia, with all amenities except for a TV. The food was excellent, a combination of Italian, local Creole, and international dishes. Favorite fare: fresh-from-the-water fish, lightly coated in a tasty dusting of flour and fried to perfection.

Evenings meant meeting at the bar in the resort, the

perfect place for an after-dinner drink. We relaxed with a cocktail and the sound of the waves. Socialising in the bar at night or by day on the beachfront created convivial, relaxed atmospheres where guests could meet and relax in each other's company.

In and Out of Breath: An Adventure

So, there I was at BIT, bumping into Sandro—yes, the one from the Seychelles trip. We reminisced about the sun and surf. The next night was the epic Valtur summer bash: colleagues, cocktails, and confetti. It went on until 3 am, and I was a wreck the next day.

In the midst of all that, I was deep in conversation with Emanuela and Andrea Sarto from Trieste Airport. We were hatching plans to boost regional contributions to our flights. Mission 'Fund Flights from Israel' was in full swing. Italy trips with Livia became our regular thing, spawning new ideas and projects that were both adventurous and fun.

Madeira: The Bank Heist of Fun

Fast forward to my next mission: organising an incentive trip to Madeira for a bank that I'd wooed the previous year. Flights were booked, inspections done in Lisbon with the bank managers, and voila, a late summer adventure was set. Even my parents joined in, swapping their usual Austrian getaway for Madeira's charm. They loved the island—every scenic bit of it.

Cruise Control: My Maiden Voyage

By year-end, Livia booked us a two-week cruise from Miami through the Panama Canal, stopping in Ecuador and Peru, where in Lima, we got into a civil rights demonstration and finally landed in Santiago de Chile, followed by 10 days exploring Chile. My first time on a cruise ship, and I was hooked. Not those gargantuan ships, mind you, but a cosy, smooth-sailing one. Chile was a whirlwind—wineries, urban Santiago, and the bohemian buzz of Bellavista. Highlights included Plaza de Armas and Sky Costanera's jaw-dropping views. The food? Absolutely delicious.

We flew south to Puerto Montt, the gateway to the lakes and fjords of Chilean Patagonia. Picture this: a waterfront by the sea with snow-capped volcanoes. Seafood markets, national parks, and the stunning Lake District filled our six idyllic days of early rises and Pisco indulgences.

Back at our hotel, Boaz called to break the news: Tommy was heading our wholesale department. I knew Tommy—he'd faced bankruptcy that year. That very afternoon, we jetted back to Santiago. With fresh memories of our blessings, we made our way back to Tel Aviv via Madrid.

And there you have it—a whirlwind of adventures from Seychelles nostalgia to Italian escapades and Chilean charm.

CHAPTER 17
The New Millennium—
2000-2004

Y2K and a New Beginning:

As the new millennium began, there were widespread concerns about the Y2K bug, a computer glitch expected to cause problems with date-sensitive systems. Fortunately, most issues were minor or non-existent. I recall watching TV to follow the global events and noticing that our company was on high alert the next day. However, everything turned out fine, even for Ophir Tours.

The Pope in Israel

In March 2000, Pope John Paul II made a historic visit to Israel, arriving on March 21 and departing on March 26. This momentous event presented a unique opportunity for the travel industry, and I took it upon myself to capitalise on it. I initiated negotiations with Italian charter operators to secure exclusivity for 7,000 seats in the Israeli market between March 19 and March

27, specifically targeting the influx of pilgrims and tourists.

We committed to purchasing 6,000 seats at a rate of $200 each. However, due to favourable airport tax conditions, we effectively paid only $175 per seat. This strategic move allowed us to offer these seats at a competitive price while maintaining healthy profit margins. Even better, we managed to acquire the remaining seats at the cost of airport tax only, significantly enhancing our profit potential.

My meticulous planning and hard work paid off when we successfully sold approximately 3,500 seats at $250 each. This resulted in a substantial profit, affirming the success of our strategy. The available destinations included captivating cities, such as Catania, Palermo, Bari, Milan, Rome, and Naples. Our offerings catered to a variety of interests, encompassing guided tours, fly-and-drive packages, and even ski vacations, ensuring there was something for everyone.

The organisation of coordinating such a large-scale operation was complex, involving precise scheduling, coordination with tour operators, and ensuring the seamless transportation of our clients. Our team worked tirelessly to provide exceptional service from the moment of booking to the final return home.

Despite our success, the company underwent restructuring under the leadership of Boaz, who shifted the focus to low-cost operations. This strategic change impacted the quality of our services, as cost-cutting measures often led to compromises in customer experience. It was a challenging transition, but it underscored the importance of balancing profitability with quality service. Reflecting on this period, it stands out as a testament to the power of strategic planning, negotiation, and the ability to adapt to changing circumstances. The experience not only provided significant business growth but also valuable lessons in the dynamics of the travel industry.

Background of the Situation

The early 2000s were a turbulent time, marked by significant geopolitical events that impacted travel and business operations worldwide. Two key moments stand out from this period.

The Second Intifada

The second intifada began in late September 2000, leading to escalating violence between Israelis and Palestinians. The heightened conflict created an environment of uncertainty and risk for travellers. Recognising the potential dangers and logistical challenges, I successfully negotiated the cancellation of our commitments with Valtur for their club in Marrakesh and with the airline. This strategic decision was crucial in minimising potential losses and ensuring the safety of our clients.

The September 11 Attacks

The world was shaken by the terrorist attacks of 11 September 2001 by al-Qaeda. They caused global airspace closures, including in Israel, that were like nothing else. The first days left thousands of travellers trapped around the world, a logistical mess for the tourism industry.

In the face of this crisis, our team worked around the clock to provide support and solutions for our stranded clients. Our priority was to ensure their safety and facilitate their return home as smoothly as possible. Despite the challenges, we managed to secure arrangements with airlines to cover all the additional expenses incurred. This effort demonstrated our commitment to our clients and our ability to navigate through extraordinary circumstances.

My Parents' Wedding Anniversary Planning

As we planned for my parents' 50th wedding anniversary, Livia and I decided to rent out an entire restaurant, Rothchild, in the Neveh Zedek area for a special celebration. We reserved the venue for a Friday afternoon event on February 3rd of the following year.

Meeting Nahela and a Cross-Country Adventure

Later that year, in December, Livia and I took a memorable cross-country trip. We started in New York with Joe and his new girlfriend, Nahela, who would become his wife. Nahela, an amazing woman born in

Afghanistan and raised in Thailand and Kenya, met us for a wonderful dinner. We discussed several topics without going too far into politics (which made sense considering the circumstances). We saw the Rockefeller Center's new Christmas tree and went to the place where 9/11 had occurred, a memory we all took.

From New York, our adventure took us to Las Vegas. After spending two exciting days in Sin City, we embarked on our cross-country drive. Our first stop was Williams, AZ, from where we travelled along the historic Route 66 to Albuquerque, NM. In Santa Fe, we immersed ourselves in the vibrant arts scene, explored historic adobe architecture, and enjoyed the rich cultural heritage. We visited museums and galleries and even met Chabad Rabbis, who were giving away dollar coins for Chanukah.

Continuing south through snowy landscapes, we reached Roswell, NM, famous for the alleged 1947 UFO incident and its extraterrestrial lore. We enjoyed a river cruise on the Pecos River, admired the holiday decorations, dined on delicious meals, and listened to live country music.

Our journey then took us to Carlsbad, NM, renowned for the breathtaking Carlsbad Caverns National Park with its spectacular underground caves and rock formations. After an overnight stay in Fort Stockton, TX, we headed to San Antonio, TX.

In San Antonio, we spent three delightful nights. We

visited the historic Alamo, known for the 1836 battle during the Texas Revolution, and explored the scenic River Walk, where we had a lovely dinner along the water. Our explorations also took us to the San Fernando Cathedral and Market Square (El Mercado), where we experienced the lively Mexican marketplace.

From San Antonio, we drove to Houston, TX, for a brief stop before continuing to New Orleans, LA, where we stayed for three nights. In the French Quarter, we enjoyed the vibrant architecture, strolled along Bourbon Street, visited Jackson Square and St. Louis Cathedral, and explored Royal Street, known for its street performers. At Café du Monde, we indulged in beignets and coffee. We also visited Preservation Hall for live jazz and experienced the lively Zydeco music scene. Our culinary adventures included local delicacies like raw oysters, gumbo, jambalaya, and étouffée.

Our journey continued to Tallahassee, FL, with stops in Baton Rouge, LA; Biloxi, MS (where we stayed overnight); and Mobile, AL. We arrived in Tallahassee in the early evening and continued the next morning to Vero Beach, FL, where Livia's mom had recently moved to an assisted living unit. We spent a relaxing week there, taking a break from our travels and reflecting on the exciting experiences we had enjoyed.

It was a wonderful journey filled with unforgettable memories. However, as with any trip, there were moments of tension, and Livia found herself upset with Elizabeth once again.

A Special Year

2002 was a special year for us. We had just celebrated my parents' 20th wedding anniversary, which was an enormous success. There were around thirty people including family and friends of my parents. I made a great speech, and others just enjoyed the meal, and the atmosphere.

The Terror Attack in Netanya

All this travel was happening against the backdrop of problems in Israel. In the Passover massacre, on 27th March, a suicide bombing at the Park Hotel in Netanya killed thirty people during a Passover Seder. This happened the same week that Hamas's reprisal operation, Operation Defensive Shield, started. Despite these challenges, work continued to flourish.

Israelis are remarkably resilient and somehow manage not to dwell on trouble for long.

Business End

Professionally, 2002 was a busy and successful year; the Futura Airlines flights to Spain continued to progress well. We had decided to end flights to Vitoria, which had been greatly oversaturated, and new expansion was in the pipeline. We introduced the Neos Air flights to Verona.

We also created a new program of escorted tours in Northern Italy, based at the Holiday Inn Verona Congress Centre, a 4-star hotel located less than two kilometres from the airport and providing all the facilities required by our market—and not to mention a shopping center.

Winter destinations were also on the rise, particularly the destinations in the Valtur resorts of Marilleva and Sestriere.

Trip to the Marche Region

Later that fall, we flew to Italy for a trip I remember until today. We started in Rome, taking in the city's antiquities, then picked up a car and drove north up the coast to the spectacular Marche region. We rented an apartment in Ascoli Piceno, the regional capital, and everything about Marche was wonderful. The region has beautiful hilltop towns and whitewashed beaches—so beautiful that you would need a month to explore its arts, history, and culture. The UNESCO-listed Renaissance architecture of Urbino took our breath away, while days lost in medieval villages, such as Offida and Loreto, felt like a time warp.

On other days, we lay on the Adriatic beaches in Senigallia and Sirolo. In the evening, we ate fresh seafood and truffles from the woods, then bought a few regional bottles of wine from vineyard tours. Marche had it all.

Day to Day

On a personal level, we all remained friends, deeply so with Avi and Terri, and I stayed in touch with Ian, who had divorced Pitty and moved to Tel Aviv, where I used to visit him every Thursday evenings during the time Livia was playing Majoun. All in all, it was an incredible year, albeit with its fair share of ups and downs.

Travels to Vero Beach and Cruise

We returned to Florida and Vero Beach again, this time as a base for our next cruise: a visit to Livia's mom, and a gift to them from us (and us again) with a trip to Orlando to enjoy Universal Studios and Epcot. This cruise to the Caribbean was even better than the one we had taken to South America. The ship felt more luxurious than the last one, and we had a fun time. Of course, it was with *Celebrity Cruises.*

2003: A Year of High Drama, International Conflict, and Tragedy

The roadmap for peace, a joint plan by the United States, the European Union, the United Nations, and Russia to resolve the Israeli-Palestinian conflict and create a Palestinian state beside Israel, was launched. Like most such road maps, it was easier to unfold than to follow.

Implementation hit pothole after pothole, and while terror attacks were less frequent than they were in 2002, they were still an issue.

February 1, 2003: Tragedy of Space Shuttle Columbia

On February 1, 2003, the Space Shuttle Columbia disintegrated during re-entry, killing all seven astronauts on board, including Ilan Ramon, the first Israeli astronaut. The mission faced issues after a piece of foam struck the shuttle's wing during launch, damaging its thermal protection.

This damage led to the shuttle breaking apart as it re-entered the atmosphere. The disaster highlighted the risks of space travel and the need for rigorous safety protocols. The loss of Columbia was a profound tragedy, particularly for Israel and the global space community.

In March 2003, the United States, along with the United Kingdom and a coalition of allies, launched a military invasion of Iraq to remove Saddam Hussein from power. The invasion, known as Operation Iraqi Freedom, was justified by the US and UK governments on the grounds that Iraq possessed weapons of mass destruction, had links to terrorist organisations, and needed to be liberated from Hussein's oppressive regime. Despite extensive searches, no significant stockpiles of WMDs were found in Iraq, leading to widespread controversy and debate over the legitimacy of the invasion.

Challenges With Futura Airlines and CSA

In the meantime, as we returned to our daily operations, we faced a significant challenge. We had overcommitted with Futura Airlines, securing more flights than we could realistically sell. The market demand did not meet our expectations, leaving us with an excess of unsold seats. After careful consideration and analysis, we realised that the only viable solution was to downsize our agreement with Futura Airlines. This decision could not be an easy one, as it involved renegotiating terms and reducing the number of flights for which we had initially planned.

Tommy, who had been heavily involved in securing the original deal, was understandably upset about the downsizing. He had invested considerable effort and optimism into the partnership, and scaling back felt like a setback. However, given the circumstances, it was the prudent course of action to prevent further financial losses and to realign our resources with actual demand.

Things took a turn for the worse when our system failed to load one of the flights to Prague. We suddenly found ourselves with just two days to sell an entire aircraft's worth of seats. Despite the significant loss, we managed to achieve the mission.

Changes in the Office

In 2004, global events took a back seat as work became my priority. That year was marked by significant changes. Boaz fired Tommy, which was a tough blow after three years of success. One bad year can change everything. Boaz became more cautious, avoiding large-scale flights and sticking to sporadic or guaranteed ones. We continued working with Futura Airlines, but not as intensely, losing our market exclusivity. We relied more on scheduled carriers and subcontracted with other tour operators for charter flights. Competition increased, and Boaz became obsessed with price as our main competitive strategy.

Roxy and Trade Shows

Before departing for BIT, we faced a heartbreaking moment. Our beloved labrador, Roxy, developed a throat tumour and could no longer eat or drink. I had to take her to the vet to be put to sleep. It was devastating for Livia, who adored Roxy. Despite the pain, Livia accompanied me to BIT the next day.

That year, I travelled extensively: I attended FITUR, the Madrid international tourism fair, in January, WTM (World Travel Market) in London in November, and visited Italy twice for TTG in Rimini and meetings at the Valtur offices in Milan.

Valtur New Openings and Meetings

Valtur invited Ophir Tours to a meeting with international representatives at their Pollina club in Sicily, and I took Boaz with me. It was his first experience at a Valtur club, and it turned out to be quite an eye-opener.

During my spring inspection, I was captivated by the club's pristine location, elegant amenities, and the promise of an unforgettable vacation experience. The beaches were lined with fine golden sand, and the clear blue waters invited visitors for a refreshing swim. The club itself featured beautifully designed rooms, a range of dining options offering local and international cuisines, and various recreational activities that catered to both relaxation and adventure seekers.

Understanding the club's potential, we launched an aggressive marketing campaign in Israel. We highlighted the unique features of the Bodrum Club, emphasising the perfect blend of relaxation and excitement it offered. Our collaboration with insurance companies made the travel packages even more attractive, ensuring peace of mind for our clients.

To truly cement Bodrum's place in the Israeli holiday scene, we organised a spectacular familiarisation trip. Renting a plane, we flew in prominent Israeli celebrities and key travel agents for a weekend stay. The purpose of this trip was to allow them to experience firsthand what made the Bodrum club so exceptional.

The familiarisation trip was a phenomenal success. The celebrities and travel agents left with glowing reviews, and their enthusiastic endorsements spurred a surge in bookings. This strategic move not only established the Bodrum club as a top holiday destination for Israelis but also strengthened our partnership with Valtur, paving the way for future collaborations.

Bodrum became synonymous with top vacations, and our efforts played a significant role in transforming it into a beloved getaway for many Israeli travellers.

Crystal Cruises

In 2004, Livia and I enjoyed a luxurious Crystal Cruises trip at the rate of $50 a day, thanks to Livia's travel agent connections and Ophir Tours being Crystal's exclusive representative in Israel. We flew to Miami and sailed to Tortola, St. Barts, St. John, and other extraordinary places. After returning to Miami, we rented a car and drove to Livia's mom's house in Vero Beach for the rest of our vacation.

We then flew to New York to visit Joe, Nahela, and their new baby, Gabriella, who was born on June 19. They had recently moved to Brooklyn. Staying with them meant adjusting to a new-parent schedule, with lights out at 10 PM. Gabriella, a cute six-month-old, allowed us to experience a different side of New York City.

On one Saturday, Joe rented a car, and we drove to Yorktown to visit Raymond and Vicky. It was wonderful to reconnect after all those years. The drive was scenic, and we enjoyed catching up on the latest happenings in each other's lives. Our visit was filled with laughter, stories, and the joy of rekindling old friendships.

Gabriella brought a special charm to our stay, her giggles and playful antics providing a heartwarming backdrop to our trip. Brooklyn, with its vibrant neighbourhoods and diverse culture, offered us a refreshing perspective on city life. Even the simple moments, like strolling through local parks and discovering cozy cafes, became cherished memories.

Overall, our trip to New York was a delightful blend of family bonding, nostalgic reunions, and new experiences.

Flying with Swissair on Christmas Day got us a complimentary upgrade to first class on our return flight, with a stopover in Zurich. There, we learned of the devastating Indian Ocean tsunami, which occurred due to a 9.3 magnitude earthquake, causing massive waves that affected fourteen countries, including Indonesia, Sri Lanka, India, and Thailand.

CHAPTER 18
My 50th Birthday—2005

So, you're 50, and that mountain—that hill, whatever you call it—you're up there. And the best views are from here. So, here's everything I want to share with you about that year: I celebrated my 50th birthday, went travelling, and I was up for drama in the office, if you will.

It all started in February when I went on a business trip to Rome. Emanuela and I met there and attended the BIT trade fair in Milan. We also had a pleasant chat with Corrado, the Arena di Verona's marketing director in Rome. This meeting would pave the way to the main event of my 50th birthday—a celebration in Verona!

Highlights of a Visit

The girls came in and out of Emanuela's office each week to make up for their lost days. The Dead Sea was a new sight to many people: the esthetic beauty of the desert. One of my favourite parts of these tours was the jeep ride that I gladly led. The journey was a wild trip, brimming with breathtaking views and thrilling experiences.

The best example of this—and a highlight of our journey—was the jeep tour. Paola, Emanuela's friend, was wearing black Armani from head to toe. As we navigated the sandy terrain, Paola's pristine outfit quickly became a canvas for the desert's fine grains of sand. The sight of her, typically so elegant, now dusted in sand was both funny and poignant. It was a jolting reminder that fashion doesn't always go well together in the desert!

Despite this haphazard, somewhat hilarious episode, the trip went smoothly. We came back from the desert with stories, people, and memories we'd never forget. Paola's 'sanding' became a story we often told each other, always laughing.

50th Birthday Celebrations

Livia and I flew to Verona in July and rented a vintage rental car to Villa del Quar in Valpolicella. The villa's private pool and garden made for an ideal weekend break.

When we got there, we learned that Corrado had booked tickets for Aida and La Bohème at the Arena di Verona. We were thrilled! We dined in the hotel's Arquade restaurant and had local dishes and local wines.

The following day, we went to Sirmione's Scaligero Castle and explored the old town. After a pleasant lunch in the medieval village of Borghetto sul Mincio, we made our way back to the villa to set up for the evening.

That evening, we met Emanuela in Piazza Bra for an aperitivo before seeing the *Zeffirelli Aida* at the Arena, conducted by Maestro Daniel Oren. During the intermission, we drank prosecco under the stars. After the opera, we went to dinner in Piazza Bra, where Corrado had brought Maestro Oren and three performers to our table for a birthday drink.

The next day, we took a boat on Lake Garda to Riva del Garda, where our friend, Luigi, had offered us a lakeside lunch. We drove to Limone and Malcesine, then back to Sirmione and then to the villa. The evening, on Sunday night, was spent at a local pizza parlour with Emanuela and Corrado, drinking, eating, and talking.

On Monday, we sat around the pool, ate some light open-air lunch, and went to a lavish evening opera performance for La Bohème at the Arena. I loved the show, and we went to a local restaurant for dinner.

Umbria and Tuscany Get Away

This fall, Livia and I made it to Umbria, Tuscany, and Milan after years of planning. In Umbria, we stayed in a villa that served as our base for day trips. Our first stop was Assisi, where we went to mass in the magnificent Basilica of St Francis.

Giotto and Cimabue's bright frescoes were spiritually inspiring. We spent the afternoon strolling through the pretty town of Spello, with its narrow stone streets and flower-decorated balconies, a sight Livia loved.

The following day, we walked around the medieval town of Gubbio, which Herman Hesse wrote had an 'unreal and perturbing' effect. We stopped by the Palazzo Dei Consoli and the Basilica of Sant' Ubaldo, where Livia took exquisite rooftop photographs. Then we had lunch at a nearby enoteca with wonderful wines.

We drove on to Todi, a hilltop town overlooking the Tiber Valley. We strolled through its quiet medieval structures, like the Piazza del Popolo, Palazzo Dei Priori, and the Romanesque Cathedral. In Norcia, the gastronomic capital of black truffles and aged meats, we ate our way through the cuisine and trekked in the Monti Sibillini National Park.

It was a rainy day in Spoleto, but we enjoyed the summer jazz festival, Roman Theatre, and Rocca Albornoziana. On our last day in Umbria, we took a chocolate tour of Perugia. We gazed at the Fontana Maggiore and walked along Corso Vannucci.

Paola booked us a room in Viareggio's Grand Hotel Principe di Piemonte in Tuscany, an opulent coastal town. From there, we toured the lovely streets of Lucca, took in the breathtaking coastal walks on the Via dell'Amore in Cinque Terre, and marvelled at the medieval citadels of San Gimignano.

Viareggio itself, with its secluded beaches and

bustling harbour, added to Tuscany's appeal. We concluded the trip with a successful day in Milan where I was able to wrap up a business deal with Valtur. Life never slowed down, and I enjoyed every moment of it!

New Manager

There was upheaval at work, too. Boaz installed a new head of wholesale and a new general manager. I wasn't thrilled with the new head of wholesale—she exuded the confidence of someone at the top of a gradient whose mostly voluntary followers obediently claimed it as flat. But, if flights and packages continued to run on time, I'd give her a chance to prove herself.

That winter, however, we halted all our sales of Valtur Sestriere (happily, the Torino Winter Olympics had taken over the region the following year).

The Situation in Israel

In Israel that year, the disengagement plan, a unilateral move of Israeli Prime Minister Ariel Sharon, involved withdrawing all Israeli settlements and military bases from the Gaza Strip and four others in the northern part of the West Bank. The pullout triggered great controversy inside Israel, with demonstrations in both camps inciting a storm of protest and political animosity. Some saw it as a bold step toward peace, while others considered it a dangerous concession.

CHAPTER 19
The Years 2006-2008

Political Changes

To that extent, last year felt like a foretaste of what we could expect in the years ahead, politically as well as globally. In Israel, Ariel Sharon's stroke in January 2006 had left him incapacitated. So, he was replaced as the prime minister by Ehud Olmert. Everyone wondered what might come next.

Visit of Italian Friends

Corrado, Emanuela, and Giorgia (Emanuela's little sister) came to Israel in February, having attended the BIT in Milan. I was behind on a debt of hospitality, so I planned a good trip for them. We started in Nazareth, where we went to see the Basilica of the Annunciation, that beautiful, golden Catholic church built on the presumed site where Gabriel appeared to Mary to tell her that she was going to give birth to the Son of God so that the Word would become flesh and dwell among us.

Next, we returned to the Sea of Galilee, where we travelled to the beautiful Mount of Beatitudes, where Jesus gave his Sermon on the Mount. Views from here are stunning, between Capernaum and Ginosar. Then we drove to Tabaha on the shore of the Sea of Galilee, where Jesus is believed to have performed the miracle of feeding the five thousand. Here, too, is the Church of the Multiplication, modern but containing remnants of the original church, including the mosaic floors. We visited the Tomb of the Twelve Apostles, saw Peter's House, and, on our very last day, took a late afternoon drive north to Tiberias. For cocktails at the Scots Hotel on the Sea of Galilee, our view was as soothing as the drinks.

We returned to Haifa for dinner. On our way back, the drive was so pretty that we decided to do it in reverse. The four of us—Emanuela, Corrado, Giorgia, and I—met almost every night in Tel Aviv, and I took them to a very nice Georgian restaurant, which everybody loved. The food was wonderful, and the atmosphere was warm. We also met at my office in Tel Aviv, so I managed to squeeze some business into it as well.

Slovakia Flights

It was a busy year for Ophir Tours. We started selling Slovakia in 2005, with flights scheduled to begin in the summer of 2006 with an airline, Air Slovakia (which in the early days was still trying to run to schedule). We wanted to make our destination portfolio interesting with some new, more interesting destinations. Along came a low-cost airline called 'Sky Europe Airlines' that was operating in Central and Eastern Europe and bravely promising cheap airfares all over Europe. I flew over to Bratislava to have a look at them, and, after shaking lots of hands ecstatically, we signed a contract for 2007 and went on an exclusive basis. More clients started coming our way, and we got more bookings for the spa in Piešťany. Thanks to the cheap flights to Bratislava, Austria seemed not that far away, especially since it could now be combined with an escorted tour, too.

2006 Situation

In that summer, the Second Lebanon War broke out. It began in July after Hezbollah kidnapped two Israeli soldiers in a cross-border raid, firing a barrage of rockets on north Israel, and Israeli jets launched a bombing campaign on southern Lebanon. The fighting was tense but eventually ended in August with a UN-mediated ceasefire. Italy won the World Cup that summer for the fourth time, providing much-needed celebration.

Hotel Hunting in Italy

Due to a downturn in business, Boaz asked me to travel to Italy to scout for hotels that could be included in our upcoming winter season packages. Recognising this as an important task, I eagerly accepted the challenge. Livia and I flew to Verona, with our first mission being to drive to Vicenza and Bassano del Grappa. These picturesque towns offered a delightful mix of history and charm. Vicenza, known for its Palladian architecture, provided a visual feast, while Bassano del Grappa, famous for its strong grappa and scenic wooden bridge, added a touch of rustic beauty to our journey.

The itinerary was packed and fast-paced. After soaking in the local flavours and securing potential hotel partners, we made our way to the majestic Alps. Our destination was San Sicario, where we assessed the Hotel Majestic, a stunning establishment built for the Olympic Games. The state-of-the-art facilities were impressive, and the breathtaking views of the snow-capped mountains were a definite bonus. We also explored the Olympic Village at Sestriere, envisioning it as an ideal location for ski enthusiasts looking for an all-inclusive winter getaway.

Back in Israel

As soon as we returned, I jumped right back into work, developing all the new places we had visited into a viable product for the upcoming winters. I contacted ski schools and equipment stores, securing final prices for the season. I integrated these into new packages, resulting in a great season with high demand for the ski trips I had put together.

Atlantic Cross Cruise, Florida, and New York

On the personal front, Livia and I decided to shake things up with a trip to Barcelona, followed by a 10-day cruise to Miami. With only two ports of call in Lisbon and Madeira, it sounded like a dream. However, my stomach had other plans, and I decided to stage a full-blown rebellion.

Picture this: Livia trying to enjoy the cruise while I am waging a war with my insides, leading to an emergency visit to the ship's doctor. Meanwhile, I was lying horizontally in our cabin, trying to negotiate peace with my gut.

After a few days, I was back on my feet and ready to explore Lisbon and Madeira. Both ports offered a much-needed respite and a chance to stretch my legs. We soaked in the sights, sampled the local cuisine, and pretended like the earlier gastrointestinal mutiny never happened.

Upon our arrival in Miami, where we picked up a car and drove to Vero Beach for Livia's mom's birthday dinner in Palm Beach. The food was delicious, and the company was even better! After celebrating in style, we flew to New York to visit Joe and his family. They had moved from Brooklyn to a beautiful new house in Maplewood, New Jersey. Gabriella, now a very animated two-and-a-half-year-old, provided endless entertainment. It was heartwarming to see them all so settled and at peace.

Events in Winter 2007

The beginning of 2007 was intriguing due to the shifting markets and the onset of a new global crisis. Tensions between Israel and Gaza did not stop for several months. We saw an almost daily cycle of rocket hits on southern Israel and retaliatory strikes by the Israeli air force. Underway was the usual preparation for the winter season, which was going well so far, and for next summer's preparations.

The Empty Leg New Trend

We found a creative way to utilise empty legs on charter planes, ferrying tourists into Israel and then flying out empty to destinations like Valencia, Sevilla, Pamplona, Genoa, Bari, Linz, and Salzburg. This not only maximised efficiency but also opened new travel opportunities for our clients.

Our close relationship with Sun D'or Airlines, El Al's charter division, positioned us at the forefront of these new projects. This partnership was crucial in maintaining balanced books and offering bespoke escorted tours at the lowest possible prices. It allowed us to secure the best deals and prioritise new, exciting itineraries.

While part charters to Spain continued, they were not on the same scale as in previous years. However, our strategic use of empty-leg flights helped us keep costs down and provide unique travel experiences. This approach ensured that we remained competitive, offering diverse destinations without compromising on quality.

During these changes, we navigated the challenges of the industry with innovation and adaptability, always aiming to deliver the best possible service to our clients. The empty-leg flights became a key part of our strategy, displaying our ability to turn logistical challenges into opportunities for growth and adventure.

Livia created a lucrative venture for AACI, focusing on high-quality Kosher tours, which became a very interesting project since it was growing so much each year.

Me and the Manager

I did not like the manageress who was brought in to replace Tommy. She was arrogant, thought she knew everything, and created a toxic atmosphere. She seemed to delight in stirring up antagonism between the different managers. Boaz, the owner, shared my dislike for her. After numerous complaints about her behaviour, Boaz and I decided to act.

One evening, Boaz asked me to go to her office and remove work documents and sensitive information. I did so, and the next morning, Boaz confronted her and asked her to leave the company. She was furious and stormed out, looking like the last burglar in town. Her departure was a relief to everyone, and it marked the end of a particularly unpleasant chapter at the company. I was not sorry for my actions.

A New Itinerary From Trieste to Rome

Instead of travelling to the States, Livia and I spent five days driving around Italy. We flew to Trieste and rented a car to explore Friuli Venezia Giulia. In Trieste, we strolled through Piazza Unità d'Italia and visited the Castello di Miramare. Polenta and fontina cheese became Livia's favorites in Udine and San Daniele, famous for its prosciutto. We also visited Cividale del Friuli, known for its Lombard heritage, and the Ponte del Diavolo and San Floriano del Collio for vineyard views and the Ribolla Gialla wine.

Next, we drove to Venice and stayed at the Boscolo Hotel Dei Dogi in the Cannaregio District. We explored the Rialto Market, the Venetian Ghetto, the Ghetto Nuovo, the synagogues, and the Jewish Museum of Venice.

After Venice, we spent three days at the TTG travel trade fair in Rimini. From there, we headed to Radda in Chianti and stayed at the four-star My One Hotel Radda. Our first stop in the Chianti Classico zone was Via delle Volte in Castellina in Chianti, where we enjoyed panoramic vineyard views. In Greve in Chianti, we explored the triangular main square and a wine bar near the wine museum. Panzano in Chianti offered a Sunday food fair and a visit to the famous butcher, Dario Cecchini. We also visited Badia a Coltibuono, a former abbey now turned winery, and the medieval village of Volpaia for wine tasting.

We continued to Saturnia for the thermal waters of Cascate del Mulino, to Montemerano for its medieval streets and Chiesa di San Giorgio, and to Pitigliano, known as 'Little Jerusalem,' for its historic Jewish community. We visited Sovana, rich in history but still off the beaten track.

On the way to Rome, we stopped in Scansano for local wine, reached Porto Ercole for spaghetti alle vongole with white wine, and then headed to Fiumicino airport via the old Appian Way.

Global Situation

The global financial crisis, which began in 2007, intensified in 2008. Major financial institutions collapsed, leading to widespread economic turmoil and a severe global recession. Again, I travelled to Milan for the BIT and got some new leads there, finding a hotel in the region of Verona since the Holiday Inn was not suitable for our needs any longer. I found the expo near the airport, with which I finalised a direct contract.

20th Wedding Anniversary Escapades

In early April, Livia and I embarked on our anniversary trip to the Basque regions of France and Spain, A reminder of the old business in which I was a pioneer. We flew to Pamplona. Our adventure began in the French Pyrenean village of Saint-Jean-Pied-de-Port, with its medieval buildings and cobbled streets transporting us back in time. We visited the Notre-Dame de Bout du Pont church, feeling the weight of countless pilgrims who had passed through on their way to Santiago de Compostela.

The next morning, we drove to Espelette, known for its red peppers adorning whitewashed houses. After strolling along river paths and enjoying traditional Basque food, we headed to Saint-Jean-de-Luz. We explored Place Louis XIV and the Maison de L'Enfant before having a glorious seaside lunch.

Our journey continued to Biarritz, a surfing mecca. We enjoyed its beautiful beaches, visited the lighthouse, and savoured local dishes like moules-frites. Livia lost herself in Halles, the local market, with its fresh produce and gourmet goodies.

Crossing into Spain, we arrived in Hondarribia, a charming town with ancient, cobbled streets and traditional houses. We soaked in its vibrant street life and scenic views. From there, we visited San Sebastián, enchanted by La Concha Beach and Monte Igueldo's stunning views. We indulged in pintxos in the lively Old Town before returning to Hondarribia for a peaceful night's rest.

The next day, we drove through the Cantabrian landscapes to Bilbao. We explored Casco Viejo, the city's Old Town, and dined at the Guggenheim restaurant. The following morning, we visited the iconic Guggenheim Museum, admiring its architecture and exhibits. A walk along the Nervión River and the Zubizuri Bridge rounded off our day.

We then drove to LaGuardia, the heart of the Rioja Alaves region. We visited local wineries, enjoying both modern and historic experiences. After a night at a charming boutique hotel, we continued our wine tour at Bodegas Marqués de Riscal and strolled through Logroño.

As our trip wound down, we returned to Pamplona. We explored Calle Estafeta, known for the Running of the Bulls, and enjoyed lunch at Café Iruña. A relaxing walk to La Ciudadela and Parque de la Taconera capped off our journey.

Seeing Livia happy and full of joy made me truly content. Our anniversary trip through the Basque Country was a journey full of discovery, culture, and unforgettable moments.

Futura Airlines Crisis

In that year, Futura Airlines faced severe financial difficulties, nearing bankruptcy by September. As a result, our commitments to Spain were lower and eventually stopped altogether. This decision was tough, not just from a business perspective but also on a personal level. I had friends at Futura Airlines, and the situation deeply affected me. The loss of these friendships was a constant reminder of the airline's struggles and the broader impact on the industry.

This period highlighted the fragility of business relationships and the personal bonds intertwined with professional commitments. It was a sobering experience, underscoring the importance of adaptability and resilience in the face of adversity.

Expanding to Other Destinations

Other destinations played a crucial role in our travel plans. We continued to operate flights with Sky Europe to Bratislava, capitalising on the growing interest in this vibrant city. Bratislava, with its charming old town, stunning Danube River views, and rich history, attracted a diverse range of tourists.

Our flights to Trieste were flexible, changing airlines based on the most competitive prices available. This approach allowed us to maintain cost efficiency while still providing excellent travel options to our clients.

In Italy, Verona and Trieste emerged as our main destinations. Verona, renowned for its historic architecture and romantic ambience and as the setting for Shakespeare's 'Romeo and Juliet,' was a favourite among tourists. Trieste, with its unique blend of Italian, Austro-Hungarian, and Slovenian influences, offered a fascinating cultural experience.

By strategically selecting these destinations and adjusting our partnerships, we were able to cater to a wide array of travel preferences, ensuring that our clients had diverse and exciting options to choose from.

Livia's Prosperity With AACI

Livia was thriving in her role with the AACI, significantly expanding their travel offerings. She worked diligently to increase the number of groups and cruises, ensuring a wider array of travel experiences for their clients. Her hard work paid off as she successfully added four new and exciting destinations to their itinerary.

Thailand, with its rich culture, stunning temples, and beautiful beaches, became a popular choice for travellers seeking an exotic getaway. Australia's diverse landscapes and vibrant cities attracted those looking for adventure and unique experiences. New Zealand's breathtaking scenery and outdoor activities appealed to nature lovers and thrill-seekers alike.

Livia also added more familiar destinations, such as Spain and Italy, to the roster. Spain, with its enthusiastic flamenco, historic landmarks, and delectable cuisine, offered a delightful experience for tourists. Italy, known for its art, architecture, and culinary delights, continued to be a beloved destination for travellers.

Through her efforts, Livia ensured that the AACI could cater to a diverse range of travel preferences, providing enriching and memorable experiences for all its clients. Her success not only boosted the AACI's reputation but also brought her immense professional satisfaction.

Livia's 50th Birthday Celebration

August marked Livia's 50th birthday, and I wanted to make it truly special. She had always gone all out for my birthdays, so I decided to celebrate her in a memorable way. I decorated our rooftop like a Christmas wonderland, with lights and candles hanging from every inch, creating a magical atmosphere. I also bought her a beautiful necklace as a special gift.

That evening, I came home early to prepare. I lined the stairs to the roof with candles and hung lights from the poles to the corners of the floor. For dinner, I prepared a menu just for her: ceviche of white fish for the first course, followed by a grilled rack of lamb with asparagus and potatoes on the barbecue. For dessert, I served the ice cream I had bought earlier.

Livia positively glowed when she walked in and saw the candles. As she climbed the stairs, she teasingly mentioned that she thought she might be getting a pony, which was exactly the reaction I had hoped for.

I paired the meal with a chilled bottle of Pinot Grigio for the ceviche and a 1998 Barolo I'd been saving for a special occasion. Romantic music by Dean Martin played in the background, making it a perfect evening filled with stories of our life together. It was the most special birthday gift I could give her.

December Adventures in Tuscany

In December, Livia and I flew to Rome, rented a car, and headed to a villa in Tuscany to spend a week with Joe and Nahella and Gabriella . On the way, we stopped overnight in the charming hill town of Pienza. The owner welcomed us with a fantastic dinner of homegrown wine and food. The next morning, we explored Pienza's Renaissance architecture and stunning views of Val d'Orcia, sampling pecorino cheese to prepare our palates for the delights of Tuscany.

Our next stop was Fattoria La Loggia in San Casciano in Val di Pesa. Ivana, the owner, had everything ready for us in a cosy three-bedroom apartment. We arrived a day before Joe, Nahela, and little Gabriella, settling in and preparing for their arrival.

When they arrived, Gabriella made a beeline for the attic, only to climb down quickly after realising it was not entirely safe. That night, we enjoyed pizza, Gabriella's favourite, as snowflakes floated through the air.

The next morning, we visited San Gimignano, where snow began to fall. Gabriella was fascinated by the market's colours and crafts. We climbed a tower for breathtaking views and enjoyed a leisurely lunch. After a quick visit to Volterra, we returned to the villa for a family dinner of pasta and sausages, laughing and enjoying each other's company.

The following day in Siena, Gabriella ran joyfully through Piazza del Campo. She marvelled at the frescoes in Palazzo Público and the mosaics in Siena Cathedral. We ended the day with a cosy trattoria lunch and gelato, followed by a visit to the Museo di Storia Naturale.

In Florence, we visited the Uffizi Gallery, admired Il Duomo, and enjoyed Tuscan cuisine near the Ponte Vecchio. Gabriella loved the carousel in Piazza della Repubblica and the view from Piazzale Michelangelo.

We continued to Greve in Chianti, which had transformed into a Christmas wonderland with its festive market and nativity scene. The next day, we had a delicious Bistecca Fiorentina and Gabriella's favourite, Pizza Margherita.

On Christmas Eve, we enjoyed a traditional seafood dinner and attended Midnight Mass. Christmas morning was filled with joy and gifts. We savoured a hearty Tuscan Christmas lunch before saying goodbye to Joe, Nahela, and Gabriella as they headed to London. Livia and I continued our journey to Emilia Romagna.

Castelvetro di Modena Adventures

Our final stop was Castelvetro di Modena, staying at Locanda del Feudo, a charming boutique hotel. After a long drive from San Casciano, we took a nap and woke up just in time for dinner. We strolled around the cold town, bundled up in layers, before enjoying a delicious meal at a nearby restaurant.

The next day, we visited the Ferrari Museum, where I felt like a kid again, marvelling at the classic cars. We then bought a 30-year-old bottle of balsamic vinegar from a local producer and enjoyed a traditional lunch of tortellini in brodo with Lambrusco wine. In the afternoon, we explored Modena's beautiful centre, shopped, and dined at a Modenese trattoria.

Early the following morning, we visited a small farm near Guastalla to buy Parmigiano Reggiano and then drove to Parma. There, we explored the Teatro Regio and Piazza Duomo, admired the Cathedral's frescoes, and had a wonderful lunch before heading back to our hotel. We booked a special New Year's Eve dinner at Locanda Del Feudo, enjoying a multi-course meal featuring local Emilia Romagna products.

The dinner was exquisite, with antipasti of local cured meats and Parmigiano Reggiano, followed by handmade tortellini in brodo and a succulent roast with lentils. We drank Lambrusco and indulged in Italian holiday sweets. At midnight, everyone raised their glasses to toast the New Year, and we ended the night with a grappa before turning in.

On New Year's Day, we drove to the quaint village of Reggio Emilia. The town was quiet, with a holiday stillness in the air and snow gently falling. We explored Piazza Prampolini, visited the Duomo and Palazzo del Comune, and enjoyed a leisurely lunch of pasta Bolognese and red wine. We strolled through the narrow streets, savouring espresso and pastries at a small café.

Reggio Emilia felt like a place removed from time, a perfect way to start the year. We returned to Locanda Del Feudo for our last night, packed our bags, and the next day, drove to Verona airport to fly back home.

CHAPTER 20
A Very Significant Year—
2009

My Father

Then 2009 hit. Our celebrations in Italy had just ended, and as soon as we returned home, we rushed to see my dad. When we arrived at his apartment, I was struck by how thin he looked compared to the last time I had seen him just three weeks earlier. My father's health was rapidly declining, and within a few days, he was admitted to the hospital.

I visited him daily, hoping for improvement, but in March, his condition deteriorated. Despite my explicit instructions to the doctors not to proceed without my approval, one night, they decided to intubate him because he was struggling to breathe. When I saw him the next day, he was unresponsive, intubated, and unable to speak or communicate. Seeing him so helpless, motionless, and attached to a breathing machine was devastating.

Intubation meant a tube had been inserted in his windpipe to ensure his lungs received oxygen, but it also meant that I couldn't speak to him, hear his voice, or share a moment of clarity. His better days were far outweighed by the bad ones. I was livid with the doctors, knowing this was the beginning of the end.

In early April, they finally removed the tube, but it was too late. He couldn't breathe on his own, and his other systems were shutting down. One night, as I sat with him, I asked how he felt. His response made me cry. "Better," he said, "if you'd shave me." It was so human, so intimate. I went out to get shaving cream, a razor, and some aftershave. When I returned, I shaved him, fussed over his comfort, and whispered goodnight. A small thing, yet everything.

The next day, on Passover Eve, Jews around the world were preparing for the upcoming celebration. I had just returned from work when I received the most frightening telephone call of my life until that day. The hospital asked me to come immediately. I knew what it meant. Livia and I rushed there. When we arrived, they told me that my father had passed away 45 minutes earlier.

I had to recognise him. He looked so calm and composed. I kissed his forehead and spread his arms. That was it; he was no more. But nobody ever prepared me for this, and there were so many things to do. I had never done anything like this before, and suddenly, I had to organise a funeral, arrange a cemetery plot, and notify relatives and friends. My mother, who had prepared a real meal for the Seder table, broke down in tears, but she held up with superhuman strength.

Livia was crying, a rare occurrence for her. She was the backbone of the situation as much as possible. But it felt like a dream. Grief is paralysing, loss is heavy. When we received the news, I wanted to believe it wasn't real, that it was a dream, and I would wake up and it would all go away. I needed that love more than ever on those sleepless nights.

His burial was set for April 11. It was a big turnout—family, friends, and co-workers. Even though it goes against Jewish law to sit Shiva during the holiday, we did so at my mom's apartment.

'Sitting Shiva' refers to the practice of mourning one's loved one after burial. Shiva is a Hebrew word for seven, so the family 'sits Shiva' during the seven days the immediate family of the deceased is in mourning. The family stays at home surrounded by the accoutrement of grieving, mostly to make time to think, but also possibly in anticipation of the flood of visitors who will likely arrive to pay condolences and offer support. In our case, we sat Shiva while the holiday festival continued, and we returned to work.

Livia

Within weeks, Livia complained of discomfort in her nose and swelling in her neck. Our family doctor examined her and found no problem, so we went to a private specialist who referred us to a surgeon. He suggested immediate surgery to investigate further. In late May, after the operation, the surgeon told us it was probably cancer and that we should see a specialist. Within 24 hours, we were consulting a professor at Ichilov Hospital in Tel Aviv. The diagnosis was lymphoma: cancer that originates in the tissues of the lymphatic system, a network of tissue and organs that help to fight infection by producing white blood cells.

Following a biopsy, we learned that Livia had a Stage 2B tumour, an aggressive, non-Hodgkin lymphoma. This would require a series of six chemotherapy treatments, using terribly harsh drugs to kill cancer cells. Chemo was no picnic either. It often made Livia sick. I remember one morning after her second treatment when she came out of the shower crying, with tufts of hair in her hands. That was truly shocking. She shaved her hair and got a wig, which she hated very much.

It was my turn now to be her steady support. I went with her to every treatment. When we got back from them and were too tired to think, she'd just put her head on my lap and fall asleep. I'd try to stay composed and do all the cooking and shopping while she rested. Livia was amazingly strong. Although the treatments knocked the living daylights out of her, she'd be back at work the day after each one like it was nothing. And so, we future-planned trips and promised each other we'd enjoy our lives to the full.

When the chemotherapy was over, Livia was given a month of radiation. She was very sick—stage 2 cancer—but after the radiations and a PET CT follow-up scan, it was clear she'd beaten the cancer. She got a wig that she always wore out of the house, but at home, she never bothered. In mid-September, we started making plans for a trip to the States. We wanted to get back to life.

Work and Getting Back

Meanwhile, Livia was working as usual, and her business grew steadily. She was promoted to manager of the Ophir Tours branch in Ra'anana, a 10-minute drive away. Thanks to the technological and defence industries, Israel's economy kept growing despite the global financial crisis of 2009.

My Work

I, too, was busy, moving into another office in a new building that Boaz had bought and helping Sharon, the manager of the new wholesale department, to organise things.

We sold only flights for Bratislava and Verona and packages to Rhodes, Crete, Santorini, and Cyprus. In winter, we sold flights to Torino and Sofia. A small ski resort in Bulgaria was a new destination. Everyone knew that Sky Europe could go bankrupt by 2010, so I tried to find another carrier for Slovakia. I eventually signed with a small Bratislava-based aircraft company, Seagle Airlines, and operated two planes; I agreed to distribute the 2010 season flights.

Trip to Rome, Florida, Amalfi Coast

That year, we embarked on an incredible journey that took us to Florida, Southern Italy, and a festive Rome.

Rome Adventures: We stopped in Rome for a couple of days before Christmas. The city was turned into a festive wonderland, and Piazza Navona was a magical Christmas market. We soaked up the atmosphere and did some Christmas shopping. We strolled through the narrow, cobblestone streets, our excitement rising with every step. The Pantheon, with its ancient charm, was our next stop. Meeting my dear friend, Emanuela, for lunch, we felt like locals. Our day continued with a visit to the ruins of Largo di Torre, Argentina, where cats reign supreme. We then wandered through the Jewish Ghetto, one of the oldest Jewish quarters in the world. Tired but happy, we returned to our hotel to recharge.

Florida Fun: Next, we flew to Miami for fifteen days, with plans to return to Italy. We were in a hotel by the beach, and it was a blast seeing Joe, Nahela, and Gabriella, who joined us for the weekend. Watching them have fun in the pool was a joy. After some fantastic days in Vero Beach, filled with restaurants and fun places for Gabriella, we said goodbye to them and drove to Miami for two nights. We spent a delightful day with Terri and visited the Vizcaya Museum and Gardens, a peaceful and beautiful retreat. A stroll through Little Havana added a dash of culture to our trip before we settled into the Epic Hotel, marvelling at its contemporary design and rooftop pool.

Amalfi Coast Magic: After our Florida stint, we flew back to Rome and drove to Castellammare di Stabia, staying at the lovely La Medusa Hotel. This became our base camp for exploring the Amalfi Coast. We visited Sorrento, with its cliffside beauty and bustling streets. After enjoying a leisurely lunch overlooking the sea and a stroll through the picturesque Marina Grande, we admired the frescoes in Sorrento Cathedral and walked along the stunning coastal paths.

Next, we drove to Positano, a town that seemed to tumble into the Tyrrhenian Sea with its mosaic-like streets. We sipped espresso at a quaint coffee shop and enjoyed an aperitivo on Spiaggia Grande. A ferry ride took us to Amalfi, where we were captivated by its historic charm and vibrant streets. We visited the impressive Amalfi Cathedral and savoured a fantastic lunch at Ristorante L'Abside. Our journey continued to Ravello, a serene and elegant town perfect for relaxing and enjoying the views.

One afternoon, we strolled along the Lungomare di Castellammare, the December breeze reminding us of the chill in the air. The festive lights in town added to the charm. This trip was special, as it was our first since Livia's chemo and radiation. We took it easy, cherishing every moment and looking forward to the future. After a beautiful week on the Amalfi Coast, we drove back to Rome and flew to Israel, ending the year on a high note.

CHAPTER 21
A New Period in My Life—
2010-2013

2010 Highlights: A Year of Highs and Lows Major Event:

In 2010, the Israeli military intercepted a flotilla of ships trying to break the naval blockade of Gaza. The raid on the Mavi Marmara, the largest ship in the flotilla, resulted in the deaths of nine Turkish activists and strained relations between Israel and Turkey.

Livia

As Livia's health improved, she resumed her pastimes with Majan and her friends. I stayed by her side during hospitalisations, trying my best to comfort her.

Work Endeavors

On the work front, it was a whirlwind of activity. The first low-cost carriers, EasyJet and Wizz Air had arrived in Israel, rapidly filling their planes with budget-friendly flight slots. This aligned perfectly with Boaz's new strategy: package low-cost carriers ASAP. Our flights to Bratislava, operated by Seagle Airlines, continued smoothly.

That summer, I prepared a proposal for a large senior citizens organisation—the former employees of the Israeli Aircraft Industries. We were planning a travel for 7,000 people during the low season (May-June). This involved meticulous coordination, from doorstep pickups to managing thousands of passengers' flights and belongings.

I had to negotiate with El Al to use a jumbo jet with no more than 460 seats to Budapest. During the summer of Livia's frequent check-ups, my main activity was securing planes for our operation, aiming for completion by August 2010 for implementation in 2011. Unfortunately, Livia and I did not travel together that year.

I attended industry events alone—BIT in Milan, TTG in Rimini (where I learned Seagle Airlines was going bust), WTM in London, and a trip to Greece in search of a new destination (Evia Island did not pan out). Finding a new Bratislava airline became my top priority.

New Partner

We needed a plane in Bratislava departing for Tel Aviv at midnight and returning at 6 am, offering seven days but paying for six nights. The problem was

Slovakia's airlines had either gone bankrupt or ceased operations. Eventually, I discovered a Czech airline with one plane based in Bratislava for the summer. I flew to Prague on December 24 to sign a contract with Travel Service, and on Christmas Eve, I sealed the deal and returned to Israel.

2011 Beginnings

In early 2011, Livia's cousins, Peter and Jacky, visited Israel. We met them in a Jerusalem restaurant, giving them a taste of Israel.

Events in Israel

That summer, mass protests erupted in Israel over the high cost of living, housing prices, and economic inequality. The 'tent protests' symbolised the public's demand for social and economic reforms, drawing hundreds of thousands to Tel Aviv.

Back to Work

At work, I was busy with the successful operation of my Travel Service. I initiated new vacation destinations, like Crete, Kos, and Naples. The senior citizen operation was going perfectly. We began negotiations for the 2012 season, offering Croatia/Slovenia or Romania. They chose Romania, so I contacted Targu Mures airport and El Al subsidiary Sun d'or for flights. I secured a significant discount from the airport, which greatly impacted our pricing.

An inspection trip to check hotels and services

introduced me to Florin, who organised all the ground services. Livia was thriving at her AACI job, earning several bonuses.

Provence and Piedmont Trip

That fall, we embarked on an adventure to the Provence and Piedmont regions. We flew to Marseilles and picked up a rental car for two weeks.

Provence

Our first stop was Avignon, where we stayed at Hôtel La Ferme, a charming rural hotel surrounded by greenery on Île de la Barthelasse. The relaxed atmosphere was perfect. We explored Avignon's Gothic palace and the Pont Saint-Bénézet bridge, enjoyed lunch at a café in the lively Place de l'Horloge, and wandered through the cobblestone streets of the old town.

The next day, we drove to Gordes, one of Provence's most beautiful hilltop villages, and strolled its narrow streets and markets. We had lunch at L'Artegal, with stunning views of the Luberon Valley, and then continued to the quieter hilltop village of Joucas.

The following day took us to Châteauneuf-du-Pape for wine tasting. We visited vineyards like Domaine du Vieux Télégraphe and Château de Beaucastel, enjoyed a delicious lunch at Le Verger des Papes, and explored the village before heading back to our hotel.

We left Avignon with a sense of accomplishment and

drove toward the French Riviera, stopping in St Tropez for a delightful seafood lunch. The drive along the Côte d'Azur was breathtaking.

French Riviera

We arrived in Vence, a medieval town with cobblestone streets, art galleries, and cafés. We stayed at La Maison du Frene, a charming boutique guesthouse with a mix of modern art and classic French interior. It was Livia's first time on the French Riviera, and she was so excited about the whole trip.

We took trips to Saint-Paul-de-Vence, a medieval hilltop village known for its art galleries, and visited the Fondation Maeght, a modern art museum. Back in Vence, we got eyeglasses for Livia and enjoyed a Pernot at a nearby brasserie.

We also explored Tourrettes-sur-Loup, known for its violet production, and took a peaceful walk through the village. Another day, we drove to Gorges du Loup, a beautiful green gorge with waterfalls and rocky walls, and continued to Antibes to visit the Picasso Museum and stroll through the old town.

Piedmont

Next, we drove to Italy, passing through San Remo and Savona and finally arriving in Torino. We stayed at the Opera35 Boutique Hotel, a cosy place with modern touches and friendly service. We enjoyed a fantastic local dinner with great wines.

We visited Mole Antonelliana, now the National Museum of Cinema, and took in panoramic views of Turin. Despite the rainy weather, we savoured Bicerin, a traditional hot beverage, and explored the Museo Nazionale dell'Automobile and Eataly Torino, a megastore specialising in high-quality Italian food.

After visiting Alba, we continued to Grinzane Cavour, a historic castle nestled in a renowned wine-growing region. From there, we explored tranquil towns like La Morra and Barolo, visiting wineries and indulging in wine tastings that showcased the area's rich heritage.

Our visit coincided with the white truffle season, a time of year that highlights one of Italy's most coveted culinary treasures. White truffles, rare and incredibly expensive, are prized for their distinctive pungent aroma and unique flavour that is almost indescribable. Though they can be found in various parts of Italy, their heartland is Piedmont, particularly the Langhe region, slightly south of where we were exploring.

My earlier experiences with truffles were limited to rare occasions in Eastern Europe, where only the most exclusive restaurants offered a taste of these luxurious delicacies. Since we were now in the heart of the truffle country during its peak season, we decided to seize the opportunity to savour this exquisite treat again.

One evening, we dined in Alba, a charming town famous for its truffles. At a local restaurant, I enjoyed a meal that was a true celebration of the season: pasta with butter and truffles, followed by a risotto infused with the delicate flavour of white truffles. Both dishes were perfectly paired with Barolo wine, enhancing the entire experience.

That same evening, across the grand piazza in front of our hotel, a truffle auction was taking place. The atmosphere was electric as bidders competed for these treasures, with prices for white truffles rivalling the value of gold.

As our journey continued, we drove north through Milan, where we concluded our adventure with a flight back home, leaving behind the enchanting flavours and memories of Piedmont.

That trip was a great one, memorable for our wonderful and fun experiences.

My Eye Problem: A Comedy of Errors

That year, one evening after work, I noticed a disturbance in my left eye. It felt like I was seeing pesky black floaters darting around. When I got home, Livia and her friends were sprawled on the floor, smoking and laughing—so stoned and drunk that the scene resembled a comedy sketch. I tried to tell Livia about my eye issue, but she laughed so hard she almost threw up. Her laughter was so infectious that I can still vividly remember it. Seeing that no one was paying me any attention, I decided to call it a night and went to bed.

The next morning, I mentioned my eye problem to Livia again. She brushed it off with, "Ah, don't worry, it will pass." By Saturday evening, my eye had worsened significantly, and I had to rush to the emergency room. The doctors diagnosed a tear in my retina and instructed me to return the next day for laser treatment. I spent hours in the waiting room before finally getting to the procedure.

This scenario repeated itself about ten times. Each visit involved eye drops to dilate my pupil, a long wait, and then more laser treatment. The whole ordeal became a tiring routine. Now, every time I see a black spot, I have flashbacks to those endless appointments. My left eye has never been quite the same.

The Start of Livia's New Health Experience

So, 2011 came to an end, and a new beginning with 2012 began. Unfortunately, Livia was not feeling good again; she found two lumps on her neck, on the opposite side from where the first one was. Livia's health was not yet where we both wanted it to be. She needed to get a bone marrow transplant. With a bone marrow or stem cell transplant, you replace damaged or diseased blood-forming cells in your bone marrow with healthy cells. It's also used to treat some non-cancerous conditions, notably aplastic anaemia. She had an autologous transplant, where doctors collect your own bone marrow or stem cells before your treatment and infuse them back into your body after your treatment is over. Doctors perform a transplant if you have lymphoma; it is a very used method with pretty good results. That healthy cells are put back into your body. They get into your bloodstream through an IV line, travel to your bone marrow, and then start making new healthy blood cells.

All the time, she was on the lookout for infections or graft-versus-host disease (when the new cells reject their host by attacking its tissues), and she had to go once a week for a check of her blood cell counts to make sure her new bone marrow was producing a normal range of them. She had to go back to the hospital three or four times a week for two months, and she was exhausted.

One day, they suspected that Livia was sick with the flu and immediately brought her down to a different unit of the hospital there. She was not as comfortable as before, and it took about five days to move her back. Through it all, she never once complained. Livia faced the procedures as if they were no more than the flu, coming and going. She was in the closed section of the transplant department in the hospital, and everything had to be clean and sterile. Livia had a number of Pet CTs after, and she was clean again. We both hoped and prayed that this time, the cancer could finally be beaten. I stayed with her, sleeping in her room where I had a bed and a computer on which I could work from a distance during hospitalisations, doing my utmost to comfort and help her. Regardless, after spending a month in the hospital with Livia, she went back home, where she relaxed for another 3 weeks.

Winter and Travel Service's New Idea

The winter season was set, with firm bookings for hotels and flights to Italy. However, the forecast predicted little to no snow. Despite this, Valtur experienced a generous snowfall, providing us with a unique marketing challenge. We had to vigorously promote our packages, assuring customers that snow was guaranteed. Our marketing team crafted messages emphasising the snowy experience and enticing people to book. We pulled it off, and bookings continued to pour in. Flights operated as scheduled, and all commitments were honoured. The season turned out to be a success, much to our relief and excitement.

Meanwhile, during the summer, we decided to take a bold step and extended our routes, increasing the frequency of flights to Bratislava to three times a week. This move allowed us to accommodate 560 passengers weekly. It was a risky decision, but we managed to keep Travel Service on their toes and showcased our marketing prowess.

Our success can be attributed to a few key strategies:

Market Research: We conducted thorough market research to understand our target audience's needs and preferences. This allowed us to tailor our offerings to meet their expectations.

Collaborations: We collaborated with local

businesses, ski schools, and equipment stores to provide comprehensive packages. This not only added value to our packages but also created a sense of community among our partners.

Promotions: We ran targeted promotions and discounts, making our packages attractive to a wider audience. This helped boost bookings and ensured a steady flow of customers throughout the season.

Customer Engagement: We actively engaged with our customers through social media and email campaigns, keeping them informed about the latest updates and offers. This helped build trust and loyalty among our customers.

As a result, our efforts paid off. The risky move to increase flight frequency to Bratislava proved to be a success. Our strategic marketing, coupled with our partnerships and customer engagement, helped us navigate the challenges and come out on top.

Dreams and Reality

Time was racing. There wasn't much time left for me, caught between visits to hospitals, Livia at home, and work. I wanted to travel more—a plan I've always had: to pay a visit to Brazil. I want to dance to the samba and see the football, the beautiful beaches, and the forests of the Amazonas. The crime, the poverty in the favelas—all this scares me, but Brazil has always called me, and one day, I'll go there. Dreams...

Trip to New Jersey, Connecticut, and Rome

That winter, we were planning to go to New York, Connecticut, and then a weekend in Rome. In December, we flew to New York and spent a few days with Joe. It was wonderful to be with family again. Gabriella had grown and was even more fun than before. We had the visits of relatives, including Livia's cousin, Elisa, and her brother, John, who flew in from Chicago to see her. Our evenings were filled with dancing and playing games with Gabriella.

We drove to the Bronx one afternoon, took in the Bronx Zoo, and had dinner on Arthur Avenue at a famous Italian restaurant, Dominick's. This family-style, cash-only restaurant has been a staple in the neighbourhood for decades. Dominick's is famous for its communal seating, classic Italian American dishes, and a casual, old-school atmosphere. We shared plates of pasta and homemade ravioli, roast beef (a family tradition), and fresh cannoli from the local bakery. We walked through the old home where Livia's grandmother and uncles had lived. It was a great moment to remember, especially for Livia, who was so fond of the routs.

Then we went to Waterbury in Connecticut to stay at the Courtyard by Marriott because that's where Livia's mother now lived, following yet another move. It was about a 15-minute drive from her place, so it provided that good balance between being close enough and far enough away. We went on walks, stayed outside, and went shopping at the malls because her mother's home was very dark and not something we wanted to spend a lot of time in.

Then, after three or four days, we flew to Rome, where we stayed at The Inn at the Roman Forum, a superb hotel with gorgeous rooms and ancient Roman ruins built into the structure. We walked down Via Cavour, viewed Michelangelo's Moses at San Pietro in Vincoli, and visited the cat sanctuary in Largo di Torre, Argentina. We had a light lunch near Piazza Navona and then returned to the hotel, and then, we had a wonderful dinner at a nearby Roman restaurant.

But the next day, a thick layer of snow covered Rome. Knowing that snow disrupts everything in Italy, we checked out of the hotel two days early and tried to make our way to the airport to get back to Israel. Holly Molly! Changing our flights was a nightmare. It was Alitalia! It took me forever, but I got the flights changed. Good Lord! It was a nightmare trying to find a taxi in a snowy city. Welcome to Rome! But I did get lucky. And driving in Rome in the snow was beautiful; it was romantic. And that was the end of 2012.

Livia's Health

By 2013, Livia was weak again. She had a fever and felt terrible. After tests and a PET-CT scan, doctors recommended six more cycles of chemotherapy, followed by a month of radiation. They told us this would be the last time they could administer either treatment—her body simply could not take it anymore. Livia was crushed, her faith in the process at an all-time low. We were devastated, unsure of what to say to each other. We had so many plans.

I tried to make her smile, to lift her spirits with the many things we would do together. But the hospital visits, the treatments, the pain—it had left her broken. Encouraging her to stay positive felt like a disservice, knowing the ordeal she was facing. The next five months of chemotherapy and radiation were gruelling. We were so tired of it all that I wished I could erase the memories from my mind. Yet, she completed the treatment with remarkable strength and dignity. Despite everything, she continued to get up and go to work every day, even driving herself to the office after radiation treatments. Truly, a lioness.

Back to Work as Much as Possible

Meanwhile, at work, I had my own battles. I fought hard to retain the exclusivity of our relationship with the Valtur clubs, but they threatened to pull the contract because sales outside the winter clubs were weak. We lost that battle but managed to keep our exclusivity for all clubs still under contract. In aviation, we started booking flights with Wizz Air, incorporating them into our packages for destinations in the former Eastern Bloc.

On the bright side, Livia was excelling at her job.

She received praise from the entire AACI board and Boaz and even earned a surprise bonus of $3,000.

Slovakia Journey

At the end of the summer holidays, we flew to Bratislava, Slovakia, hired a car, and drove to the High Tatras. We stayed at the Grand Hotel Kempinski on the banks of the beautiful glacial lake Štrbské Pleso, with stunning views of the surrounding mountains. It was the perfect place for us to relax and enjoy nature's beauty. This grand hotel with modern facilities was one of the world's top destinations in 2013.

We stayed for seven days, spending our mornings walking by the lake. One day, we drove about 1.5 hours to Zakopane in Poland, a small, cosy town with wooden houses, local markets, and restaurants. It was nice to soak in the local atmosphere. Zakopane is also known for its skiing and walking destinations.

One morning, we took a half-hour drive to Pepard in the High Tatras, strolling through picturesque streets, shops, and cafés. Another time, we drove about an hour to Spiš Castle, one of the largest castles in Central Europe. The monumental ruins and stupendous views were breathtaking. Spiš Castle is a UNESCO World Heritage site, a stark reminder of the region's medieval history. We had lunch in the castle, but the walk left Livia so exhausted that she had to rest for the remainder of the day. I tried to cheer her up with small gestures, but it was hard seeing her so tired.

On our last day, we drove back to Bratislava to catch our flight home. We spent seven hours in the city, visiting Bratislava Castle and its grounds, which offered panoramic views of the city, the Danube River, and the hazy horizons of Austria and Hungary. We also visited the Slovak National Museum located in the castle and then went to St. Martin's Cathedral, an outstanding Gothic building where Hungarian royalty were crowned for centuries.

Finally, we strolled through the quaint little streets of Bratislava's Old Town—a walkable area with historical architecture and beautiful squares. We ate lunch in a typical Slovak restaurant, trying bryndzové halušky (potato dumplings with sheep cheese and bacon), kapustnica (sauerkraut soup), and roast duck. Our last walk was along the Danube River, where we could observe the UFO Tower on the SNP Bridge—a sci-fi-looking observation deck on an important landmark in the city. We left for the airport after the sunset and flew back to Israel. It was a bittersweet trip—the beauty of the place, the stimulation of new sights and sounds, the food and wine, offset by Livia's growing frailty.

Beginning of December Trip

After a few months of hard work, Livia and I travelled to Belgium and the Netherlands, specifically Bruges and Amsterdam. We flew to Brussels and took the train to Bruges. Our first day started slowly, which was just perfect. We meandered through Markt Square, bustling with people and adorned with festive Christmas decorations. The Belfry of Bruges rose above us like a proud clocktower. I remember squeezing Livia's hand as we stood there, feeling like we were shaking ourselves free from time.

We spent the evening in a cosy bistro off the Burg, enjoying Flemish stew with dark Belgian beer. The candlelight inside was warmer than the chilly night air outside. We drank wine and talked about everything and nothing, feeling like the only people in the world as the streetlights cast a golden glow over the cobblestones.

The next day was dedicated to art and history. We spent several hours in the Groeningemuseum, marvelling at Flemish paintings. We stood in awe before van Eyck's Madonna with Canon van der Paele, captivated by its depth and beauty. We hardly spoke, simply moving from room to room, immersed in the art.

That evening, we found tranquillity in Minnewater Park, also known as the 'Lake of Love.' We sat on a quiet bench, watching swans glide across the water. It was a place to just be together, without distractions, where the past and future seemed to fade away.

Our final stop in Bruges was the Basilica of the Holy Blood. We sat in silence, contemplating the history and reverence within the small church. One evening, we feasted on mussels prepared with beer and butter at a local restaurant, accompanied by Belgian beer. We made a final stop at a chocolate shop, leaving with a small box of pralines.

As the train pulled away, I watched Bruges disappear, already feeling pangs of sadness for the things I wanted us to do. Bruges provided us with time and space, a promise of getaways that I wanted to stay with. We changed trains in Brussels and headed to Amsterdam.

Amsterdam greeted us with its magical Christmas decorations. The streets were lit up with festive lights, shop windows adorned with wreaths and candles. The reflection of the lights on the canals made the city especially picturesque.

Our first day in Amsterdam involved walking along the canals and visiting the Anne Frank House. The sombre mood inside contrasted with the holiday spirit outside. We held hands, navigating the crowded streets of Jordaan. Later, we found a candlelit café, where Livia enjoyed a joint, and we people-watched through the window while sipping warm coffee and sharing a slice of Dutch apple pie.

On our second day, we embraced the holiday spirit at the Christmas markets. The Rijksmuseum provided a peaceful respite from the bustling streets. We spent time gazing at the Dutch Masters, particularly Rembrandt's *Night Watch*. The Van Gogh Museum's vibrant canvases offered a temporary escape from the grey winter skies.

That night, we took a canal cruise. The boat was heated and cosy, drifting through Amsterdam's waterways adorned with holiday decorations. The bridges and houses glittered with lights. We snuggled together, feeling like we were in a Christmas card. We ended the evening with a splendid dinner at an Indonesian restaurant near our hotel.

On our final day, we visited the Flower Market, surrounded by Christmas trees, poinsettias, and tinsel garlands. Eventually, we headed to the airport, the Christmas lights of Amsterdam fading behind us. We carried the promise of Christmas with us, taking a piece of Amsterdam home.

This trip was a celebration of Christmas, love, and the simple joy of being in the most beautiful city in the world with the person I love.

This was the end of 2013, a year I will remember until my last day.

CHAPTER 22
Livia, Livia, and Livia
Again—2014

Final Trip to the States

In January, Livia and I took what would be her last trip to see all her friends and family. We flew into New York and drove to Waterbury, Connecticut, where we stayed at the same little hotel as before. On our first day, we had dinner and drinks at a local restaurant with Livia's childhood best friend, Deirdre, and her successful plastic surgeon husband, Terry, who had driven in from Albany. After dinner, we moved the party to a local bar where the women reminisced about their youth over drinks, sharing stories of summers spent at Deirdre's house on the New England beach and laughing about their youthful mischief. The night stretched into the early hours, filled with joy and nostalgia.

The next day, while walking through town, Livia's vision in her left eye began to deteriorate. She saw dark spots and had trouble seeing—a disturbing reminder of my own eye problems. I took her to the local hospital, where they quickly repaired her retinal tear. It was uncomfortable for her, but she was determined to see Joe the next day.

At Joe's place, we had a whirlwind of activities. We walked around a huge mall, visited Italian bakeries, and tasted various baked goods. Joe made us pasta with broccoli di rabe and Italian sausage, pizza for Gabriella, and roast beef, just like our grandmother used to make. We finished with fresh cannoli and fruit, all paired with wine and grappa. It was a family feast that had Livia beaming.

In the evenings, we hung out in Joe's newly renovated basement, which turned into a playroom for Gabriella, complete with a couch, projector, screen, and Netflix. We played cards, listened to music, and enjoyed stimulating conversations with Nahela's cousins about Israel. It was wonderful, but our departure came too soon.

On the morning we were set to leave, a snowstorm struck, blocking the roads. Not knowing how to drive in the snow, the trip through the snow was a nightmare, taking over three hours. After returning the car, the rental company drove me back to Maplewood. We took a taxi to the airport and flew back to Israel.

My Mom Moves

Since my father's death, we visited my mom every

week to ensure she was okay. We took her out to restaurants and had good times together. Eventually, she needed twenty-four-seven care, so we moved her from her apartment in Bat Yam to Herzliya, closer to us. We rented a new, nice apartment just 10 minutes away and bought new fixtures, furniture, and appliances. By the end of February, she had moved into her new apartment, making it easier for us to visit her.

Livia's Health Deteriorating

We didn't even unpack our luggage in Israel before heading to another doctor. I had scheduled an appointment for Livia with a private eye doctor to check on her retinal tear. We were relieved to learn it was healing nicely, but then we got a frantic call from Livia's oncologist. The cancer had returned, and another bone marrow transplant from a new donor was the only option.

Livia was devastated, screaming, "Eric, what should I do? I'm tired of being sick and doing this again and again. I just want to live my life."

We decided to go home and talk about it, trying to make sense of it all. The doctors drew blood and asked for a family member who might be a donor. We called Joe, who got tested and was found to be a match—ready and willing to help.

The Situation in Israel

In June, Hamas kidnapped and murdered three

Israeli teenagers in the West Bank, leading to a massive search and Operation Protective Edge. The conflict between Israel and Hamas from July to August resulted in hundreds of fatalities and thousands wounded. Rockets from Gaza and heavy Israeli airstrikes dominated the news. Meanwhile, the World Cup in Brazil provided a much-needed escape from reality.

Joe Comes to Israel

Amidst all this, Joe travelled to Israel for the first time to help with Livia's bone marrow transplant. It was supposed to be a ten-day visit, but the war escalated everything. It was a chaotic yet beautiful time because Joe was there. We picked him up at the airport, and although he looked frazzled, it was great to have him with us.

I set up blood-donation appointments for Joe over the next few days while I had to work. Livia stayed by his side. Once the doctors were satisfied with the blood donations, we took Joe on a sight-seeing tour of Israel.

We started in the Old City of Jerusalem, walking the Via Dolorosa and visiting the Church of the Holy Sepulchre. We explored the underground tunnels beside the Western Wall, and Joe was impressed with the history. We had lunch at an excellent Arab restaurant specialising in hummus, visited the Western Wall, and walked to the Temple Mount. The Temple Mount complex, with Al-Aqsa Mosque and the Dome of the Rock, moved Joe deeply.

We visited the Tower of David near Jaffa Gate. For dinner, we stopped at Dalal Restaurant in Neve Tzedek, one of Tel Aviv's oldest and prettiest neighbourhoods, known for its fusion of Mediterranean and French-inspired cuisine.

The next day, we drove to Nazareth to visit the Basilica of the Annunciation, followed by lunch at Diana's, a restaurant renowned for its traditional Arab cuisine. Then we drove to Tzfat, known for its mystical reputation and art colony, and attended a session on Kabbalah.

We headed north along the Hula Valley, stopping at a lookout above the sea in Rosh Hanikra, a seaside grotto at the northern tip of the country. "Israel is gorgeous here," Joe remarked.

We continued to Akko, a city rich in history and culture. We ended the day with dinner at Uri Buri, a world-renowned seafood restaurant by Chef Uri Jeremias, combining local produce with global influences—a perfect end to a long day of discovery.

Livia's Birthday

On 10th August, we celebrated Livia's birthday in style. We decorated the roof with lights from her 50th birthday, set up music, arranged a long buffet table, and barbecued various meats. Livia made salads and bought fresh dips and veggies. We stocked up on mineral water, wine, beer, and some hard liquor. After two days of preparation, the guests arrived, and it was a fantastic party. Everyone had a great time, and Livia was extremely happy, especially with Joe being part of the action. The party lasted until 1 am, and Joe and I did most of the cleaning up, leaving the rest for the next day.

The Second Bone Marrow Transplant

Two days later, Joe flew back to the States. Soon after, the hospital called to schedule Livia's bone marrow transplant for the eve of Rosh Hashanah. Just before the procedure, we attended her last concert together with Avi and Terri—and what a concert it was! Tony Bennett performed in Tel Aviv, singing all the songs Livia and her grandmother loved. It was an evening to remember.

The next day, I drove her to the hospital. The procedure, where her blood was replaced, lasted the entire day. It was torturous, but Livia remained courageous and upbeat. She was hospitalised for four weeks, during which her body began accepting the transplant. I visited her every weekend and night after work, staying late and sometimes watching movies on the computer.

Terri also visited before leaving for Florida to meet her daughter, who was about to give birth to her third child.

The Final Days and the End

When Livia was finally discharged, we thought the

worst was behind us. But three weeks later, she took a sudden turn for the worse. I rushed her back to the hospital, where she was admitted again. Her kidneys had failed, and the doctors recommended starting dialysis, knowing it marked the beginning of the end. I stayed by her side, but she could barely speak or eat. After four agonising days, Livia passed away in my arms at around 4 am. I was there to hold her head and kiss her goodbye.

In those final days, Ian and Avi took turns staying with me. Avi brought meals, and Ian stayed close. We played music for Livia, hoping she could still hear. When Livia passed, I called Ian and Avi first, and they came to the hospital immediately.

Then I called Joe, who wrote: "My sister, Livia Berman, died last night (early this morning—Israeli time) after a long and fierce battle with cancer. She was 56. I am flying back to Israel this evening to be with her great husband, Eric."

And indeed, he came.

A heartbreaking moment followed when we decided to change Livia's Facebook page into a memorial page. Those days were incredibly difficult. We shared drinks and talked about Livia, her childhood, and the things she always longed for. I took out all her jewellery and asked Joe what he wanted to take back home for Gabriella, thinking she would get Christmas presents from Livia for the next 20 years.

Joe wrote: "Livia had been battling lymphoma for four years and ultimately succumbed to complications related to Graft-versus-host disease after a stem cell transplant.

Livia lived in Israel with her husband, Eric. Her passing was deeply felt by her family, who remember her fondly for her vibrant life and the love she shared with them."

At the funeral that Sunday, I read the following:

"Livia, Always the sunshine of my life, now and forever. Her grandfather used to sing a song to her when she was young, and it went like this: 'You are my sunshine, my only sunshine. You make me happy when skies are grey. You'll never know, dear, how much I love you. Please, don't take my sunshine away.' She was the love of my life, the light of my existence, the force that lifted me and kept me moving forward. She never gave up and loved her work, and family meant everything to her. Holidays and family gatherings were always cherished moments that she would embellish in her memories. Her friends were her second family, each one holding a special place in her heart. And then, as Pink Floyd said, 'We're just two lost souls swimming in a fishbowl.' Love, love, love, forever and always, my lioness."

David London also read a eulogy for Livia:

"Dear Livia, You would not like this day. It's grey and overcast; there is no sun shining, no view of the sea, and no glass of wine in your hand. One of my favourite memories of you, Carole, and myself is sitting at a restaurant in the port of Tel Aviv, basking in the sunshine. You were always a private person, and I only got glimpses into your life between all our brainstorming and organising trips. I know you'd be happy to see Eric and your brother, Joe, together today. I know how much you treasured the time you spent with Joe on his recent trip here. You were so proud of him, showing him around Israel for the first time.

"Eric was the love of your life. You told me once, with such pride in your voice, how he always stood by his word, professionally and personally, and that you couldn't imagine a better husband. He was there for you through every terrible moment of this battle with cancer.

"Livia was a true professional. She loved Italy—the culture, the style, the food. Last year, she organised a trip to Pitigliano, the 'Little Jerusalem' in Italy, and she was so excited about it. It was one of the many wonderful trips she planned, but there was one trip to France that she was especially looking forward to—one she hoped to take with Eric. Sadly, that trip was not meant to be. I didn't know many of her friends, but I know she cherished her Thursday night gatherings for wine and fun with them. She loved animals, especially George the cat, and she always wanted the best experiences for everyone. Her last fully planned trip to South Africa will undoubtedly be a great success, just as she would have wanted."

Terri sent a letter to be read by Fran:

"How does one define friendship? I'm sitting here, trying to make sense of it all—why certain people pass through our lives and what it all means. I once read that everyone hears what you say, but true friends listen to what you don't say. That was you, Livia. My friend, my confidante. It's hard to believe that we won't have another cup of coffee together, or share another meal, or play another round of Mahjong. How many challenges did we face together, adjusting to our new lives in a foreign country, until we found happiness? Those Thursday night games became more than just fun—they were a bonding experience, a sisterhood. We laughed, we cried, we argued. You were always there. You were a loving and devoted wife. You lived by a code of commitment and loyalty. You loved your work, appreciated art and music, and found joy in simple moments. Lunch on your rooftop with a good book and a bottle of wine—those were your moments of peace. You touched all our lives, and I hope you knew just how much you were loved. I'll miss you forever, Livia."

At the funeral, I played our song, *"Stand by Me,"* followed by *"Wish You Were Here."*

When we returned home, we had a quick lunch before preparing for the shiva. It was long, and after three days, Joe left. I was alone. The stress and emotional toll were heavy, and I developed psoriasis on my elbows and knees. The doctor prescribed some cream, but I felt lost and directionless. It was as if the world had stopped, and I didn't know where to go next.

The Trip to Joe

Later that year, I got tickets for a flight to visit Joe, Nahela, and Gabriella for the Christmas and New Year holidays. We drove one Saturday to visit Livia's mom, and I brought her Livia's laptop. Spending the holidays with family was wonderful. It reminded me how much I cherish them.

CHAPTER 23
Life After Livia, Meeting Iris—2015-2019

Back to Israel

When I came back home from the States, one of the first things I did was take all of Livia's things away: clothes, shoes, toiletries, jewellery—anything that reminded me of her. I called her mahjong friends and asked them to help me clear her room, and they kindly took almost everything. I wanted a blank canvas to start anew.

Boaz and His Moves

I turned to myself, trying to see my mom more often and find rock concerts—a world I was eager to re-embrace. I kept working but without much enthusiasm. Livia had taught me to manage the AACI account, and I kept it going along with the tours and groups, but never with the same excitement. Eventually, Boaz decided that perhaps I wasn't the best person to lead the project. He slowly let it go, and I watched it wither, as no one except Livia cared for it the way she did. Boaz also made me angry during Livia's illness by asking for the company-leased car to be returned. Livia refused, but the day after her funeral, they came from the office and took the car.

Iris

I began to attend shows in Israel and abroad, consuming concerts at an intense pace. At one show, I met Iris.

Iris was an enigma wrapped in allure—a woman whose presence captivated me from the very first moment. A tattooed and pierced divorcée with a daughter living in the US, her wild and eclectic appearance was a magnetic force. Her striking makeup accentuated her expressive eyes, while intricate tattoos wove stories across her skin—each one a piece of art begging to be admired. A dazzling array of piercings added to her vibrant tapestry of rebellion and creativity.

Beyond her stunning exterior, Iris was a whirlwind of energy and passion. She wasn't just pretty and sexy; she exuded a vivacious spirit that was impossible to resist. Her laughter was infectious, her zest for life was contagious, and her adventurous soul turned every moment into an exciting escapade. She had an incredible ability to make even the mundane feel extraordinary, and her enthusiasm for life's little things was truly inspiring.

Deeply connected to the music scene, Iris shared my love for concerts and live performances. Music became the soundtrack to our blossoming connection, with each melody and beat bringing us closer together. We lost ourselves in the rhythm, dancing and singing with unbridled joy. Her passion for music matched mine, creating a bond that felt almost electric.

Her eclectic style and bold personality made her stand out in any crowd. Being around her was like being swept up in a whirlwind of colour and energy. Iris had a way of making me feel alive, pushing me to embrace life with the same fervour that she did. She was more than just a companion; she was a muse—a source of inspiration and excitement that reignited my passion for life.

Concert Fever

We met at an Asaf Avidan concert, which was an unforgettable experience. The atmosphere was electric from the moment the lights dimmed and Avidan took the stage. His presence was magnetic, and he captivated the audience with his unique voice. One evening, Iris and I went for dinner together and began spending our time concert-hopping.

Prague Adventures

We went to Prague to see Sting and Paul Simon. It was supposed to be a quick weekend trip, but ended up taking much longer. We left on a Friday afternoon and arrived in the city of spires and red roofs. We checked into our hotel and headed out into the winter evening. Our first stop was Old Town Square, a fairy-tale setting of Slavic folklore. The Gothic Týn Church towered over us, and we watched the much-photographed astronomical clock. It's strange to wander among the baroque statues and street performers and even stranger to watch the clockwork procession of 12 apostles every hour, halting tourists in their tracks. It lasts only a minute.

The next morning, we made the arduous climb up to the castle district. We started in Malá Strana, a quaint neighbourhood with charming, cobbled streets rising steeply to Prague Castle. The Gothic St Vitus Cathedral greeted us with its towering spires. From the castle's terrace, we could see all of Prague—a mix of old and new buildings centred around the meandering Vltava River.

In the afternoon, we visited the Jewish Quarter, Josefov. The history was poignant as we walked along the streets in silence. We ended up in a little restaurant off Wenceslas Square, eating goulash with dumplings and roast pork washed down with Pilsner. Simple but good, with rustic decor and old wooden furniture.

On the last morning, we explored the quiet backstreets to see some less-touristy areas. Before heading to the airport, we stopped at a cafe for one final Trdelník, a dough pastry coated in sugar and cinnamon. We sat on a bench overlooking the river, watching the world go by. Oh, and did I mention the concert was canceled because Sting got sick? No rain check.

Athens Excursion

Later that spring, we flew to Athens for Israeli Independence Day. We stayed in Glyfada, a blend of coastal beauty, luxury, and vibrant energy—perfect for a two-day escape. Whether lounging on pristine beaches, exploring chic boutiques, or enjoying the local nightlife, we left Glyfada relaxed with a taste of the Athenian Riviera lifestyle.

More Concerts and Celebrations

Back home, Iris and I attended several concerts in Tel Aviv, including One Republic in the park. Led by Ryan Tedder, their high-energy performance spanned their biggest hits, electrifying the atmosphere. Shortly after, we went to Terri's birthday party—a strange gathering considering how close Terri was to Livia. We continued to see each other periodically, and within a couple of months, we flew to Berlin to celebrate my 60th birthday.

Berlin Adventures

In Berlin, I'd booked tickets for Santana, and the anticipation was electric. He started with his trademark Latin-influenced rock, mixing old and new favourites from Corazón. Our days in Berlin were spent visiting historical markers—the old Jewish Quarter, the Holocaust Memorial, poking around Alexander Platz, and dining in some of the best Italian restaurants along Kurfürstendamm.

We also attended a concert by Mark Knopfler, which was an absolute masterclass in musicianship. The next night, we saw the Blue Man Group, a visual and musical spectacular. The theatre was high-tech and futuristic. We had five wonderful days in Berlin, feeling rejuvenated and thrilled by the experiences.

Renovation of the Apartment

Iris and I decided then to try to live together. I renovated it completely, and Iris moved into my apartment. The only original room in the apartment was the bathroom. The contractor was there for two months, giving me advice on the furnishings. I redid the living room and bedroom, painted everything, and got a new TV, a wine refrigerator, and an expresso maker with it is own grounding. At the end of it all, it felt like a new apartment.

Meeting Eden (Iris's Daughter) in Italy

We flew to Bologna later that year for one of my annual trips to my TTG conference in Rimini. We picked up Iris's daughter Eden and her husband, Wesley, at Bologna airport; we were going to stay in a villa in San Casciano Val di Pesa, an area I know well, and they were both so impressed by how pretty it was.

Eden is a beautiful young lady with captivating brown hair that cascades in soft waves and striking green eyes that shine with intelligence and kindness. She is tall and lean, moving with a grace and elegance that naturally draws admiration. Her presence is both calming and invigorating, a blend that makes her unique.

Eden is an art major, and her passion for creativity is evident in everything she does. Whether she is painting a vibrant canvas or crafting a delicate piece of pottery, her talent and dedication shine through. She is also a future teacher of nutrition education, committed to helping others lead healthier lives. Her dedication to this field stems from a genuine desire to make a positive impact on people's well-being.

Like her mother, Eden is very emotional, displaying a depth of feeling and empathy that endears her to everyone she meets. Her ability to connect with others on an emotional level makes her a cherished friend and a supportive confidante. She has a natural warmth and charm that makes her interactions with others feel genuine and heartfelt.

Eden currently lives in Missouri, USA, where she continues to bring her unique blend of warmth and creativity to every aspect of her life. Her home is a hub of activity and inspiration, filled with her artistic creations and the sounds of laughter and conversation. Eden's presence is a beacon of positivity, and she leaves an impression on everyone who has the pleasure of knowing her.

Eden is married to Wesley, a blond guy with his own set of green eyes that sparkle with mischief and kindness. Wesley is pretty tall and has an engaging personality that matches his vibrant looks. He is a talented drummer, bringing rhythm and energy to any setting. His excellent command of English adds to his charismatic presence. Together, they make a very fun and dynamic couple, sharing laughter, adventures, and a genuine bond that is palpable to everyone who meets them.

Our Adventures in Tuscany and Beyond

Our first stop was the Uffizi Galleries in Florence. Eden, an art major, was ecstatic. For the next hour, we marvelled at masterpieces by legends, such as Botticelli's *The Birth of Venus,* da Vinci's *The Annunciation*, and Michelangelo's *Doni Tondo.* Eden and Wesley were captivated by the fine details and beauty of the paintings.

Next, we walked to the Ponte Vecchio, where Iris was amazed by the jewellery shops on the bridge. We continued to the Palazzo Pitti and wandered through the Boboli Gardens, taking a coffee break before heading to the Duomo. Brunelleschi's dome, the Baptistery with Ghiberti's Gates of Paradise, and Giotto's Campanile left Wesley and Eden wide-eyed with wonder.

After lunch, we visited the Great Synagogue of Florence, appreciating its beautiful architecture and Jewish history. Then we explored the Medici market, where Iris found paradise among the leather goods, sharing her joy with me. We had dinner in the old town and returned to the villa, satisfied with a bottle of wine to share before bed.

The next day, we drove to Siena, stopping first at Piazza del Campo and the striking Torre del Mangia. We continued to the Duomo di Siena, admiring its black-and-white façade, sculptures, and artistic masterpieces inside. We enjoyed a lovely lunch of pici pasta, local greens, and coffee with cantucci. Our day ended with a dinner in Tavarnelle Val di Pesa, featuring Bistecca alla Fiorentina, risotto con fungi, and copious amounts of red wine and conversation. We then headed back to the villa to relax.

The following morning, I arranged a day trip to Cinque Terre. We drove to La Spezia and took the train to the five villages, starting with Rio Maggiore. The colourful buildings and marina were beautiful, and Iris captured many shots with her camera. A boat tour along the coast offered wonderful views of the villages clinging to the cliffs, made magical by the cool sea breeze.

In Vernazza, we strolled the streets, drank coffee at a harbour-front café, and enjoyed the lively bustle. After a brief stop in La Spezia, we headed to Pisa, where we saw the Leaning Tower and walked the streets in the early evening. We finished the day with dinner at a roadside trattoria on our way back to the villa.

The next day, we drove to San Gimignano, known as the 'Manhattan of the Middle Ages' for its remaining

14 towers. We explored the beautifully preserved medieval town, sampled Tuscan produce, and ate gelato at the Gelateria Dondoli, a winner of the Gelato World Cup. Iris indulged in her favourite fetish—shoes. We had dinner at a restaurant near the villa.

On our last day, we returned to Florence, visiting the Accademia Museum to see Michelangelo's David. We ended the day with dinner at a local trattoria, enjoying crostini, ribollita, pasta with sausages, a Tuscan almond cake, and coffee and grappa.

The next day, we drove Eden and Wesley to the Bologna airport and then flew back to Israel. The emotional goodbyes were intense, as Eden and Iris had not seen each other for about three years. I was happy to bring them together once more.

Mia

As soon as we returned, Iris wanted to get a dog. So, we contacted SOS and adopted a four-year-old Amstaff named Mia. She was a mix of scary and gentle, the sweetest yet most fearful dog I ever had. Despite her affectionate nature, Mia was easily frightened by noises. However, we always kept her on a leash because she was ready to attack any cats or dogs she encountered. She was incredibly cute but also very aggressive.

Due to her temperament, we couldn't leave her alone with other dogs. Every time we travelled, we needed a dog sitter to stay at our home. We hired a girl to take Mia out four times a day and sleep over at our house to ensure Mia was well taken care of in our absence.

Birthday Cruise Adventure

Since Iris's birthday was on 1st January, I arranged an upscale Miami-to-Eastern Caribbean Sea cruise with Oceania Cruise Line as a silent gift for her. We flew from Rome to Miami on her birthday and had dinner at a local restaurant, enjoying great food and service.

In Miami, we checked into the W Hotel downtown and visited the market at Brickell. Later, we partied the night away at a nightclub in Little Havana, immersing ourselves in Cuban culture.

The next day, we boarded the cruise ship, which had amazing rooms and a massive balcony, adding to the luxurious feel of the trip.

Ports of Call

- **Grand Turk, Turks and Caicos:** After a leisurely day at sea, we spent the day on Grace Bay Beach, sipping cold beer and admiring the gorgeous view.

- **San Juan, Puerto Rico:** We took a half-day trip to El Yunque National Forest, the only tropical rainforest in the US National Forest System. The lush greenery, cascading waterfalls, and exotic flora were enchanting. In the afternoon, we walked around Old San Juan, where I shared memories of Livia with Iris.

- **Gustavia, Saint Barts:** I rented a Mini Cooper convertible, Iris's dream car. We visited Saline Beach and Flamands Beach, had lunch at a seaside restaurant, and indulged in some shopping. It was a day to remember.

- **Philipsburg, Saint Maarten:** We toured the mountainous Loterie Farm, hiked the tropical rainforest, and explored the Dutch/French island border. We enjoyed lunches, beers, and reggae bands at a lively marina, ending the day with a romantic sunset on top of the mountain.

- **Tortola, British Virgin Islands:** We took a ferry to Virgin Gorda, exploring the rock formations and grottos at The Baths. We spent the afternoon on Cane Garden Bay beach and had dinner at the captain's table, enjoying an exquisite meal with different wines.

- **Nassau, Bahamas:** We shopped at Downtown and the Straw Market, visited Fort Fincastle and the Queen's Staircase, and ended our trip at a bar, reminiscing about our cruise memories.

We sailed back to Miami the next morning and then headed to the airport for our flight to Israel. It was a terrific vacation, and upon returning, Mia was anxiously waiting for us, giving us the faces of an angry dog.

More About Iris

Iris would mess up my name on purpose when I'd call her Livia, like a reminder of how hard she worked. A self-made woman who loved her shoes and handbags. She had been married previously but was lonely (probably because her husband was absent so often).

She is really the full figure of the perfect partner; she does accept my crazy behaviour, and she is always ready to help and keep us together. She is nine years younger than me. She had a sister in Israel, Lee, who often invited me and my mom to family dinners. Also, among her parents, her father was already sick with Parkinson's and Alzheimer's diseases, which were just starting to be recognised. Her mother is still going strong, but is now dealing with dementia.

Concert Frenzy

We attended several remarkable concerts in Israel in 2016. The most important was the trip to Barcelona to see Bruce Springsteen and the E Street Band in an unprecedented concert that lasted for more than 3 hours. The tour was called *The River*, and it was just magical. Walking back to our hotel, we could not stop talking about it.

Back in Tel Aviv, we were treated to one of Israel's most famous rock bands, Mashina, fronted by Yuval Banai, singing many of their classic rock, punk, ska, new wave, oriental, and Eastern melodies.

The second was a concert by Robert Cray, who is one of the greatest blues guitarists and singers of our time. He performed in Tel Aviv and played a mix of old and new songs. His perfect guitar playing bounced off his soulful voice. Beautiful and classy, the golden sounds of his playing hit the notes, accompanied by the powerful beat of the band.

Later, we were off to a Joe Bonamassa concert in Tel Aviv, which, for blues and rock fans, was a masterclass show of both intensity and virtuosity.

Morrissey, who has a long history with Israel, rated his Tel Aviv show as one of his favourite performances of the year. He said that he was being moved by the way he felt Israeli audiences connected with his music.

When Camel—the band known for creating a fusion of rock, jazz, and classical influences—created a setlist from their legendary self-titled album through Nude (1981), the Israeli audience responded loudly to their signature sound. Camel's music became the blueprint for others in the genre, and their popularity proves that they are still the leaders in the field, enjoying the dedication of fans formed decades after the release of their debut album.

Garbage performs in Israel during their Strange Little Birds tour. The US alternative rock band—featuring the captivating lead singer Shirley Manson—performed at the Zappa Amphie Shuni in Binyamina as part of their Strange Little Birds tour. It must be mentioned that the Israel shows were always the star or the end of a tour for any performer due to the political situation.

Unfortunately, Iris sprained her ankle on the roof that summer, and she missed some of these concerts. She was at home for a month, and I tried in vain to pressure her to use the crutches and not be like a sitting duck, but with no prevail. She really got angry with me since I was telling her, "You can go with the crutches." She was just so afraid.

She didn't make it to Beth Hart, who came to town as part of her Better Than Home tour for her 2015 album of the same name. So I took Ian with me.

However, Iris did make it to Buddy Guy's concert at Caesarea Amphitheatre, in a wheelchair. Buddy Guy is one of the last of the bluesmen of Chicago, a master of heavy string-bending guitar playing, a singing bluesman with a powerful, visceral stage presence. This year's list of concerts was never-ending, and I had made up for the years Livia was sick and couldn't go to shows.

The Trip to Sorrento With Friends

Inspired by a suggestion that fall, we decided to spend the holidays together in Italy. Avi, Silvian and his girlfriend, Ayelt, and Avi and Terri—my friends—all agreed, and we rented a villa in Sorrento for 10 days. We flew to Naples, and I rented a minivan for 9 people. Instead of driving straight to Sorrento, I followed the GPS, and it took us through the narrow streets of

Sorrento. Manoeuvering the minivan was challenging; the car's rearview mirrors had to be folded in to squeeze through. A lot of panic broke out, but Avi managed to steer us out of it. This became a running joke: 'How did I manage to shrink a minivan into a Fiat 500?'

Once settled in, we found the villa beautiful—three bedrooms and three bathrooms on the second floor, a large living area, and a well-appointed kitchen. The beautiful gardens were perfect for breakfast. In the afternoon, we walked to a nearby market to buy yogurt, milk, coffee, cheeses, and pasta. Then, we took a bus downtown to Sorrento, walking through Piazza Tasso and Corso Italia, sampling local lemon products, including the famous limoncello.

The next morning, after breakfast, we drove north to Caserta to visit the Reggia di Caserta (Royal Palace of Caserta). The palace, once the home of the Bourbon kings of Naples, is an impressive Baroque and Neoclassical masterpiece, comparable to Versailles. We toured the palace and its enormous royal gardens. Afterwards, we had lunch at a family-run trattoria with pasta alla sorrentina and ended the day at the big outlet mall near Caserta.

The following day, we took a day trip to Pompeii. Visiting the ancient city, frozen in time by the eruption of Mount Vesuvius in the year 79, was fascinating. We walked through well-preserved streets, ruins of houses, temples, and public buildings and were amazed by the frescoes and mosaics.

Next, we drove to Positano, walked through beautiful villages, and visited Amalfi. We parked beside the beach, visited the centre, and admired the cathedral. We hiked to a viewpoint on the mountain and then returned to the center for lunch. Afterwards, we visited Livia's favourite restaurant between Amalfi and Atrani and then drove to Ravello to see Villa Rufolo. On the way back, Terri and Iris got carsick from my driving, so Avi took over for the rest of the trip.

We spent a full day in Naples, exploring its vibrant and energetic streets. Despite its reputation, we found Naples charming. We enjoyed sfogliatelle, divine food, and finished the day with different types of Neapolitan pizza. We also visited some of the city's monuments, all masterpieces in their own right. Exhausted from our day trip, I cooked dinner once we returned to the villa.

On our last day, we took a ferry to Capri and spent the day exploring the island. We walked through picturesque streets, visited lookouts, and admired the famous cliffs and crystal waters. Capri was the highlight of our trip, a perfect ending to a beautiful week.

We flew back to Israel the next day. Workwise, I was still very much involved, but I slowed down the pace. I was madly in love. I wanted to give Iris everything she wanted or imagined. It was as if I had not loved Livia enough before, and I was making up for it now. It was my way of getting over her.

I was soon going to the gym twice a week; I loved it.

My working week became 10 am to 5 pm to the letter: no late-night at the office, no midnight calls, no working on the weekend. All my time would be for her.

And for 2017, I had big plans. I bought tickets for us to see *Chris Cornell, The Pretenders, Al Di Meola*, and *Joss Stone*, all in Tel Aviv.

A Short Weekend in Madrid

I got flight tickets for another trip back to Madrid to visit with Eden and Wes before they flew to Israel. It was a really busy year—manic a lot of the time—but Iris loved spending 10 days with Eden in Madrid and not just in Israel. Eden and Wes loved being in Madrid. They loved everything they were taking in, from the city's famous museums to its vibrant food and wine scene.

When they came to Israel, they stayed with us, and I borrowed a big mattress from Ian and put it in the living room. They stayed for a week or so. Any time we went to Iris's parents, we would all go together. We all went to a Dag Nahash concert, the rap band, a big, big band here in Israel.

That summer, Iris sliced her right hand. She was cutting a watermelon, and by mistake, the knife went into her hand, leaving a bloody mess. Needless to say, she had to get stitches and surgery to repair the tendons. It was terrible, but she survived.

Slovenia, Croatia, and Italy Trip

After Iris recovered and the concerts were over, we went on holiday to Slovenia, where we stayed for a week in a quaint little hotel in Bled, surrounded by lakes and mountains. We took trips and enjoyed the mountains' fresh air. We then went to Croatia, not before stopping in Ljubljana for a short visit, and stayed for a couple of days at Kempinski Hotel Adriatic in Istria, one of the five-star luxury resorts on the coast next to the town of Umag, with a breathtaking view of the Adriatic Sea and a private beach.

Kempinski Hotel Adriatic in Istria is a true paradise of tranquility, Mediterranean architecture, design, and a first-class spa. From there, we took daily trips to Pula and the Adriatic coast. One day, in Porec, a beautiful town by the Adriatic Sea, it started raining so badly that we had to get cover and lunch within the cover to wait for the rain to stop.

Next, we drove to Italy, passed an Outlet mall by Venice, and then ended up in Rimini for the annual TTG travel show with its endless meetings and networking sessions. From there, we drove to Bologna airport and flew back home, feeling rejuvenated after our adventure through Slovenia, Croatia, and Italy.

Arezzo Weekend

This was the same winter I travelled to another trade show in Arezzo, which was quite dull—apart from the joy of exploring the charming streets of Arezzo itself.

Eden Comes Again to Israel

Around the same time, Eden came again when Lee's daughter, Stav, got married. What a lovely affair it was—the bride and groom wearing white and the smiles on the faces of their assembled family and friends lighting up the holy surroundings of the traditional religious ceremony followed by a party where guests enjoyed themselves. How could they not, with such charming and delightful people all around? And this was the last big party that Haim, Iris's father, managed to attend. Iris was ecstatic, floating on clouds, seeing Eden for the second time in one calendar year.

The New Year

In March, our old partner, Valtur, went bankrupt. Given our agreement with Ophir Tours, we found ourselves with a mess to sort out. The bankruptcy happened right at the end of the winter season, and we had a couple of weeks' payment outstanding when we believed that we could make it through to the end of the season without disruption. We owed money to both the airlines and the club itself. It was a tense period. Fortunately, the last of our customers returned happy and we could wrap up, although it was agony.

To make matters worse, the management at Ophir Tours unjustly blamed me for the situation, even though they didn't really have any grounds to do so—it was just convenient for them. And that was just one of the several added stressors to my year.

The Lisbon Flight Issue

We also had some fun: Rod Stewart was playing at Tel Aviv Park, so we went to see him—a great concert even with the terrible traffic after the show. During that time, I was in negotiations for a new route for the summer of 2019 from Tel Aviv to Lisbon in Portugal. There was a lot of talk, back and forth, over who would sign the contract, who the clients would be, and when, and why not, and all that sort of thing, and I subsequently lost the job with Ophir Tours over the frustrations involved in this deal.

Eden, and Missouri Trip

As all this was unfolding, we had another good piece of news: Eden was pregnant, so we were going to have a grandchild born sometime in late January or early February of 2019. We made plans to fly to Fayetteville, Arkansas, and booked tickets for the end of January 2019. I was still on track to get the Lisbon deal, but the discussions were stuck. They weren't moving forward, so I wasn't able to get it. Still, coming up was this visit with our grandchild, and we were looking forward to that.

CHAPTER 24
Eden, Wes, and Lilith—2019

Becoming a Grandfather in Missouri

I booked an apartment in Joplin, Missouri, just 20 minutes from Neosho, where Eden and Wes lived. After arriving by plane, we drove straight to Eden's house to see her before checking into our apartment. Eden, heavily pregnant, greeted us with a radiant smile. Despite her big belly, she moved around with ease, even though Wes worked nights and she was alone. Their home sat on a large lot with plenty of land out back, and they had three dogs and a rabbit, which added a sense of warmth.

The following day, we spent time with her. That evening, she asked us to stick around as Wes was working again. Her water broke that night, and we were in the right place at the right time. Wes sped home, and we all drove to the hospital in Joplin. A few hours later, Eden delivered a beautiful daughter, Lilith Marie—my first grandchild. Becoming a grandfather filled me with a deep sense of belonging.

We spent the next few days revolving around Lilith and Eden, cherishing every moment. We bought new dishes, glasses, and appliances for their home to help them settle in. After three weeks, it was time to return to Israel, and the goodbye was bittersweet.

The End with Ophir Tours

Upon my return, I was called into a meeting at work where Boaz, my boss, informed me that he had been disappointed in me for years, citing the Lisbon flight as the final straw. After 26 years of passion and dedication, I was being let go, and my age—64—probably played a role in the decision. I felt hurt and unsure of how to react, but Boaz offered me a part-time position at his other company, ETS Avia, at half the pay. I accepted, becoming the marketing manager for Rwanda Air in Israel, which was about to launch direct flights to Tel Aviv.

Rwanda Air

Rwanda Air's flights were politically motivated, initiated at the request of the Israeli prime minister to the president of Rwanda to help manage unwanted immigration from Africa. My role was to attract business clients, a task I had never undertaken in my 41-year career. Despite the challenges, I found some success and became involved in various projects for the airline.

In July 2019, I travelled to Rwanda for four days, immersing myself in the culture and gaining a deeper understanding of the airline's operations. The trip was an eye-opener, as I had the opportunity to experience Rwanda's vibrant atmosphere and rich history firsthand. I visited Kigali, the capital city, where I marvelled at the country's rapid development and modern infrastructure. The hospitality of the Rwandan people was heartwarming, and their resilience and optimism were truly inspiring.

During my stay, I attended several business meetings and networking events to promote Rwanda Air's services. These interactions allowed me to forge valuable connections and explore potential partnerships. I also toured the Kigali Genocide Memorial, a poignant reminder of the nation's tragic past and its remarkable journey towards healing and reconciliation.

The experience broadened my perspective and added a new dimension to my professional journey. It taught me the importance of adaptability and the value of embracing new challenges. I returned to Israel with a renewed sense of purpose and determination to contribute to Rwanda Air's success, knowing that my efforts were part of a larger mission to strengthen ties between our countries.

During that time, my life revolved around the news and photos of Lilith.

Vacation in Italy

In September 2019, Iris and I took a vacation to Italy. We flew into Trieste and booked Agriturismo

Millefiori, a place near Rovigo in the Veneto region. From there, we embarked on day trips to nearby cities. Our first stop was Chioggia, often referred to as Little Venice. We strolled along the Corso del Popolo, the town's vibrant main street lined with cafes and shops.

Iris picked out a pair of new glasses at a local store, and since they would be ready in two days, we had a quick lunch before heading back to Rovigo.

In Rovigo, we wandered through Piazza Vittorio Emanuele II, the town's bustling centre. Iris found a beautiful wool sweater at a boutique, and we enjoyed a classic Italian aperitivo—Spritz and local wine with Venetian-style snacks—at a nearby cafe. Dinner followed at a local restaurant, where we savoured wild boar paired with an excellent red wine.

The next day, we drove to Mantua, starting at the Ducal Palace, the historic seat of the influential Gonzaga family. From there, we walked to Piazza dell Erbe, the lively heart of the city. After a meal at a charming trattoria, where we enjoyed local specialties, like Tortelli di Zucca, we headed to Ferrara. There, we wandered through the medieval streets, particularly the atmospheric Via delle Volte, and stopped for dinner to sample the famous Cappellacci di Zucca before returning to Rovigo.

After picking up Iris's glasses, we strolled through Canal Vena in Chioggia, admiring the views from Ponte di Vigo and watching the boats go by, a perfect glimpse into the town's maritime history.

One day was fully dedicated to Padova. We started at the beautiful Prato della Valle square, visited the Basilica di Sant'Antonio, and marvelled at Giotto's frescoes in the Scrovegni Chapel. We ended the day shopping and enjoying an Aperol Spritz before dinner.

On our last day, we explored Verona. Starting at Piazza Bra, we visited the arena, an ancient Roman amphitheater, and took a quick walk to Juliet's Balcony, an iconic stop. After wandering through Verona's streets, we indulged in gelato before heading to Piazza delle Erbe, where a beautiful exhibition of antique cars was on display amidst the historic buildings. It was magical for me, and Iris enjoyed it just as much. Most of my trips with Iris felt like a nostalgic journey where memories of the past with Livia resurfaced. Each destination, each adventure, carried echoes of the times I had spent with Livia, whom I loved so deeply.

Travelling with Iris

Travelling with Iris was a beautiful blend of new experiences and cherished memories. Whether we were strolling through the picturesque streets of a quaint Italian town or marvelling at the breathtaking vistas of a remote beach, I often found myself reminiscing about similar moments shared with Livia. The joy, the laughter, and the sense of wonder that accompanied those past journeys seemed to intertwine with the present.

Iris, with her vivacious spirit and zest for life, brought a fresh energy to these trips. Her enthusiasm for exploring new places and her ability to make every moment special added a new layer of enjoyment. Yet, amid the excitement of discovering new destinations, there was always a comforting familiarity—a reminder of the love and adventures I had once shared with Livia.

In essence, travelling with Iris allowed me to create new memories while honouring the old ones. It was a continuous journey of love and remembrance, making each trip a poignant and enriching experience.

A Bizarre Return

Upon my return to Israel, I encountered an unexpected situation. I was informed that I should have asked for permission from the Rwanda manager in charge before undertaking my trip. This was dumbfounding, as it seemed like an unnecessary bureaucratic hurdle. Despite this setback, we pushed on.

The flights were operational, but I faced another challenge. The travel agents weren't forthcoming with potential clients, leaving me to find new leads on my own. This required a great deal of perseverance and creativity. I reached out to various business networks, attended industry events, and leveraged my connections to generate interest in Rwanda Air. Each new client brought a sense of accomplishment, reinforcing my belief in the airline's potential.

Navigating these challenges taught me resilience and the importance of persistence. It was a complex task, but the support from the Rwandan team and my determination to succeed kept me motivated. The experience ultimately strengthened my skills in client acquisition and broadened my professional horizons.

CHAPTER 25
COVID-19 Years: 2020-2022

IMTM Travel Exhibition 2020

In February 2020, the IMTM (International Mediterranean Tourism Market) Travel Exhibition in Tel Aviv was set to take place. This event is one of the most important tourism fairs in the region, attracting exhibitors and visitors from all over the world. The exhibition serves as a significant platform for promoting tourism, networking, and business opportunities within the industry.

Our team was allocated a booth at the exhibition, meticulously prepared to showcase Rwanda Air's services. The booth was strategically designed to attract attention and provide visitors with comprehensive information about our flights and destinations. We adorned our space with vibrant visuals of Rwanda's scenic beauty and cultural richness, aiming to captivate potential clients and partners.

Throughout the exhibition, we received numerous inquiries about flights, highlighting a keen interest in our offerings. The interaction with visitors was dynamic and engaging, allowing us to explain the benefits of flying with Rwanda Air, such as our competitive pricing, exceptional service, and convenient connections.

The exhibition also provided an invaluable opportunity to network with other industry professionals. We connected with travel agents, tour operators, and representatives from other airlines and tourism boards. These interactions opened doors for potential collaborations and partnerships that could further enhance Rwanda Air's presence in the market.

In addition to engaging with visitors and industry peers, we attended various seminars and workshops held at the exhibition. These sessions covered a range of topics, including the latest trends in tourism, sustainable travel practices, and innovative marketing strategies. The knowledge gained from these sessions was instrumental in refining our approach and staying ahead in the competitive landscape.

The IMTM Travel Exhibition was a resounding success for Rwanda Air. It not only boosted our visibility but also reinforced our commitment to providing excellent service and forging strong relationships within the industry. The positive reception and the wealth of inquiries we received underscored the potential for growth and the exciting opportunities that lay ahead. There, we were informed about the beginning of the strange pandemic that was starting to influence the world.

COVID-19's Impact in Israel

Out of nowhere, COVID-19 struck, and everything came to a halt. The country went on lockdown: there were no flights, no movement. All came to a standstill. This was one of the toughest times of my life. Events, such as Passover, birthdays, and celebrations, were canceled; there was no way of visiting my mom.

The pandemic's arrival in Israel was swift and unforgiving. The government imposed strict lockdown measures to curb the spread of the virus, leading to the closure of borders, suspension of international flights, and restrictions on domestic movement. The bustling streets of Tel Aviv turned eerily quiet, and the once vibrant city became a ghost town.

The lockdown measures were stringent: people were required to stay at home, non-essential businesses were closed, and social gatherings were banned. The impact on daily life was profound. Families were separated, and individuals were confined to their homes, grappling with the uncertainty and fear brought on by the pandemic.

The healthcare system faced unprecedented challenges. Hospitals were overwhelmed with COVID-19 patients, and healthcare workers worked tirelessly to provide care under extremely difficult conditions. Eventually, the Israeli government implemented a rapid response, including the development and distribution of vaccines, which played a crucial role in controlling the spread of the virus.

The economic impact was severe. Many businesses struggled to survive, and unemployment rates soared. The tourism industry, in particular, was hit hard, with travel restrictions and fear of the virus keeping tourists away. Rwanda Air, like many other airlines, had to suspend its operations, leading to significant financial strain.

The emotional toll was also significant. The inability to visit loved ones, the cancellation of important events, and the constant fear of contracting the virus took a heavy toll on people's mental health. The sense of isolation and uncertainty was palpable, and many struggled to cope with the new reality.

Despite the challenges, the resilience and adaptability of the Israeli people shone through. Communities came together to support each other, and innovative solutions were found to navigate the new normal. The pandemic was a test of endurance and strength, and while it brought unprecedented hardship, it also highlighted the importance of unity and solidarity.

Rwanda Air stopped flying, so I was let go once again.

Reflecting During the Pandemic

The sudden halt brought by COVID-19 gave me an unexpected opportunity to reassess my life and consider the future. Being an optimist, I sought ways to find a new rhythm amidst the chaos. Walking Mia every day became a source of strength and solace. Her companionship was invaluable, especially during our nearly 7,000 steps each day, which helped keep me grounded and focused.

Job Search and Routine

With the world at a standstill, I dedicated most of my time to searching for a job on LinkedIn. Creating a structured timetable gave my days a purposeful routine, ensuring that I stayed productive and motivated. The job hunt was a challenging endeavour, but it provided me with a sense of direction during these uncertain times.

Staying Connected With Mom

Visiting my mom became particularly difficult due to the lockdown restrictions. However, I made a concerted effort to stay connected with her through regular phone calls and video chats. These virtual interactions provided both of us with comfort and reassurance. When restrictions eased slightly, I made short, cautious visits to ensure her safety. These visits were a reminder of the importance of family bonds and provided much-needed emotional support.

Staying Connected With Iris's Parents

The same applied to Iris's parents, who lived in another city. Maintaining contact with them was crucial, as they also faced the challenges and isolation brought about by the pandemic. We ensured regular communication through phone calls and video chats, keeping them informed and connected. These conversations helped bridge the physical distance, providing a sense of normalcy and emotional support during these uncertain times.

When restrictions allowed, we made careful visits to Iris's parents, taking all necessary precautions to keep them safe. These visits were filled with warmth and affection, reinforcing the importance of family connections. Iris's parents appreciated the effort to stay in touch, and the moments we shared, however brief, were deeply cherished.

Balancing Connections

Balancing the needs of my mom and Iris's parents was a delicate task, but it underscored the significance of family and the strength found in these relationships. Both sets of parents provided a sense of continuity and love, reminding us of the enduring bonds that hold us together. These connections became lifelines, offering support and a shared sense of resilience in the face of adversity.

Emotional Impact

The pandemic, with its widespread uncertainty and fear, highlighted the importance of staying connected with loved ones. The isolation imposed by lockdowns made these connections even more valuable. Our efforts to maintain contact with our parents not only provided them with comfort but also strengthened our own emotional well-being. The regular interactions, whether virtual or in-person, reinforced our sense of belonging and community.

Finding New Rhythms

As we adapted to the new normal, finding a balance between staying connected and ensuring safety became a routine. We developed new ways to stay close, whether through creative virtual gatherings or socially distanced visits. These efforts were a testament to the resilience of our relationships and the unwavering support of our family.

Personal Reflections and Growth

This period of enforced pause allowed me to reflect on my past experiences and the lessons I had learned. I came to appreciate the importance of adaptability and resilience, qualities that had seen me through various challenges over the years. The pandemic reinforced the need to stay positive and find new ways to cope with adversity.

I also took the time to cherish the small moments that brought joy and solace. Whether it was the simple pleasure of walking Mia or the deep conversations with loved ones, these moments became the silver linings during a time of widespread uncertainty.

Rediscovering Passions

With more time on my hands, I revisited old hobbies

and discovered new ones. I started reading more, delving into books that had long been on my to-read list. I also explored creative outlets such as writing and photography, which provided a welcome distraction and a way to express myself during the lockdown.

Community Support and Solidarity

Witnessing the resilience and solidarity of the community during the pandemic was truly inspiring. People came together to support one another, whether through volunteer work, mutual aid groups, or simple acts of kindness. This sense of community and shared purpose helped me stay optimistic and reminded me of the importance of human connections.

Adapting to the New Normal

As the situation evolved, I adapted to the new normal, finding ways to stay connected and engaged despite the physical distance. Virtual meetings, online events, and remote collaborations became the norm, and I embraced these changes as opportunities to stay active and involved.

In essence, the pandemic, while challenging, became a period of introspection and growth for me. It provided an opportunity to recalibrate my life, appreciate the present, and prepare for the future with renewed strength and resilience.

Navigating Work During the Pandemic

At the same time, Iris was working full-time and,

indeed, non-stop from home in an essential business. Hour after hour every day, she was glued to Zoom meetings, often working overtime and weekends. She told me not to disturb her, and I understood how challenging her job was. Her dedication and hard work were commendable, and I tried to support her by ensuring she had a quiet and comfortable working environment.

Seeking Opportunities

While Iris was occupied with her demanding job, I focused on finding new contracts for travel representation. Invitations from companies in Israel started coming in, and the prospect of new opportunities made me enthusiastic. However, with the country in lockdown, it was difficult to sell my skills effectively. Despite the interest from five companies who were eager to bring me on board, making significant headway proved challenging.

Challenges in the Travel Industry

The pandemic posed unprecedented challenges for the travel industry. The shutdown meant that I couldn't travel to explore new destinations or meet potential clients in person. This was particularly frustrating as the Emirates had just opened for Israeli tourists, presenting new opportunities that I couldn't fully capitalise on. I often felt a step behind other operators who might have had more resources or different circumstances.

A Promising Contract

Eventually, I landed one contract that seemed promising. The initial success was a beacon of hope amid the uncertainty. However, after a month, the company stopped paying me despite some bookings. This was a bitter loss after all the effort and enthusiasm I had put in. It felt like a significant setback, but I tried to remain optimistic and continued to seek new opportunities.

Adapting to New Realities

The experience taught me the importance of adaptability and resilience. It was a period of intense learning and growth as I navigated the complexities of the industry under unprecedented conditions. The pandemic forced me to rethink my strategies and find new ways to connect with clients and showcase my value.

Supporting Each Other

Throughout this time, Iris and I supported each other. Despite the pressures of our respective work, we found solace in our shared moments. Whether it was a brief walk with Mia or a quiet dinner, these moments provided a sense of normalcy and connection.

Iris's Visits to the US

The visits were a cherished opportunity for Iris to reconnect with Eden and witness Lilith's growth and milestones firsthand. During her stays, Iris managed to work remotely, often keeping very unusual hours due to the time difference. Despite her busy schedule, she engaged in various activities with Eden and Lilith, creating lasting memories together. From playing with Lilith to helping Eden with daily tasks, Iris's time was filled with joy and connection.

Each day, Iris would share stories and photos with me, filling me in on all the delightful moments she experienced. Hearing about Lilith's latest achievements and seeing their smiling faces in the photos brought a sense of warmth and happiness.

My Time With Family

Meanwhile, my time with my family was equally valuable. Although I didn't join Iris on her trips, we stayed connected through regular phone calls and video chats. These conversations allowed us to share our respective holiday experiences and maintain our close bond, even when miles apart. I cherished the moments spent with my own family, finding comfort and joy in our time together.

Whether it was celebrating holidays, sharing meals, or simply enjoying each other's company, these moments were a reminder of the importance of family. The distance between Iris and me during her visits to the US didn't weaken our connection; instead, it strengthened our appreciation for each other and our families.

Iris's trips were a reminder of the importance of

family connections and the joy of reuniting with loved ones. These moments, although we spent them in different places, enriched our lives and strengthened our relationship.

My Mom and Her Eventful Days

My mom became increasingly difficult to check on as she could no longer venture outside on her own. To ensure she received the care she needed, I organised 24/7 support and eventually found the right candidate: a gentle lady from Moldova who spoke Romanian along with Russian. This made my mom feel much better, as she was comfortable communicating in her native language.

However, my mom suffered a hard fall and had to be rushed to the hospital. Due to her lack of exercise, she had become very heavy, making it difficult to get her up off the floor. In the hospital, they discovered that she had broken her hip and needed surgery to replace it. She was 90 years old, and I was deeply concerned that she wouldn't make it through the operation.

Thankfully, she did.

She began a three-month rehabilitation program, and I visited her every day. A caregiver took her in the morning, and I picked her up in the evenings to take her home. During rehab, they diagnosed her with a lung condition and prescribed the use of a BiPAP machine to help her breathe at night. It was a struggle, especially because she couldn't get used to the mask, but it was necessary for her survival. Explaining all of this to her was a constant battle.

After rehab, she came back home, but we were still struggling with her use of the BiPAP. This period was very challenging, as we tried to assure her how important it was for her survival. Ensuring she understood the necessity of the machine and convincing her to use it regularly was a daily effort.

Navigating Life During the Pandemic

Around the same time, Iris changed jobs. She had been employed at a company where the increasing workload drained all her energy, leaving little time for anything else. Switching to a position at Neopharm, a company that manufactured surgical equipment and tools, was a welcome change for her. She now enjoyed a better work-life balance, which brought a sense of relief and renewed enthusiasm to her days.

Living in Fear of COVID-19

Being so afraid of catching COVID-19, I did not go to the movies or attend any large gatherings for more than two years. I was so homebound that I forgot about all the good things life has to offer. I lost two years of my life, doing only what I could with Iris and Mia, barely seeing relatives or interacting with people. It was a period of silent depression and anxiety, feelings that I kept bottled up inside.

Seeking Connection

To fill the void, I turned to social media, communicating with people I didn't know and who had nothing to do with me. With men and women alike, these virtual interactions were a desperate attempt to feel connected. The very air felt heavy with the weight of solitude. How many times could I tell myself that I needed to keep going, that what I felt was not the truth of things? As the world outside took on a locked-down, half-dark facade, my job disappeared, and I saw no end point, plunging me into a sense of powerlessness. The void inside kept growing.

The Crushing Solitude

What bothered me the most was not so much the lost wages or postponed plans but the solitude. It felt like the walls were closing in. I did my best to maintain some kind of routine—taking Mia for walks, looking for work, trying to stay optimistic—but depression seemed to creep up on me in the quiet moments. It felt like walking through molasses, each step draining more energy than the one before. I woke up feeling the weight of the day before it even began. It wasn't just sadness; it was numbness. Sometimes, it felt as if the world didn't even matter, as if everything that went on wasn't really life but more like the motions of a day.

Struggling With Depression

Even though Iris was beside me, the long hours she spent working from home, buried in Zoom calls, made me feel even more isolated. I didn't want to burden her, but I couldn't help feeling the dread and gnawing anxiety that I couldn't get a handle on my life. There were days when I lay in bed, staring at the ceiling, wondering if I had already succumbed to depression. Days when taking Mia out for her walk felt impossible, as if depression had trapped me in a cycle of failure.

Finding Moments of Light

Despite the darkness, there were moments of light. Small victories like landing a contract or having a meaningful conversation provided glimpses of hope. The support from Iris and the unconditional love from Mia were lifelines that kept me afloat. Slowly, I began to realise that it was okay to feel what I was feeling and that I didn't have to carry the weight of the world on my shoulders.

Moving Forward

The journey was tough, but it taught me resilience and the importance of seeking help.

Connecting with people, even strangers, on social media reminded me that I wasn't alone. The pandemic had thrown the world into disarray, but it also brought a deeper understanding of our shared human experience. As I navigated through the darkness, I found strength in the small moments of connection and the unwavering support from those who cared.

CHAPTER 26
A New Beginning—2022

The Unexpected Opportunity

Right before my scheduled operations for my sinuses and eyelids, I got a call from Yair di Castro, the owner of Solo Italia, a travel company. He asked if I was available to meet at his office to discuss an opportunity. His travel company needed someone to run group operations. Since we knew each other from all the trade shows, especially the BIT in Milan and the TTG in Rimini, I eagerly accepted. The position was mostly home-based, with in-office check-ins twice a week, and it started in March 2022. This job was like a lifeline, rescuing me from the depths of loneliness and depression.

I didn't mind the challenging conditions. I liked working again; I liked the feeling of being useful and appreciated. It gave my soul an infusion of oxygen and banished all the dark spells I'd been under. I passed all my surgeries with the dynamism of a lion, breathing new life into myself.

Mia's Struggles

At this time, our dog, Mia, was not well. She had first lost sight in one eye and then the other. She also had epilepsy and was on medication that made her wobbly and fragile. I took her for walks several times a day, even though I was working from morning until 9 pm, sitting at my computer. Despite being manically busy, I was thriving, exuberant, and on cloud nine with every creative achievement. I even got calls on weekends, which reminded me of the old days in Ophir Tours.

Family Visits

That fall, Eden, Wes, and their daughter, Lilith, booked flights to visit Israel. This made my life even more exciting. Over the summer, I hired a contractor to build a work and guest room on the roof. The first contractor did shoddy work, so we had to bring in a second contractor to fix it. We also landscaped the front of our house, installed a new irrigation system, and planted new shrubbery, making everything look lush and new.

We bought a sofa bed, a television set, a refrigerator, and various other items, like new plate sets and glasses. Iris bought new chairs, plastic dishes, cups, and a futon, all to make our three-and-a-half-year-old granddaughter feel as if everything was new and wonderful. An air-conditioning unit was installed, and the new space was ready for their arrival.

The Exciting Visit

In October, their visit finally came. Iris and I picked them up at the airport, taking Eden and Lilith home with us, while Iris took Wes and her mom, who wanted to personally welcome them home as well. We had a wonderful time together. Lilith, having lived on an army base in Neosho, Missouri, without many friends, loved going to local parks to play with other kids. She met a new child every time, effortlessly overcoming the language barrier.

We went to the safari once, where Lilith adored the animals as much as her toys and clothes. She's a bright, quick-thinking, and not-so-quiet child, prone to occasional fits. It's hard to judge whether she's picked this up from Wes's presence or from her surroundings. We also visited Iris's father, whose condition was worsening daily. He needed to be moved with a home crane, unable to express feelings or emotions. It was pretty sad to see him like that. Both Eden and Wes were shocked by his appearance, and Lilith was afraid of him.

New Friends and Family Gatherings

One evening, we took the girls to see Lee's daughter, Stav, who had a child, Kim, the same age as Lilith. The two girls clicked instantly, and we had an entertaining (albeit loud) concert on the keyboard and guitar. As long as the kids were content, so was I.

We had a huge family gathering on the roof before they left. Iris's mother, sister, her husband, Oren, their daughters, Stav and Sapir, as well as several of Iris's uncles, and Avi and Terri, all attended. All told, about 18 people. I took over the grill, preparing a variety of meats and some vegetarian options for Eden and Sapir. We drank, ate, and drank some more. Wes, a former alcoholic, stuck to bubbly mineral water and coffee. He smoked cigarettes and joints, took Mia out for walks, swept the floor, and cleaned up. He kept busy.

A Happy Home

Iris and I slept in the new rooftop room while they were here, giving our bedroom to Eden, Wes, and Lilith, who slept on her futon. Everyone was happy, close, and re-energised.

Before they left, I booked a unit in Florida for us to be together again next February. I was busy with work and happy with my new room on the roof, where I could stay as long as I wanted without being bothered. The only thing that upset me was that I couldn't bring my mom to see everything. I was so proud that I made a video for her to see. She was happy for me, too. Her health was still okay, even though she was nearing ninety-four years old. Her mobility was really down, and she still fought me over the BiPAP machine.

A Challenging Year

And so, 2023 came along, which turned out to be a really difficult year. But amidst all the challenges, there were moments of joy and connection that made the journey worthwhile.

CHAPTER 27
A Year Not to Be
Remembered—2023

A Year of Highs and Lows

The year started with a bang. First, it was Iris's birthday, then the next day, my mom's. Shortly after, we flew to Miami, where we stayed with Wes, Eden, and their four-year-old daughter, Lilith, in a rented apartment in Hallandale Beach for two weeks. We alternated between the beach, the pool, and exploring new places in and around Miami.

Exploring Miami

We visited the Miami Zoo, the Frost Museum of Science, and the Seaquarium. We drove to Coral Gables for a lively yet relaxing street fair with music. One memorable afternoon, we visited Wynwood Walls, where the graffiti art came alive, turning the area into an open-air museum. Wynwood Walls was perhaps the most beautiful part of Miami.

Lilith, being too young to sit still, would often get frustrated. To prevent any meltdowns, we had to keep moving, taking her to different places to keep her entertained. After a full day of activities, she would fall asleep in the car, exhausted but happy.

Connecting With Friends

During the trip, we spent some time with Avi and Terri, who had a second home only 20 minutes from our apartment. We had a fun time together for two weeks before driving them home and seeing them off at Ft Lauderdale airport.

We then packed for our own return to Israel, having breakfast with them one last time before leaving.

Back to the Grind

With barely time to unpack our bags, we got straight back to work. Iris and I were both already stretched to the limit, with work getting busier and busier. I was managing new groups and getting more involved in various projects. I even hired a personal trainer—the same one Iris had. But I quit after a couple of weeks because I didn't like her personality and the fact that she kept three cats in the fitness room. I switched to visiting a private Pilates teacher instead.

Political Unrest

At the same time, the country was imploding. The government was looking to enact reforms that would curb the dominant power of the judiciary, including the

Supreme Court. These reforms brought hundreds of thousands of Israelis onto the streets to protest what they saw as an assault on the rule of law. The weekly protests dramatically polarised society.

Joe's Visit

In the midst of this, Joe came to Tel Aviv for a business trip and to attend the Dan David Award ceremony at Tel Aviv University. He stayed with us for two nights before the event. We picked him up at the airport, and he immediately noticed all the changes since his last visit. We took him out for dinner on Friday and lunch on Saturday, making him feel at home in our upstairs room.

Joe, looking very thin and well, wasn't even drinking, just a glass of wine at dinner. Gabriella had just finished her first year of college—a real prize! Joe was excitedly talking about their new Italian citizenship, which he and Gabriella both acquired through his father's and grandmother's Italian roots. They even got a small apartment in Florence where Gabriella was going to study Italian that summer. What a wonderful father.

Family Time

We stopped in to see my mother first thing on Saturday morning and again in the afternoon before Joe left. Avi and Terri also visited. The next day, I drove Joe back to his hotel in Tel Aviv before his business meetings began.

Loss and Grief

Then, on 6th August, my mom's maid called to say that she wasn't moving. I was there within 10 minutes. She was cold, eyes wide open. She had passed in her sleep. I closed her eyes and kissed her face one last time. It was a surreal moment, filled with a profound sense of loss.

I had to deal with the formalities—getting the doctors to pronounce her death, coordinating with the police who confirmed it was natural, and planning for her burial, which had to happen the same day, in accordance with Jewish tradition. Iris was with me through it all, and her support meant the world. Her presence was a comforting anchor in the storm of emotions.

After notifying family and friends, the hardest part began—dealing with the emotional weight of losing her. Once the shiva was over, I had to clear out, clean, and paint my mother's apartment that she had rented until the end of her life. It was an arduous task, each item a reminder of her life and our memories together. I sold most of her things, a process that felt like erasing parts of our shared history, and drew a line under that part of my life. It took about two soul-depleting weeks.

At the end of it, the realisation that I now had only one aunt—Miricel—and two cousins that I was close to was excruciatingly painful. The profound loneliness settled in, a void that felt impossible to fill. The house, once full of life, now seemed emptier than ever.

Despite the challenges, I tried to focus on the positive moments. Iris's constant support and the small acts of kindness from friends and family were lifelines. They reminded me that even in the darkest times, there is light and love. This period, though immensely tough, also taught me the value of resilience and the importance of cherishing the moments we have with our loved ones.

More Heartache

A few months later, Iris's father was taken to the hospital. His condition was critical, and Iris, along with her sister, Lee, sat with him night and day as he struggled. Despite the physician's predictions that his time was near, his passing was still a shock. He died peacefully after a week, the morphine having closed down his pain centres, allowing him a painless departure.

In the final days, Iris was inconsolable, weeping copiously as she faced the imminent loss of her father. The reality of his death hit hard, leaving her devastated. The funeral was a small, intimate affair, attended largely by relatives, Iris's early colleagues, and friends of Lee and her husband, Oren. The sense of loss was palpable among everyone present.

Following the funeral, the family observed two days of shiva—a traditional period of mourning. During this time, friends and family visited to offer their condolences and support. Despite the comfort of their presence, the grief was overwhelming. The end of shiva marked the beginning of a new, challenging chapter for Iris as she adjusted to life without her father. The swift return to everyday life after the brief mourning period left a lingering sense of emptiness and sorrow.

Hamas Attack

On 7th October, Hamas terrorists launched a savage attack, murdering 1,200 people and kidnapping 252 in the biggest massacre of Jews since the Holocaust. The assault was terrifyingly different in its scale and ferocity. Hamas coordinated a multi-pronged offensive on Israel, not only launching a record rocket barrage but also breaching the Green Line perimeter to enter Israeli communities and abduct and murder civilians and soldiers.

The entire country was stunned that Hamas had been able to pull off this assault. They outsmarted Israel's spies and penetrated layers of detection technology and early-warning systems. The surprise attack was a massive blow, coming on Shemini Atzeret, a day that was supposed to be peaceful. As rockets continued to pour through the sky, militants armed with assault rifles and grenades infiltrated Israeli border communities, causing chaos and devastation.

A National Crisis

Deaths were high, and hospitals were soon overrun. The IDF declared an emergency and launched immediate retaliatory strikes against Hamas in the Gaza Strip. The country was left grappling with the aftermath of the attack, raising endless questions about the abduction of 252 people and the response to their kidnappers and murderers. When the first group of hostages was released in a truce in November, the country gathered around their television sets. The parents and families of the freed were relieved, but the rest of the population, including Iris, felt the weight of national sorrow and anxiety. Iris cried and cried.

Life in Wartime

Work came to a halt. International airlines stopped flying into Israel. The three Israeli carriers, El Al, Israir, and Arkia continued flying but had to reduce service on their flights. Many people were left without income, feeling that recovery wouldn't come anytime soon.

Helping Where I Could

So, I did what I could to help. I sorted and handed out basic necessities to displaced families in hotels or private homes, drove food to army bases, and even helped pick tomatoes on a farm near the Gaza border. The work was difficult, but my reward was knowing that I helped people in need. In wartime, it seemed important to support normality in the midst of upheaval. Somehow, life had to continue.

Indeed, we all continued to a new year, a new hope, and a new change in our lives.

CHAPTER 28
The Current End

By 2024, the Situation Had Only Deteriorated

The Hamas hostages were still alive, reduced to 140. Too many, but most of them were civilians: old men, convalescents, and children. To wake up each day and read of them was still to wince at a national tragedy. Some of the hostages were dying of illness. Others, in the course of military operations, were accidentally shot. A few managed to escape, and others were brutally killed by the Hamas terrorists. But 101 men, as of this writing, remain stuck in those tunnels, suffering the indignities of their airless confinement. Their family members at home are suffering, too, and the government appears powerless to do anything but watch as one calamity piles upon another.

From this initial group, the total has dwindled to roughly 30 still alive.

A Personal Second Earthquake

A personal second earthquake hit when Iris's

mother, Batya, who now has trouble remembering even the most basic details, was diagnosed with dementia. She had started to forget small things, then more complex things, until the point was reached when, day by day, she lost more and more. Her daughters, Iris and Lee, found themselves in the unenviable position of having a deteriorating parent on their hands and were forced, each in their own way, to cope with her decline.

Redundancy and Reflection

Against all this, I was made redundant. No groups were travelling and no tourists for the incoming ones. No stable work outside of Israel's three operating airlines, as airlines kept stopping and restarting. I started writing this autobiography, unemployed, as a means to distract myself and then to keep myself busy, filling all the mental space with the trip I hadn't realised I still had, of a life that was nearly over, that I could write about. I could take pleasure in it and make sense of it.

Lebanon Crisis

Since Hezbollah started bombing northern Israel, all the villages and towns close to the border have been evacuated to hotels. The war has been raging simultaneously in the north and the south. Israel decided to completely dismantle the entire Hezbollah organisation from top to bottom. The situation has been dire, with Hezbollah launching unprecedented rocket attacks on Israel, including Tel Aviv and Haifa. The intensity of these attacks has caused significant damage and disruption, with rockets hitting various military and civilian targets.

Displaced Israeli Citizens

For Israeli citizens, the crisis has been equally devastating. All the villages and towns close to the northern border have been evacuated, with families forced to leave their homes and seek refuge in hotels and temporary shelters. As of now, these citizens have been away from their homes for 13 months and counting, living in uncertainty and discomfort. The long-term displacement has taken a severe emotional and psychological toll on these individuals, who are now grappling with the loss of their homes, the disruption of their daily lives, and the constant threat of violence. The government has been working tirelessly to provide support and maintain a sense of normalcy for these displaced citizens, but the road to recovery remains long and arduous.

Iran's Attacks

As if the situation with Hezbollah wasn't enough, Israel has also been attacked twice by Iran. In October 2024, Iran launched a massive salvo of ballistic missiles at Israel, sending millions of people into bomb shelters. This attack was part of a broader escalation in the region, with Iran seeking to retaliate for Israeli strikes on Iranian military targets. The missiles targeted key Israeli military installations, causing significant damage and casualties.

The conflict with Iran has further strained Israel's resources and heightened the sense of insecurity. Despite the challenges, Israel's air defenses have been largely effective in intercepting many of the missiles, but the threat remains ever-present.

The current situation does not leave too much hope, but we all believe in the strength of our military and trust all will be in place soon.

I am sorry that I have to end the book with these sombre facts.

EPILOGUE

Personal Reflections

So, as I look back on my life, as I live it now in retirement, I am grateful. For I have lived a life full of work and play, knowing that I have contributed to my community and to something larger than myself. My story is a story of resilience and caring. It is a story of struggle and of triumph. It is a story that tells us that, with hard work and goodwill, anyone can survive the odds and, in their will, do good and let that good overcome. Life was a gift, and I've always tried to make the most of it.

Now, after nearly 40 years in the travel business, I have friendships spanning every continent. My knowledge of cultural and geographical diversity had enriched my life tenfold—and it was all in jeopardy. Of course, my journey wasn't all smooth sailing. I had my moments of desolation, and there were many times when I found it difficult to adequately prioritise both my career and my desire to have a family. Nonetheless, with the help of my parents, I managed to overcome these obstacles and always gave it my all.

The End

About the Author

Eric is an expert in Tourism, with diplomas in various fields. After graduating from medical school, he restarted his life in the tourism field and has been at it for more than four decades. He is an avid book reader and sport enthusiast. This is his first book.

www.ingramcontent.com/pod-product-compliance
Lightning Source LLC
Chambersburg PA
CBHW051257120626
46547CB00015B/1985